Irrigation Investment, Technology, and Management Strategies for Development

Studies in Water Policy and Management
Charles W. Howe, General Editor

About the Book and Editor

The results of investment in irrigation projects in developing countries have often been disappointing both to investors and to local beneficiaries. The editors argue that the ultimate goals of irrigation projects must be set within the larger context of general social issues. Economic efficiency must often be weighed against social gains; irrigation projects cannot be conceived simply as technical problems, and structures must be designed with reference to their continuing maintenance and operation.

Using a management model, the contributors offer new perspectives on the evaluation of investment priorities and the potential benefits of irrigation projects in developing countries. Recommendations on evaluating investments in small-scale irrigation projects, improvements in water allocation, project rehabilitation and maintenance, water pricing, government food policy, technical assistance, and project sustainability are empirically grounded in studies from India, Thailand, Pakistan, and Egypt. The analysis of specific small-scale projects suggests that there are many opportunities for improving farmer participation and thus increasing the chances of success for these projects.

K. William Easter is professor of agricultural and applied economics at the University of Minnesota, working in the general area of economic development and resource economics, with a special focus on water and land problems and resource pricing issues.

Irrigation Investment, Technology, and Management Strategies for Development

edited by K. William Easter

Routledge
Taylor & Francis Group

LONDON AND NEW YORK

First published 1986 by Westview Press, Inc.

Published 2018 by Routledge
52 Vanderbilt Avenue, New York, NY 10017
2 Park Square, Milton Park, Abingdon, Oxon OX14 4RN

Routledge is an imprint of the Taylor & Francis Group, an informa business

Copyright © 1986 Taylor & Francis

Library of Congress Cataloging-in-Publication Data
Main entry under title:
Irrigation investment, technology, and management strategies
for development.
   (Studies in water policy and management)
   Bibliography: p.
   1. Irrigation--Government policy--Developing
countries. 2. Irrigation--Developing countries--Finance.
3. Irrigation--Developing countries--Management.
I. Easter, K. William. II. Series.
HD1741.D44I77 1986   338.4'762752'091724   85-31523
ISBN 13: 978-0-367-00874-1 (hbk)

ISBN 13: 978-0-367-15861-3 (pbk)

CONTENTS

LIST OF TABLES

xiii

LIST OF FIGURES

CONTRIBUTORS

ADUL APINANTARA, Assistant Professor
Department of Agricultural Extension, Khon Kaen University,
Thailand

RICHARD L. BOWEN, Assistant Professor
Department of Agricultural and Resource Economics,
University of Hawaii, Honolulu

E. WALTER COWARD, JR., Professor
Department of Rural Sociology and Asian Studies, Cornell
University, Ithaca, New York

K. WILLIAM EASTER, Professor
Department of Agricultural and Applied Economics, University
of Minnesota, St. Paul

T. ENGELHARDT, Research Scholar
Economics Program, ICRISAT, Andhra Pradesh, India

SAM H. JOHNSON III, Assistant Professor
Department of Agricultural Economics, University of
Illinois, Urbana-Champaign

DIMYATI NAGNJU, Senior Agronomist
Irrigation Division I, Agricultural and Rural Development
Department, Asian Development Bank, Manila, Philippines

K. PALANISAMI, Associate Professor
Department of Agricultural Economics, Tamil Nadu
Agricultural University, Coimbatore, India

V. RAJAGOPALAN, Vice Chancellor
Tamil Nadu Agricultural University, Coimbatore, India

K.V. SUBBA RAO, Senior Research Associate
Economics Program, ICRISAT, Andhra Pradesh, India

RAYMOND Z.H. RENFRO, Economist
USAID, Pakistan

R.K. SIVANAPPAN, Director
Water Technology Centre, Tamil Nadu Agricultural University,
Coimbatore, India

EDWARD W. SPARLING, Associate Professor
Department of Agricultural and Natural Resource Economics,
Colorado State University, Fort Collins

JERACHONE SRISWASDILEK, Assistant Professor
Department of Agricultural Economics, Kasetsart University,
Bangkok, Thailand

YUAVARES TUBPUN, Assistant Professor
Department of Economics, Thammasat University, Bangkok,
Thailand

MATTHIAS VON OPPEN, Principal Economist
ICRISAT, Andhra Pradesh, India

DELANE E. WELSCH, Assistant Dean
Agricultural International Programs, University of
Minnesota, St. Paul

ROBERT A. YOUNG, Professor
Department of Agricultural and Natural Economics, Colorado
State University, Fort Collins

FOREWORD

This volume, the ninth in Westview's Water Policy and
Management Series, summarizes the results of a long program
of field research on the effectiveness of various irrigation
technologies and management practices in the Third World.
The determinants of the effectiveness of a technology are
shown to include not only the usual economic factors, but
also a range of social and cultural values. The complemen-
tarities of agricultural policies and agricultural research
to technology are clearly exhibited. The feasibility of ongoing operation and maintenance is a major determinant of
the net benefits from a choice of technology. The economic
environment facing the small farmer, including the method of
water allocation, is a key ingredient in the farmer's
willingness to adapt to changing conditions.
This volume will be directly useful to irrigation
planners, although their governments may not be receptive to
some of the findings. Dealing with organizational detail
and cultural diversity at the local level is difficult and,
to some at the top, less rewarding than pushing ahead with
the next large project. It is, nonetheless, the direction
development programs must go.

Charles W. Howe
General Editor

Charles W. Howe is professor of natural resource economics
at the University of Colorado and the author of several
books in the Water Policy area.

PREFACE AND ACKNOWLEDGMENTS

This book is the outgrowth of the growing concern about water resource management in developing countries at the University of Minnesota (UM), Colorado State University (CSU), and USAID. The mutual concern of these three institutions resulted in a USAID funded research project which is the foundation for this book. Many of the authors in the book worked directly on the research project and helped make it a success. The overall approach of the project was to work on irrigation problems in developing countries by collaborating with researchers in these countries. This was particularly successful in India and Thailand where we worked with Doctors K. Palanisami, R.K. Sivanappan, V. Rajagopalan, Yuavares Tubpun, Adul Apinantara, and Jerachone Sriswasdilek.

Studies were conducted in south India, northeast Thailand, Egypt, and Pakistan. The areas were selected for study based on a survey of interest among USAID country missions and the extensive contacts and experience of UM and CSU in the four countries involved. In India and Thailand the research focused on small-scale irrigation and is discussed in Chapters 6, 8, and 9. For Egypt and Pakistan the studies involved water allocation in large-scale systems and are reported in Chapters 11 and 12.

A number of the chapters in this book have been developed from papers presented at the UM-CSU-USAID Workshop on Water Management and Policy held in Khon Kaen, Thailand, September 13-15, 1983. The workshop had three purposes. The first was to report the results from the irrigation research done by the UM-CSU group and their colleagues from Tamil Nadu Agricultural University, India; Khon Kaen University, Kasetsart University, and Thammasat University, Thailand. The second was to foster interaction among a wide

range of people from developing countries on common irrigation problems. The third was to stimulate the writing of
papers which went beyond the project's scope to suggest new
vistas for irrigation research.

Several smaller workshops were held during 1980-1983 at
CSU and UM to discuss various water management and investment issues ranging from water pricing and the collection of
water fees to the constraints associated with expansion of
small-scale irrigation projects. In addition, a symposium
on "Promoting Interaction Between Farmers and the Irrigation
Systems in LDCs," held at the 1983 summer meetings of the
American Agricultural Economics Association, was a direct
outgrowth of the project. The focus of the symposium was on
the link between farmers and the irrigation systems that is
the Achilles heel of many irrigation projects. Participants
discussed a wide range of factors which influence farmers in
operating and maintaining irrigation systems. For example,
cooperation among farmers and irrigation officials is made
difficult by differences in perspective on how water should
be allocated during scarcity periods. Farmers often view
water as a substitute for other inputs, such as weeding,
whereas irrigation officials tend to view water as a complement to other inputs. In contrast, the use of tubewells,
the sale of well water, and water trading provide incentives
for cooperation in canal maintenance and repair. The purchase or sale of water by farmers provides them with a
strong incentive to minimize delivery losses. Other factors
influencing participation include: water scarcity, size
distribution of farms, project size, local customs, strong
local leadership, and the irrigation bureaucracy's experience in working with farmers.

The editor would like to acknowledge Delane Welsch's
contribution to this book. Delane helped in the original
planning of the book and was involved in the early stages of
editing. However, after Delane became Acting Assistant Dean
for International Programs at the University of Minnesota,
he was no longer able to continue with the editing. Another
key person in the research project was Bob Young who
directed the CSU research effort. Without his continued
efforts, the research would not have been completed. John
Day and Dick Suttor were both very helpful in providing
guidance for the project from USAID's perspective while Ken
Nobe and Ed Schuh gave continued support from the University
side.

Maynard Hufschmidt's comments were very helpful in strengthening the first three chapters of the book. The water management model presented in Chapter 1 is adapted from work by Bower and Hufschmidt. The editor would like to thank Leslie Small, Donald Taylor, Ed Sparling, K. Palanisami, and Sam Johnson for their helpful comments on earlier drafts of Chapters 2 and 3 and Keith Fuglie for his help with Chapter 9. Finally, I would like to thank Charles Howe and Tom Legg for their editing comments throughout the book.

During the 1984/85 academic year, while I was on sabbatical at the East-West Center, the manuscript was completely revised. A special thanks goes to Karen Ashitomi who typed the revised draft. The final typescript was completed upon my return to the University of Minnesota by Patti Schwarz. Patti deserves special recognition since she not only typed the first draft and the final typescript, her editorial assistance was invaluable throughout preparation of the manuscript. Finally, a special thanks goes to Charles Eldridge who helped Patti with a new word processing package required for the book and the laser printer.

K. William Easter

CHAPTER 1

INTRODUCTION AND CONCEPTUAL MODEL

K. William Easter

THE PROBLEM

Many irrigation schemes fail to generate expected
levels and distribution of farm output and income. Overall
system management, particularly operation and maintenance
procedures, are major contributors to poor project performance both in terms of the level of farm income and its
distribution. In some cases the irrigation systems are
poorly designed while in others the projects are not implemented as planned. Some of the difficulties are related to
the lack of capacity to properly evaluate complex water
resource development schemes and to plan, design, and implement appropriate projects and policies. In many cases,
expectations concerning output and its distribution are
unrealistic.

However, many developing countries cannot or will not
take the time to develop these management capacities before
they try complex water projects. For example, many have
argued that if Asian countries are to meet their future food
production requirements, irrigation investment will have to
be accelerated. For India alone, Sivanappan and
Rajagopalan, in Chapter 4, argue that 42.7 million hectares
will need to be brought under irrigation by the turn of the
century if food supplies are to match demands. Of the total
investment in Asian irrigation, 20 to 25 percent is planned
just for improving existing systems, but in India the
percentage is much higher. Poor performance of existing
irrigation systems is one of several serious problems
constraining efforts to increase food production in Asia.
If these irrigation investments are going to fulfill expectations, then the question of how to improve irrigation
systems must be answered.

1

Both the World Bank and USAID have recognized this need and are making sizable investments in improving existing irrigation systems worldwide. For example, USAID is investing significant amounts in technical assistance projects to improve existing irrigation. These are mainly multiple-disciplinary approaches such as the Water Management Synthesis II Project designed to improve irrigation water management. If past experience is any indication, these investments will not be used efficiently unless something is done about management from the farmers' standpoint. When the irrigation system manager and the user are the same, such as a farmer who owns and operates a tubewell, water is nearly always used efficiently from the private perspective. If the system management unit and the farmers served are not the same, then serious water use problems often arise. A number of solutions have been proposed to help bridge this gap between farmers and system management. At one extreme are recommendations to sell publicly owned and operated tubewells to farmers. At the other extreme, some have argued for strict policing and disciplining of farmers so that they must follow irrigation plans from the central water authority. A middle ground involves proposals for establishing farmer organizations to take over varying degrees of management.

Even if not all of the resources planned for irrigation development are used, and if only a subset of the problems is addressed, the task is still monumental. Yet concern for improving irrigation has been building since the late 1960s. A combination of past irrigation investments and the use of high yielding varieties to feed an expanding population has made irrigation and irrigation management a central development issue. For example, as early as 1972, three measures were suggested for improving irrigation in India. The first was to create and improve physical facilities by land leveling, improving the water conveyance system, providing water measuring devices, installing control and distribution structures, and developing water sources. The second was to adopt water application methods (sprinkler, surface, or subsurface) suitable to the crops, soil, and slope of the land. The third was to improve management by the application of water at a rate determined both by the water-holding capacity of the soil and by crop needs. This would include the use of up-to-date information on the frequency of irrigation, crop varieties, fertilizer application rates, and pest and disease control (Sharma 1972).

A more inclusive list of needed irrigation improvements would include the following elements:

1. Rehabilitation of existing projects both at the system and farm levels.
2. More intensive operation and maintenance of the improved system.
3. Improved procedures for allocation and scheduling of water deliveries which are arrived at after discussions with farmers.
4. Revised rules, regulations, and enforcement procedures governing access to irrigation water based on discussions and agreements between government and farmers.
5. Improved distribution of information to farmers concerning crops, cropping practices, inputs and water availability (Bromley, et al. 1980).

Although the task may seem overwhelming, progress has already been made in defining what has to be done. This book is another step in suggesting what types of improvements and investments in irrigation are the most effective. We have come a long way since the 1960s when the first serious work on water management was started.

IRRIGATION MANAGEMENT MODEL

One of the problems associated with most studies of irrigation is the absence of a whole system perspective. There is a failure to perceive the vital nature of the various stages of irrigation management. Consequently, a conceptual model is used in this book which takes a whole system approach. It is adapted from the water management model developed by Bower and Hufschmidt (1984), which includes three major components: (1) a management process involving five stages, (2) a management system with three elements, and (3) a set of linked activities and tasks. Each component provides different and important insights into water management problems.

Management Process

The first component considers water management as a process involving various stages starting with planning and ending with operation and maintenance (Figure 1.1). The emphasis in this book is on the planning stage, which is discussed in Chapter 2, and the last stages of operation and maintenance (O&M). Design and construction are not ignored since the difficulties involved in providing O&M are depen-

4

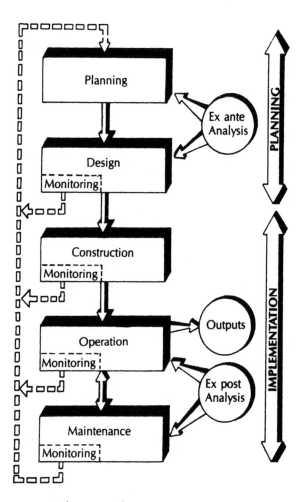

□ □□ : Information Flows

Source: Adapted from Bower and Hufschmidt (1984)

Figure 1.1 The five stages of irrigation management process

dent on the project design and how well the project is constructed. A well-designed and constructed project will require much less O&M to achieve the same level of irrigation efficiency as one which is poorly designed or constructed.

The management process can also be divided into the two broad categories of planning and implementation. It is during the planning stage that ex-ante analysis is used to help select projects and designs for construction. During the implementation stage, which is the focus of Chapter 3, monitoring and ex-post analysis become important. Information must be collected concerning a wide range of factors including water deliveries, acres irrigated, crops grown, crop yields, input use, water fees collected, and costs of operating and maintaining the system. Analysis can then help evaluate project performance and suggest possible changes in water allocation procedures, maintenance schedules, or organizational arrangements.

Management System

The second facet of the model involves water management as a system which includes a set of facilities, implementation tools, and institutional and organizational arrangements which are used to capture and deliver water to farmers (Figure 1.2). The system requires inputs of labor, materials, land and management skills which, along with the irrigation facilities, institutions, and implementation tools, are used to provide the desired "intermediate" output of water. If the system is managed efficiently water is delivered at the time and in the quantity which produces optimum agricultural production with minimum adverse environmental effects.

In the water management system the institutional and organizational arrangements as well as implementation tools are just as important as the physical parts of the irrigation system. For example, Chapter 13 highlights the importance of who actually makes the investment in the facilities (farmers or government) and the property relationships which are created in the process. To be successful a range of organizational arrangements and implementation tools may be necessary to obtain a high level of indirect irrigation investment by farmers. Another example involves the rules and incentives which govern the collection of irrigation water fees and/or the provision of farmer labor for system maintenance which are a central concern in project implementation. The organizational side of the problem

6

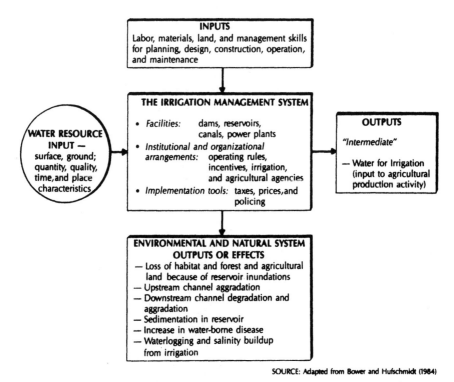

INPUTS
Labor, materials, land, and management skills
for planning, design, construction, operation,
and maintenance

THE IRRIGATION MANAGEMENT SYSTEM
• *Facilities:* dams, reservoirs,
canals, power plants
• *Institutional and organizational
arrangements:* operating rules,
incentives, irrigation,
and agricultural agencies
• *Implementation tools:* taxes, prices, and
policing

WATER RESOURCE
INPUT —
surface, ground;
quantity, quality,
time, and place
characteristics

OUTPUTS
"Intermediate"
— Water for Irrigation
(input to agricultural
production activity)

ENVIRONMENTAL AND NATURAL SYSTEM
OUTPUTS OR EFFECTS
— Loss of habitat and forest and agricultural
land because of reservoir inundations
— Upstream channel aggradation
— Downstream channel degradation and
aggradation
— Sedimentation in reservoir
— Increase in water-borne disease
— Waterlogging and salinity buildup
from irrigation

SOURCE: Adapted from Bower and Hufschmidt (1984)

Figure 1.2   Irrigation management system with inputs and outputs

includes the government agencies and farmer organizations
which are involved or should be involved in project
operation and maintenance.

There are a whole set of institutional and organizational arrangements which determine the success of irrigation projects. These range from the organization of
national irrigation agencies down to the rules for
establishing water user organizations (WUO). Are there
procedures for coordinating activities of the irrigation
agencies and the agencies in charge of agriculture and
extension? Is there a national effort to help farmers form
WUO and improve water management? The success of this
latter effort will be partly contingent on institutions
governing land and water rights. For it is these institutions which will determine who benefits directly from the
improved water management.

Finally, a serious national policy concerning efficient
water use may be more important than building another irri-

gation dam. Many countries, particularly in Asia, already
have a large number of irrigation projects and have
developed the best sites. And much can be gained from
improving the efficiency of existing irrigation systems
through better water management.

Activities and Tasks

The third component of the water management model
involves a set of linked activities and tasks which are
necessary for water delivery. Water management is sub-
divided into specific steps which government agencies,
farmer organizations, or individual farmers must perform if
the desired outputs are to be obtained. One can visualize a
surface water irrigation system as beginning with a watershed from which water is collected in a storage reservoir
(Figure 1.3). The water is then taken through canals and
delivered to farmers' fields and a system of drainage canals
drain off excess water. Investments must be made which make
these deliveries possible. Many of these investments will
be indirect investments by farmers as described in
Chapter 13. Others will involve direct government action
and policies which facilitate farmer investments as
discussed in Chapters 4, 7, and 11. The optimum mix of
investments will vary from area to area but the role of
small-scale irrigation such as those considered in Chapters
6, 8, and 9 is likely to grow in importance in the future.
Within each component of the six stages, activities and
tasks are required to assure effective water delivery. For
example, to operate the canal system effectively rules must
be established to allocate water among different parts of
the system and dates must be set for water release and shut-
off. A system of water charges may also be necessary such
as the ones discussed in Chapters 3 and 12. Flexibility
should be built into the delivery schedules if farmers are
to make mutually beneficial water trades similar to those
discussed in Chapter 11.
In the final stage the important question is how to
market the products and supply the necessary inputs for the
irrigated crops. This is another key part of the "total"
irrigation system. Without adequate transportation and
markets in which to sell products, prices will not match
expectations. The increased output will depress prices and
the net project benefits will be low. Provision must be
made for adequate markets and transportation if farmers are
to sell their increased production at reasonable prices and
inputs are to reach them at the appropriate times. In

8

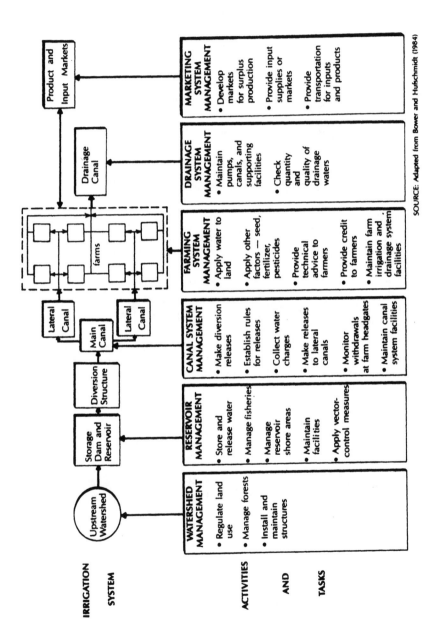

Figure 1.3 Water resources management activities and tasks for a surface irrigation system

SOURCE: Adapted from Bower and Hufschmidt (1984)

IRRIGATION SYSTEM

Upstream Watershed → Storage Dam and Reservoir → Diversion Structure → Main Canal → Lateral Canal → farms → Drainage Canal → Product and Input Markets

ACTIVITIES AND TASKS

WATERSHED MANAGEMENT
• Regulate land use
• Manage forests
• Install and maintain structures

RESERVOIR MANAGEMENT
• Store and release water
• Manage fisheries
• Manage reservoir shore areas
• Maintain facilities
• Apply vector-control measures

CANAL SYSTEM MANAGEMENT
• Make diversion releases
• Establish rules for releases
• Collect water charges
• Make releases to lateral canals
• Monitor withdrawals at farm headgates
• Maintain canal system facilities

FARMING SYSTEM MANAGEMENT
• Apply water to land
• Apply other factors — seed, fertilizer, pesticides
• Provide technical advice to farmers
• Provide credit to farmers
• Maintain farm irrigation and drainage system facilities

DRAINAGE SYSTEM MANAGEMENT
• Maintain pumps, canals, and supporting facilities
• Check quantity and quality of drainage waters

MARKETING SYSTEM MANAGEMENT
• Develop markets for surplus production
• Provide input supplies or markets
• Provide transportation for inputs and products

Chapter 8 Tubpun identifies markets and price incentives as one of the four factors necessary for successful tank irrigation during the dry season in northeast Thailand. An irrigation system based on ground water or pumping from a river, as discussed in Chapter 9, would be somewhat simplified. The watershed would be less important for ground water unless it is an area where the ground water is recharged. Instead of a reservoir there would be an aquifer or river from which pumps are used to withdraw water. No diversion structures would be present and the system of canals would probably not be as large since a pump would irrigate a smaller area than most surface irrigation systems. However, large pumps and many of the small tanks (reservoirs) in south India and northeast Thailand (Chapters 5, 6, 8, and 9) would serve an area of about the same size. The system of farm ditches and drainage canals would also be smaller. In fact, because of the better water control which is generally possible with pump irrigation systems, the drainage problems are likely to be much less than those in large surface irrigation systems.

THE CONTENT

The first three chapters provide an overall framework for the book. The irrigation management model presented in this chapter emphasizes the whole system approach to irrigation. Chapters 2 and 3 are also key chapters on which the other chapters build. They include a review of research studies on irrigation planning, investment, and implementation. These chapters indicate what is already known, and suggest critical areas for further study.

The authors of Chapters 4 through 6 are concerned with irrigation in India, with special emphasis on tank (small reservoir) irrigation in south India. In Chapter 4, Sivanappan and Rajagopalan give a broad overview of the wide range of problems which are plaguing Indian irrigation, while the focus in Chapters 5 and 6 is on tank irrigation. In Chapter 5, von Oppen, et al. suggest a strategy for small tank and well development for improving agricultural production in India. Finally, Palanisami and Easter use a sample of forty-nine tanks in Tamil Nadu state to develop a set of criteria for determining which tanks to rehabilitate.

The authors of the next four chapters are concerned with irrigation development in Thailand. Johnson, in Chapter 7, gives an overview of irrigation in Thailand and calls for an investment in irrigation improvement so that cropping can be intensified. Tubpun, in Chapter 8, esti-

mates the benefits from three small communal tanks in
northeast Thailand and makes recommendations for improving
the government's program of providing small tanks to supply
domestic water. In Chapter 9, the authors consider a range
of small-scale irrigation technologies in northeast
Thailand. They find that river pump irrigation projects may
not be profitable, in many cases, due to the high installation costs. In Chapter 10, Nagnju presents the results of
a pilot irrigation project which the Asian Development Bank
(ADB) installed in the lower Mekong Basin of northeast
Thailand. The pilot project appears to have accelerated
production in the whole Nong Wai Irrigation Project.

Chapters 11 and 12 include some of the results of the
extensive work done by CSU in Pakistan and Egypt. The focus
in Chapter 11 is on water trading which occurs among
Pakistani farmers on the same watercourse. The authors find
that private wells improve the opportunities for water
trading. In Chapter 12, Bowen and Young consider alternative pricing schemes for irrigation water in Egypt and find
that only with increased water scarcity does volumetric
pricing improve allocation efficiency over area-based
charges.

In Chapter 13, Coward calls for a rethinking of current
irrigation investment policies. He suggests that greater
emphasis should be placed on encouraging indirect investment
by local farmers in their irrigation systems. In fact,
heavy direct government investment may actually discourage
indirect investments by farmers.

In the final chapter, I highlight the policy and
research recommendations from the book and summarize what
has been learned. There are also suggestions by the UM-CSU-
USAID Workshop participants concerning future research
directions for irrigation management and investment.

REFERENCES

Bower, Blair T., and Maynard M. Hufschmidt. 1984.
    "A conceptual framework for analysis of water resources
    management in Asia." Natural Resources Forum 8(4):343-
    55.
Bromley, Daniel W., Donald C. Taylor, and Donald E. Parker.
    1980. "Water reform and economic development:
    Institutional aspects of water management in the
    developing countries." Economic Development and
    Cultural Change 28(2):365-87.

Easter, K. William, and Maynard M. Hufschmidt. 1985.
Integrated Watershed Management Research in Developing
Countries. East-West Center Workshop Report,
Honolulu, Hawaii, 38p.
Sharma, T.C. 1972. "On improving the efficiency of farm
irrigation." Indian Farmers Digest 5(8):50-52.

CHAPTER 2

PRIORITIES FOR IRRIGATION PLANNING AND INVESTMENT

K. William Easter and Delane E. Welsch

The literature on evaluation of irrigation planning and investment is more extensive than any other area of economic investigation of irrigation. Yet it focuses on individual project selection, i.e., benefit-cost analysis, but ignores many of the broader questions concerning irrigation planning and investment. These broader questions involve trade-offs among different types of investment including the following: government vs. private irrigation projects; wet-season irrigation vs. year-round irrigation; irrigation vs. rainfed production; expansion vs. intensification (rehabilitation) of irrigation; and large-scale vs. small-scale irrigation (Levine 1980).

In the first question, the case of government vs. private irrigation development, optimal use of water usually requires some type of government involvement or acquiescence. This may range from credit for private tubewells to actual construction of canals and dams. The more important question is what mix of private and government involvement is best for a given project? In the case of the tubewells, research findings suggest continued heavy private involvement. The major exception is when there are problems of overpumping and well interference, which may require government regulation of well spacing and/or pumping rates. It is also possible that water user organizations (WUO) could be established to regulate pumping. For large reservoir projects, there is little doubt that government will take the lead in planning, design, and construction. But interaction among farmers and the government in planning, design, and implementation of projects is critical. Currently, in less developed countries (LDCs), there is too little farmer involvement.

13

In the second question, the trade-off between wet season irrigation and year-round irrigation may not be as important an issue in Asia as it once was. With the development of high yielding varieties and improved farming practices, the returns to dry season irrigation have jumped. Although wet season irrigation in Asia once was the only way to provide insurance against droughts, other methods are now available, i.e., short-term food distribution programs and reserve stocks. In much of south Asia, after a large, intensive irrigation project with numerous canals and tertiary channels has been constructed, it is an economic waste not to grow at least two crops per year in the irrigated area. Returns in the dry season will tend to be higher than in the wet season because of lower pest damage, higher solar radiation, etc. With two crops per year, the irrigation system is likely to have a high rate of return while with the one wet season crop, the project will probably be marginal at best.

Unless the project size is dictated by physical con- siderations, the question still remains of how large should the irrigated area be. Although economics may favor a small area with two crops per year, a case can be made on an equity basis for larger irrigated areas and one season irri- gation. Thus the question of wet season vs. year-round irrigation partly involves the trade-off between economic efficiency and equity which is discussed in Chapter 3.

A related question is that of the intensity of irriga- tion water application. Many farmers, particularly those in the head-reaches of irrigation systems, tend to use too much water. The last cubic meter of water yields very little in crop production. In addition, these farmers grow high water-using crops such as rice and sugarcane. Thus there is substantial potential for considering less intensive water applications (Taylor 1980). This could allow either the expansion of the command area or the irrigation of a second crop. Yet to obtain farmer cooperation, assurance must be provided that less water-intensive crops will be grown by all farmers and that water will be available to irrigate more acres or a second crop.

To determine what the water application intensity should be will require extensive research. "Our considera- tion of irrigation water application intensity involves examining crop production responses to different levels of water application, and the returns to water from rice vs. from upland crop production" (Taylor 1980, p. 56). Once this research is completed, the findings can be used to help design, rehabilitate and manage irrigation systems. To

reduce water intensity in many existing systems will require
better water control and distribution.

The third question, concerning irrigation vs. rainfed
agriculture, carries with it the same implied efficiency-
equity trade-off as the wet season vs. year-round cropping.
The argument is that government should be investing more to
help the poor rainfed farmers and less to help the higher
income irrigated farmers. This distinction is not very
useful and can lead to the wrong questions. For example,
research projects on dry land crops, in some cases, have
even ignored work on better utilization of soil moisture
since that involved water management. The concern should be
with managing what water is available, whether it be rainfall or water pumped from the ground. Even under conditions
where no irrigation is possible, farmers are concerned about
how they can best use available water and soil moisture.
The investment problem is a micro one of comparing alternative investments in a given agro-climatic and cultural
situation (Abel and Easter 1971). The question is how to
invest in improving the use of whatever water and other
resources are available.

The two remaining issues were the most important for
the University of Minnesota-Colorado State University (UM-
CSU) project and will, therefore, be considered in more
detail. Governments and international lending agencies are
continually asking whether irrigation investment should be
large-scale or small-scale and whether the emphasis should
be on new projects (expansion) or on rehabilitation (intensification) including development of drainage and terminal
infrastructure.

NEW IRRIGATION VS. REHABILITATION

The expansion of irrigation through new systems has its
special appeal.

New systems present a sign of progress that has strong
political appeal, both internally and externally; and
which may have a more general psychological value.
Potential benefits may be more easily identified and
the requisite technical skills more easily mobilized
than in the improvement of existing systems, particularly when 'new' means large-scale and external
resources, both financial and technical, are available.
High quality central design teams can be obtained and

concentrated construction operations can be managed
more easily (Levine 1980, p. 6).

Rehabilitation will improve the water use efficiency
and the benefits from such rehabilitation will be felt
mainly by those farmers within the scheme. If the rehabilitation results in greater water delivery, the command area
of the scheme could be enlarged which would benefit more
farmers. There are also positive secondary impacts which
might be felt in the local economy from rehabilitation, but
most of the benefits will be received by the farmers in the
scheme targeted for rehabilitation.

Within an irrigation system, if rehabilitation improves
the reliability of water deliveries, the lot of the small-
scale farms will improve. When water supplies are unreli-
able and unevenly distributed, the small-scale farmers are
the ones who bear the brunt of water shortages (Bromley,
et al. 1980). Insecure water supplies lead to lower use of
inputs and the nonadoption of new technologies. Thus by
improving the reliability of water, production will be
increased and the distribution of benefits improved, even
when the total quantity of water delivered is not increased.

Deterioration of physical irrigation infrastructure is
one of the key constraints preventing many past investments
in irrigation from reaching their full potential. The
returns from rehabilitation appear to be high enough so that
they can no longer be ignored (Bottrall 1981). Investments
in canal lining, land leveling, control structures, field
ditches, and measurement devices increase the water delivered to the fields and provide for a more efficient water
utilization. Rehabilitation will be necessary in many
systems if water control and reliability is to be improved.

The spread of high-yielding varieties in the
Philippines increased the relative advantage of improving
the irrigation infrastructure over opening new land because
high-yielding varieties perform better under controlled
irrigation (Hayami and Kikuchi 1978). In contrast, under
poorly controlled irrigation, local varieties were superior.
The same need to improve water control in order to intensify
agriculture in Thailand is discussed in Chapter 7. Finally,
the Sri Lanka government has been criticized for investing
huge sums exclusively in large development projects with
little or no attention given to teaching farmers improved
management practices and helping them level, terrace, bund,
and drain at the field level (Kandiah 1978).

Few studies deal directly with the rehabilitation vs.
new projects issue. Most consider only the value of indi-

vidual rehabilitation projects. For example, a study of an Indonesian program which used national subsidies for rehabilitation focused on two small-scale, river diversion irrigation projects. The rehabilitation involved repairing and raising the height of diversion dams and lining of some canals. The subsidies were found to be substantial inducements to the mobilization of local resources, and that as a result, high rates of return were achieved from the rehabilitation (Hafid and Hayami 1978).

In contrast, rehabilitation of the 274,000 ha river-diversion Pakalen Sampean irrigation project in East Java, Indonesia had limited success. This rehabilitation primarily emphasized desilting of channels and the repair of water control structures rather than the restoration of original water-diversion capabilities. In this case, there was no immediately observable impact of the rehabilitation on production, perhaps because the rehabilitation did not improve the project's water supply by increasing its water-diversion capacity. There was a shift in cropping patterns towards growing more rice which substantially increased employment (Taylor 1978). Furthermore, one has to question the estimated net returns for irrigated crops used in the analysis which were lower than the non-irrigated returns for three out of the four crops considered. If farming conditions were truly comparable, then why would farmers irrigate if it lowered their net returns?

Farm Level Investments

Investments to improve irrigation at the farm level have shown a wide range of economic returns. For example, the economic return to investments in land leveling in Pakistan showed benefit-cost ratios of 1.7 and 1.9. The investment involved upgrading traditional land leveling to a precision level. Their findings implied increasing returns to added investments in land leveling (Johnson and Khan, et al. 1978).

A study of the effect of land leveling and fertilizer applications on the physiochemical properties of soil, water use, and yield of wheat found that leveling significantly increased phosphorus, exchangeable potassium, and the infiltration capacity of soil. They also attributed an irrigation water saving of 34 to 37 percent to leveling (Khattak, et al. 1981).

Additional benefits may be derived from a more comprehensive approach to inadequate water control at the field level by changing the location of outlets, improving control structures, and installing field channels. A pilot program in India was started in the late 1960s to improve a large gravity flow irrigation system at the farm level (Easter 1977; Kumar 1977). Both the agricultural and irrigation agencies worked together with farmers in relocating field outlets, improving control structures, and digging farm ditches. Young agricultural engineers, hired by the department of agricultural extension, worked with villagers to design the rehabilitation and to obtain the unanimous village approval. In many cases, the engineers walked the fields with the farmers to make the final decisions concerning where farmers would dig the farm ditches. The design enabled farmers to control the flow of water onto their fields without affecting the flow to their neighbors' fields. The program was found to be highly successful in increasing the area under irrigation, the cropping intensity, the production per acre, and the returns per acre.

Returns on investment in terminal or farm level systems will depend on the number of farmers served by an outlet. If only one or two are served from each outlet, the farmers can be expected to adequately allocate the water beyond the outlet. They will benefit directly from improved allocation, and government investments in farm level system improvements will likely have low returns. However, if five to twenty farmers are served by the same outlet, as Easter and Kumar found, individual farmers do not receive all the benefits from improved farm level water allocation. Farmers impose externalities on other farmers served from the same outlet. In such cases, outside assistance and funds may be necessary to improve the farm level system and should offer high returns. Because of conflicting interests, it is likely to be difficult to get groups of farmers to build their own distribution system below the outlet. Water will tend to be distributed unevenly among farmers, and some farmers will benefit more than others from the distribution system improvements.

Canal Lining. One of the most frequently proposed rehabilitation methods for reducing transmission losses is canal lining. Yet current technologies for lining, particularly concrete lining, tend to be high in cost. Studies of concrete lining do not give clear-cut conclusions concerning profitability (Taylor 1981). Several studies in India, where ordinary canals were concrete lined, found that such changes reduced water losses, increased the cropping intensity, and provided an assured supply of irrigation water to a larger area (Gupta, et al. 1973). Similar results were

obtained from canal lining in the rehabilitation of the
Subsidi Desa scheme in Indonesia (Hafid and Hayami 1978).
There is little doubt that properly lined canals can
reduce water losses, but the real question is how much is
added to the costs of providing water and what are the
benefits? Cheaper alternatives are often available to
assure a water supply. One possibility is partial lining of
the canals and or field channels.[1] An evaluation of several
methods of watercourse improvement including concrete and
masonry linings and simple earthen improvements of the
ditches with concrete control structures, junctions and
turnouts, found that the earthen improvements with concrete
structures were the best investment in Pakistan where labor
costs were low (Johnson and Kemper, et al. 1978). Recent
studies, however, suggest that the life of earthen improvements may be substantially shorter than assumed by Johnson
and Kemper, et al. Improved watercourses in Pakistan's
Punjab tend to reach their previous state of neglect in one
to three years (Renfro 1982).

In another study in Pakistan where earthen improvements
were assumed to have a three year life, lining of the upper
reaches of improved watercourses was just on the verge of
being profitable under 1977 prices. This lining was done on
the most heavily used and most porous sections of the watercourse (Ali 1980). Higher energy prices or procedures for
increasing the life expectancies of the earthen improvements
would make improvements profitable.

Fiberglass-reinforced polyester (FRP) flumes to carry
water above ground were shown to be superior to earthen
channels in Malaysia (Pang 1978). The flumes could be
installed more rapidly and require less land and maintenance. These cost savings plus the savings in water more
than offset the capital costs which were two and a half
times the cost of earthen channels. Finally, tests with
different ways of using pipes have shown some interesting
possibilities for water control (Lenton and Seckler 1978;
Gisselquist 1979).

Maintenance. Probably the cheapest method of reducing
transmission losses, where labor costs are low, is by proper
and timely maintenance of the canals (Johnson and Kemper,
et al. 1978). Inadequate organization of the water users is
one of the major reasons for the lack of maintenance. This
is a particularly thorny collective goods problem which is
characterized as having "... externalities resulting from
individual action; and vulnerability to opportunistic
behavior (i.e., water theft) by other farmers" (Sparling
1981a, p. 1). The organizational difficulties of water-

course maintenance appears to be an important cause of divisiveness among Pakistani farmers. But as discussed in Chapter 3 there is some evidence to suggest that WUO can effectively deal with these problems (Lowdermilk, et al. 1977).

Maintenance is also a basic investment problem. Little or no funds are generally allocated for system maintenance when budgets and designs are made for irrigation projects. In fact, countries may find that they have constructed more irrigation projects than can be adequately maintained. Both the lack of funds and trained people can be constraints to adequate maintenance of irrigation projects. When these constraints exist, new projects may have to be curtailed. In addition, maintenance should be included as a specific item in all project plans.

Solving the maintenance problem is not an easy task since it involves a number of interrelated problems (Figure 2.1). For example, inadequate maintenance causes inefficient water deliveries and discourages farmer participation. In addition inefficient deliveries discourage payment of fees which will reduce the funds available for maintenance. Thus, one must try to deal with a whole set of problems. Obtaining farmer participation in project maintenance is going to be difficult unless there is some assurance that all farmers will contribute. In addition, rules may have to be developed so that the water can be delivered effectively among farmers before farmers are going to be willing to pay fees which can be used for maintenance. They may also have to see that these funds are used to improve and maintain the system (accountability) before they are willing to pay water charges. Finally, if farmers are expected to take over a government irrigation system and do the maintenance themselves, they will probably require it to be in good condition. Therefore, a system may have to be rehabilitated before farmers are willing to take over the maintenance tasks.

A closely related question is the frequency of project rehabilitation. Could periodic rehabilitation effectively substitute for an improved scheme of annual maintenance? A major rehabilitation every ten years might allow project redesign which would make it more suitable to current farming conditions. An irrigation system designed to provide only supplementary irrigation might be redesigned to better meet the demands of high yielding crop varieties. The benefits gained from such a redesign must be weighted against both rehabilitation cost and net income losses

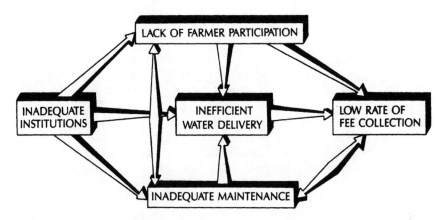

Figure 2.1   The linkage among irrigation problems related to maintenance

during the ten year period of inadequate annual maintenance. The net income losses should be adjusted for the cost savings from the reduced maintenance expenditures.

Summary. The trade-off between building new irrigation schemes and rehabilitating existing schemes is another in the series of equity-efficiency trade-offs inherent in irrigation development. The literature suggests that we have probably erred on the side of building too many large irrigation systems too fast. More now needs to be invested in rehabilitation and improved management. However, research is needed to help guide the planners in these investments. The work of Taylor, Johnson, Easter, and Kumar needs to be repeated in other areas and under different conditions. In addition, other investments in system rehabilitation need to be analyzed in the same manner as the above authors analyzed canal lining and construction of farm ditches.

LARGE- VS. SMALL-SCALE PROJECTS

Many countries must make choices as a matter of policy between large- and small-scale irrigation systems and concentrated vs. dispersed systems. Most countries cannot develop all viable irrigation supplies at once. Choices must be made between concentration of investments in limited areas, as is often the case with large-scale projects, and investment in small- or medium-scale projects scattered throughout the country. Often some aspects of a system are large-scale (diversion, storage, and main canal), while other aspects can be small-scale (control and management systems).

The Asia Development Bank (ADB) has identified small irrigation projects as a high priority. The deputy director says:

> The Bank has been particularly interested in irrigation projects which are small in size, quick in yielding economic benefits and which use appropriate technology suited to local conditions, rather than costly and more time-consuming projects requiring high technology -- such as large dams (Takase 1982, p. 8).

In some countries or regions there are relatively few sites for large multi-purpose dams and the best ones have already been developed. Furthermore, budget constraints are likely to force reluctant irrigation agencies to consider trade-offs between large- and small-scale projects. "It does seem likely ... that in the long run the availability of funds for these large projects will be influenced by their expected performance relative to the likely performance of smaller projects" (Small 1982, p. 3). Even in countries with little potential for large projects, there will be a concern for the performance of smaller projects relative to medium-sized projects.

Many countries as a matter of policy may opt for small irrigation projects in order to spread irrigation investment throughout the country. Small irrigation systems can be more rapidly developed and utilized. As will be discussed in Chapter 13, local capital and labor resources can be more fully mobilized with small projects. They minimize adverse environmental impacts and allow for adjustments when it becomes apparent that there are unforeseen impacts and costs. The potential for involvement of the local community in system operation and maintenance is greater with small projects (De los Reyes 1980).

Large projects are likely to involve irreversible changes which mean these investments should be postponed while more information is collected concerning likely outcomes. In other words, quasi-option values are involved due to irreversibilities and uncertainties concerning the projects.[2] This suggests that a more conservative decision rule should be used to select large projects as compared to small projects (Krutilla and Fisher 1985). But there is little or no research to guide decision makers concerning what the decision rule should be.

On the other hand, large projects hold several advantages:

1. Large projects frequently may be necessary for the effective utilization of a relatively large but variable water supply.
2. Large projects may permit more efficient and effective use of limited managerial and technical skills by drawing these people together to work on the same project. This advantage could be quite different if farmers are heavily involved in the operation and maintenance of the small-scale projects.
3. Large projects permit more economical use of physical elements of the system such as storage, diversion, and conveyance capacities. In other words, economies to scale are present. However, as conveyance systems increase in size there is an offsetting increase in water losses from the canals.
4. Large projects are more easily financed because it is easier to obtain external financing for large projects than for small ones.
5. Large projects generate major benefits such as employment for skilled and unskilled workers during the construction period. Yet this employment is only temporary and can also cause problems if it disrupts wages and occupational choices.

Governments have tended to choose the large project route to irrigation development. But there is a growing feeling that small projects provide greater opportunities for equitable distribution of benefits, and a greater return per hectare or cubic meter of water available. They also involve less resettlement and dislocation.

One method of modifying the adverse impacts of large-scale projects is to stage the development. Different parts of the projects are added as funds and information become available or the demand for irrigation water increases. There are three conflicting factors that enter into the decision on staging:

(1) It pays to build large increments to the system because there usually are cost savings (economies of scale) involved in increasing project size. (2) The commitment of resources to a capacity that will not be used for a long time is costly. It pays to defer investments as long as possible since future costs are more heavily discounted than present costs. (3) Maintenance of flexibility is important (Howe 1971, p. 90).

What is desired is the timing and sizes of additions to the system that will meet the demands at a minimum present value of all costs. In some problems, permitting shortages to occur but attaching a penalty to any shortage makes sense. In general, an optimum solution to these sequencing problems is difficult to determine (Howe 1971, p. 91).

The solutions involve estimating the present value of the entire sequence of costs and benefits which are tested under different assumptions. Unfortunately, large projects must be evaluated under significant degrees of ignorance. Therefore, there is a real potential for sizable unintended consequences which is another reason to favor the staging of projects or small projects. Finally, staging allows a process of incremental learning to take place, leaving more time for training of irrigation personnel and farmers.

In many cases, large irrigation projects are completed in stages but not always by design. For example, the Chao Phya river basin in central Thailand was developed in three phases.

The first involved the construction of the Chainat diversion dam and the primary distribution network; the second, the construction of the Bhumiphal and Sirikit dams and reservoirs to provide dry-season irrigation; and the third, localized on-farm consolidation and development (Trung 1978, p. 155).

An economic analysis of major and minor irrigation projects in India found that large projects often require large public investment in selected areas which benefit relatively few people (Puttaswamaiah 1977). Minor irrigation schemes generally involved lower investment cost per hectare and had a relatively slower depreciation and lower operating expenses than large projects. The time gap between creation and utilization of irrigation potential is substantially less for minor works than for major and medium projects. Finally, because of the inefficiencies in water delivery, actual irrigated areas in many of the larger projects were substantially less than the potential suppos- edly created by the irrigation system. This resulted in costs per hectare of land actually irrigated higher than the planned costs per hectare which were based on the full irrigation potential of the system.

Results of a Bangladesh government benefit-cost analy- sis showed that smaller projects with low investment cost per hectare offered higher average benefit-cost ratios than medium and large irrigation projects. Large-scale gravity irrigation and flood control projects tended to have high unit costs as well as longer gestation periods. The bene- fits from large-scale projects were found to be much below expectations (Bangladesh Planning Commission 1980).

Analysis of a wide range of irrigation projects in the Philippines suggests that communal run-of-the-river systems have had the highest pay-off. The national system and sur- face pumps had good returns, but somewhat lower than the communal irrigation. Finally, deepwell pumps have been too expensive which has resulted in benefit-cost ratios below one (Moya 1985). None of the systems analyzed could be con- sidered large-scale irrigation, as even the national system irrigated only 2,700 hectares.

In a review of studies of Sahelian irrigation projects, Sparling found "that small perimeters are more efficient than large perimeters." He argues:

That the labels large and small are misleading because important differences are organizational. Funds of social capital and human capital peculiar to each area have real economic value which can be harnessed to develop irrigation perimeters. But because these funds of capital are peculiar to each place, it is important that perimeters be developed incrementally -- without displacing farmers or requiring farmers to surrender existing agricultural practices.

The decentralization of control of agriculture leads to more efficient agriculture, but it makes extension especially important ... The organizations which surrender control of perimeters to farmers should be reoriented toward a combined extension-research and development service function (Sparling 1981b, p. 25- 26).

Similar conclusions were arrived at from the perspective of
another discipline (Waldstein 1978; Scudder 1973).
In contrast, studies of gravity-diversion irrigation
schemes in Malaysia found that economies-to-scale exist in
their construction. The large schemes also had higher
annual yields per unit of water than smaller schemes. The
cost estimates indicate that diversion headworks are generally less costly than pumping facilities. These results
suggest caution in policies to encourage small-scale
irrigation at the expense of large-scale projects (Taylor
and Tantigate 1979; Taylor 1981). However, it should be
pointed out that the schemes involved little or no resettlement, and since it was supplementary irrigation, there was
no wholesale switch in cropping.

Three Types of Small-Scale Irrigation

There are three general types of small-scale systems.
The first is the pump or ground water system, which has seen
tremendous expansion during the 1970s. Although there have
been a number of studies of tubewell expansion, there are
still important areas for research. These include the questions of regulating pumping under conditions of a rapidly
decreasing ground water stock, the impact of changing energy
costs on pump irrigation and, as discussed in Chapter 3, the
potential for conjunctive use of ground water and surface
water for irrigation.
The second type of system is the river diversion
scheme. Many of these diversions are indigenous systems
which are either locally managed or receive only limited
government assistance. These have been favorite objectives
of study by anthropologists and sociologists (Bottrall 1981,
p. 222). The literature is fairly rich in descriptions of
how these systems work effectively and the problems which
occur when government tries to take them over (Coward 1977).
A good example of government interference occurred in the
Senegal River Valley where a government agency attempted to
"help" a spontaneous irrigation scheme at Bakel (Sparling
1981b).
Further research is needed to determine ways of
managing conflict among farmers over irrigation. The con-
tainment of conflict is a prerequisite for successful system
operation and communal systems can provide ideas for reducing conflict (De los Reyes 1980). In addition, studies are
needed of the operations of small government run schemes
since few studies exist today. How do they differ from

communal systems in terms of returns, source of capital, management of conflict, and allocation rules?

The third type of small system includes tank schemes (small reservoirs) which are both indigenous and government controlled. South India and Sri Lanka have had, for many decades, a large number of tanks. In northeast Thailand the government has built over 500 new tanks during the past twenty years. The unpredictability of rainfall introduces major operational complexities into the decisions concerning water releases and the size of command area for tanks. Another major problem is the silt accumulation and damages caused by heavy rains and flooding in the watershed. These problems may be beyond the means and ability of farmers to repair or prevent. Many times it is the actions of upstream farmers from other villages which cause the erosion and flooding. The case for technical advice and support from government to overcome these problems appears to be extremely strong (Bottrall 1981).

The success of existing tanks in northeast Thailand has been below expectations in terms of increasing production and income. Although water seems to be available, little or no dry season production occurs. The Thai government as well as donor agencies would like to know why they have not reached expectations. One of the basic problems seems to be that the tanks were originally built for political or local military reasons with little concern for cost or potential irrigation benefits. These projects also tend to serve a number of purposes besides crop irrigation such as fish production and water for livestock, household use, and gardens.

What practices and policies make some small-scale projects highly beneficial and others not? Operation and water allocation should be easier on small-scale projects as compared to large-scale projects since the distance between water source and irrigated farms is much shorter. However, there may be such a diversity of operating procedures involved with small-scale irrigation that it is very difficult to generalize.

A study of five tanks in northeast Thailand found that benefits from fish culture and domestic water use were very important. With fish and domestic water use benefits included the real rates of return for the tanks ranged from 8 to 24 percent depending on the rice price and the area irrigated (Tubpun 1981). Judging from the magnitude of the admittedly rough estimates of fish and domestic water use benefits, they deserve special research attention. This is particularly true since the Government of Thailand is emphasizing the construction of small tanks which are primarily

for domestic water uses. A good approach to the problem
would be to use the travel cost or contingent valuation
methods which have been applied to the analysis of
recreation benefits. This is done in Chapter 8 where both
contingent valuation and market based methods are used in
three small tanks to estimate the value of different water
uses.

There are several other possible reasons why design
expectations are above actual performance. It is probable
that estimation procedures followed and/or assumptions made
concerning expected benefits and costs were in error.
Ex post analyses of alternative projects such as that in
Chapter 8, can help identify the procedures and assumptions
in the ex ante analysis that lead to forecasting errors
concerning project benefits and costs. In addition, an
analysis such as that in Chapter 9, provides a basis for
comparison with other investments including large-scale
irrigation and lift irrigation schemes. The distribution of
benefits from the small projects should also be estimated.
Do small-scale irrigation projects help the small farms as
Tubpun (1981) found in Thailand, or do the benefits go to
the larger, more politically powerful farmer as Easter
(1973) found in one tank irrigated village in east India?

There also may be unexpected constraints to achieving
planned performance. This might involve lack of markets,
seasonal labor shortages or limited credit. The ex post
analysis should be designed to collect information concerning these constraints so that realistic assumptions can
be formulated. Chapters 5, 6, 8, and 9 address these
questions for small-scale irrigation in south India and
northeast Thailand. The next step would be to determine if
these constraints can be eliminated and at what cost. For
example, if markets are not available and cannot be
developed for vegetables, then the project analysis should
not include vegetables as a potential output.

In summary, we need to know more about the existing
patterns of organization and operation for small-scale
irrigation projects particularly for government constructed
projects. Second, are there more effective ways of assisting and supervising small scattered irrigation projects of
any kind? Is a special technical assistance cadre needed to
help improve the performance of small-scale reservoir projects? Three related issues are: (1) Under what physical
and social conditions can large irrigation projects be operated and managed in small-scale units? (2) Are there fewer
socioeconomic problems associated with the development of
small irrigation projects as compared to large projects?

(3) Is local investment higher in smaller, locally controlled projects relative to large government projects? This latter question is addressed in Chapter 13.

NOTES

1. Field channels or watercourses are generally maintained by the farmers, while the canals are the responsibility of a government agency.
2. There is a quasi-option value to refraining from development even on the assumption that there is no risk aversion, and only expected values matter. The passage of time results in new information about benefits or alternative uses of an environment, which can be taken into account if a decision to development is deferred.

REFERENCES

Abel, Martin E., and K. William Easter. 1971. "Agricultural planning: Focus on regional constraints." _Economic and Political Weekly_, 6(30-32):1577-96.

Ali, Barkat. 1980. "Optimal watercourse improvements." M.S. Thesis, Department of Economics, Colorado State University, Fort Collins.

Bangladesh Planning Commission. 1980. _The Second Five-Year Plan, 1980-1985_, Dacca.

Bottrall, Anthony F. 1981. "Comparative study of the management and organization of irrigation projects." World Bank Staff Working Paper No. 458.

Bromley, Daniel W., Donald C. Taylor, and Donald E. Parker. 1980. "Water reform and economic development: Institutional aspects of water management in the developing countries." _Economic Development and Cultural Change_ 28(2):365-87.

Coward, E.W. 1977. "Irrigation management alternatives: Themes from indigenous irrigation systems." _Agricultural Administration_ 4(3):223-37.

De los Reyes, Ramona P. 1980. "Managing communal gravity systems: Farmers' approaches and implications for program planning." Institute of Philippine Culture, Ateneo de Manila University, Quezon City.

Easter, K. William. 1973. "The economic structure of Murethi Village." Staff Paper P73-23, Department of Agricultural and Applied Economics, University of Minnesota, St. Paul.

_____. 1977. "Improving village irrigation systems: An example from India." Land Economics 53(1):46-66.

Gisselquist, David. 1979. "Designs for a low-pressure pipe distribution system for tubewells to give a measured supply of water to individual plots." Mimeo, Ford Foundation, Bangladesh.

Gupta, D.D., A. Singh, and M.V. George. 1973. "Water management practices in sandy arid zones." Agriculture and Agro-Industries Journal 6(6):34-38.

Hafid, A., and Yujiro Hayami. 1978. "Mobilizing local resources for irrigation development: The Subsidi Desa Case of Indonesia." In Irrigation Policy and Management in Southeast Asia, pp. 123-33. A/D/C, Bangkok, Thailand.

Hayami, Yujiro, and Masao Kikuchi. 1978. "Investment inducements to public infrastructure: Irrigation in the Philippines." Review of Economics and Statistics 60(1):70-77.

Howe, Charles W. 1971. Benefit-cost Analysis for Water System Planning. Water Resources Monograph 2, American Geophysical Union, Washington, D.C.

Johnson, Sam H. III, W. Doral Kemper, and Max K. Lowdermilk. 1978. "Improving irrigation water management in the Indus basin." Water Resources Bulletin 15(2):473-95.

Johnson, Sam H. III, Z.S. Khan, and M. Hussain. 1978. "The economics of precision land leveling: A case study from Pakistan." Agricultural Water Management 1:319-31.

Kandiah, A. 1978. "Some technical and social problems in the irrigation projects of Sri Lanka." Agricultural Mechanization in Asia 9(4):49-53.

Khattak, Jehangin K., Abdur Rashid, S.U. Khan, Kermit E. Larson, and Riaz A. Khattak. 1981. "Effect of land leveling and irrigation on wheat yield." Agricultural Mechanization in Asia, Africa, and Latin America 12(1):11-14.

Krutilla, John V., and Anthony C. Fisher. 1985. The Economics of Natural Environments. (Studies in the valuation of commodity and amenity resources), Chapters 3 and 4. The Johns Hopkins University Press, Baltimore, Maryland.

Kumar, Praduman. 1977. Economics of Water Management: A Study of Field Channels. Heritage Publishers, New Delhi, India.

Lenton, Roberto, and David Seckler. 1978. "Choice of irrigation techniques under alternative physical and socio-economic conditions." Ford Foundation, New Delhi, India.

Levine, Gilbert. 1980. "Irrigation development and strategy issues for the Asian region." Draft of issues paper submitted to USAID, Cornell University.

Lowdermilk, M.K., D.M. Freeman, A.C. Early, G. Radosevich, and D. Kemper. 1977. "Organizing farmers to improve irrigation water delivery: The problems and prospects for solutions in Pakistan." Pakistan Economic and Social Review 15(3/4):152-73.

Moya, Piedad F. 1985. "Benefit-cost analysis of the different types of irrigation systems in Central Luzon Philippines." In Irrigation Management: Research from Southeast Asia, (ed.) T. Wickham, pp. 67-84. A/D/C Workshop, 1981, Kampangsaen, Thailand.

Pang, L.H. 1978. "Fiberglass-reinforced polyester flumes as tertiary channels in Malaysian irrigation development." In Irrigation Policy and the Management in Southeast Asia, pp. 39-44. A/D/C, Bangkok, Thailand.

Puttaswamaiah, K. 1977. Irrigation Projects in India: Towards a New Policy. Nrusimha Publications, Bangalore, India.

Renfro, R.Z.H. 1982. "Economics of local control of irrigation water in Pakistan: A pilot study." Ph.D. Thesis, Department of Economics, Colorado State University, Fort Collins.

Scudder, T. 1973. "The human ecology of big projects: River basin development and resettlement." Annual Review of Anthropology 2:45-61.

Small, Leslie E. 1982. "Investment decisions for the development and utilization of irrigation resources in southeast Asia." Teaching and Research Forum Workshop Report #26, pp. 1-9. A/D/C, New York.

Sparling, Edward W. 1981a. "Collective goods and conflict: An example of a positive feedback mechanism at work in rural Pakistan." Department of Economics, Colorado State University, Fort Collins.

_____. 1981b. Consulting Report: A Survey and Analysis of Ex-Post Cost Benefit Studies of Sahelian Irrigation Projects. Department of Economics, Colorado State University, Fort Collins.

Takase, Kunio. 1982. "Food production and irrigation development in Asia." ADB Quarterly Review.

Taylor, D.C. 1978. "Financing irrigation services in the Pekalen Sampean Irrigation Project, East Java, Indonesia." In Irrigation Policy and the Management in Southeast Asia, pp. 111-22. A/D/C, Bangkok.

_____. 1980. "Economic analysis to support irrigation investment and management decisions." Report of a Planning Workshop on Irrigation Water Management, pp. 39-81. IRRI, Los Banos.

_____. 1981. The Economics of Malaysian Paddy Production and Irrigation. A/D/C, Bangkok, Thailand.

Taylor, D.C., and Kanaengnid Tantigate. 1979. "Alternative strategies for developing Malaysia's irrigation resources." Kajian Economic Malaysia 16:234-94.

Trung, Ngo Quoc. 1978. "Economic analysis of irrigation development in deltaic regions of Asia: The case of Central Thailand." In Irrigation Policy and the Management in Southeast Asia, pp. 155-64. A/D/C, Bangkok.

Tubpun, Yuavares. 1981. "Economics of tank irrigation projects in northeastern Thailand." Ph.D. Thesis, Department of Agricultural and Applied Economics, University of Minnesota, St. Paul.

Waldstein, A. 1978. "Government sponsored agricultural intensification schemes in the Sahel: Development for whom?" Paper done for USAID, REDSO/WA.

CHAPTER 3

IMPLEMENTING IRRIGATION PROJECTS: OPERATIONAL AND INSTITUTIONAL PROBLEMS

K. William Easter and Delane E. Welsch

OPERATIONAL DECISIONS FOR WATER ALLOCATION

A World Bank report on the management and organization of irrigation projects calls water allocation or distribution one of the astonishingly neglected areas of research with a high potential payoff.

> Water distribution was accorded its central place in the Terms of Reference for several reasons. In contrast with other activities mentioned, it is an activity peculiar to irrigated agriculture and it has not been widely studied -- indeed, until very recently, it has been astonishingly neglected, both by academic researchers and professional practitioners. But the overriding reason was that there was recognized to be an immense potential, so far largely untapped, for improving current water distribution practices (Bottrall 1981, p.2).

There are, at least, two dimensions to water distribution. First is the technical aspect related to the appropriateness of the water distribution methods. Second is the social and political dimension which concerns the ability and willingness of irrigation officials to allocate water equitably and to resist powerful pressure to misallocate water. "Good water distribution thus requires not only a high order of technical skill but also a management system which will make it rational for irrigation officials to deny extra water to the more powerful and better located" (Bottrall 1981, pp. 122-23).

Although water distribution involves complex technical, institutional and investment questions, the potential payoff from improving irrigation systems is large. In order to simplify the discussion of research findings and future areas of work, this section is divided into three parts based on location in the system: (1) water allocation among farmers, (2) water transmission to farmers, and (3) water source allocation (Figure 1.3). Although this is somewhat of an artificial division, it helps emphasize the key role which physical design has in determining the allocation alternatives open to management.

Water Allocation Among Farmers

A wide range of procedures can be used to allocate water among farmers. These include:

1. No formal allocation procedure -- water flows continuously.
2. Rotation -- water is available for irrigation every four, seven, ten, or fourteen days depending on the crops grown and the length of rotation.
3. Farm priorities -- farms are served in order of priority based on time of settlement.
4. Market -- water users bid each period for water shares needed to irrigate their crops or buy water shares for the whole crop season.
5. Demand -- water supply for the full season is stored and each farm is allocated a fixed quantity for the season which can be obtained on demand.

Although there are rules for selecting the appropriate design for a canal there are no comparable rules for selecting the method for allocation of irrigation water. What criteria should be used to determine whether a rotation system or a demand system should be used? Maass and Anderson (1978) suggest that five objectives are important in deciding how to allocate water at the farm level: equity, efficiency, growth, justice and local control. The weight given each objective is likely to be different for water managers, farmers, and politicians. This complicates the problem of establishing criteria for selecting the appropriate method for water allocation. It is also likely that the method of allocation should change over time as farmers gain experience and can take more responsibility. For example, one may start out with a strict rotation system and change to a demand system. However, to make such a change the design capacity must be adequate to handle changes in allocation procedures. It will be possible to

change from a continuous flow system to a rotation system
only if there are adequate control structures.

Some combination of regulations and prices should be
used to allocate water. The particular mix of rules and
prices depends on a number of factors including: the value
of water, the ability to collect fees, dependability of
supply, cropping patterns, control structure, and project
objectives. The specific weights given to these factors for
selecting the appropriate combination of regulations and
prices will vary among countries and projects (Seagraves and
Easter 1983). In the rotational system (Warabandi)[1] used on
canal systems in north India, strict rules were found to
prevent the distribution of water to areas of highest need
because the times reserved for water allocation to individual farms were non-transferrable among farmers (Reidinger
1974; Malhotra 1982). One possible way to resolve this
inefficiency would be to sanction intra-watercourse markets
which allow trading of water turns or shares to take place
among farmers. But in Pakistan under the Warabandi system,
water trading use to be allowed but farmers petitioned the
government to switch to a less flexible system. The few
remaining watercourses that allow trading are small and have
extraordinary intra-watercourse cooperatives. A water
market requires coordination of turns which tends to be a
difficult task when a system is abused by the powerful
farmers (Mirza, et al. 1974). Chapter 11 discusses the
impact of water trading on Pakistan watercourses.

Incentives. The social and political dimensions of
water allocation suggest several important questions.
Irrigation systems have been called behavioral systems
because their performance is so dependent on the many people
involved. Since incentives influence people's behavior, it
is important to understand the incentives provided by an
irrigation system to all groups involved in that system
(Small 1982). This leads to several important allocation
questions concerning the compatibility of incentives.

First, there are many sub-groups within irrigation
agencies, each with different motives and responsibilities.
In fact the basic organization of many irrigation agencies
may lead to inappropriate incentives.

The improved system layout resulting from farmer input
in the design and construction stages causes better
system performance. ...and fewer operation and maintenance problems...This would appear to be a potential
incentive for the irrigation agency to incorporate
farmers in the design process. But given the usual
organization of irrigation agencies into separate divi-

sions for design and construction on the one hand; and
operation and maintenance on the other, the incentives
to incorporate farmers may exist only at the very
highest levels within the irrigation agency (Small
1982, p. 7).

In addition, where excessive water use by upstream
farmers deprives downstream farmers of water, a real conflict in objectives may occur. Only the irrigation official
may see the potential for redistributing the water while the
individual farmers can only see their own direct losses or
gains. Where there is a potential for redistributing water
without reducing production upstream, these potentials need
to be demonstrated to farmers.

Second, are the incentives for irrigation system
managers and the farmers compatible with the efficient and
equitable allocation of water? If not, how might they be
altered to increase the compatibility? For example, in
Taiwan one of the important factors upon which the efficiency of the irrigation depended was the use of management
incentives (Abel 1976). In Taiwan's case the irrigation
associations were made up of the farmers who operated the
irrigation systems themselves. The irrigation associations
hired and fired managers at their discretion. As a result
of this relationship, good managers were usually rewarded
whereas poor managers were penalized. This added to their
management efficiency which resulted in better irrigation
service. This, in turn, enhanced the users' willingness to
pay water charges and to contribute labor to the maintenance
of the system.

In contrast, India's Command Area Development (CAD)
failed to meet the compatibility of objectives test.

When CAD officials determine land localization/water
distribution policy and cropping pattern solely based
on soil, climate, and the availability of water for
maximizing cropwise production, the objectives of the
CAD and the farmer do not fully coincide
(Golpalakrishnayya 1979, p.75).

To gain participation of the farming community as an integral part of the program, the objectives of the farming
community must be taken into consideration along with
objectives of the government. Thus, institutions must be
developed so that farmers have incentives to improve water
allocation and in doing so serve their own objectives as
well as the overall project objectives.

Water Transmission to Farmers

Water losses as high as 70 percent have occurred during transmission of water through the canal system to the farmer's field. The seepage of water through the banks of canals accounts for much of the loss. If water is being transmitted over a vast area, the problem of water losses is aggravated. Therefore, an important question in transmission is how large an area should be served? This question involves a trade-off between efficiency and equity. Three things generally happen when the area irrigated is expanded. More farmers can irrigate, the transmission losses increase and the certainty of water supply decreases. One needs to compare the cost in income foregone (due to water losses and decreased dependability) with the benefits from expanding the area and the number of farm families receiving irrigation which includes taking advantage of economies to scale.

The command area of a large scale irrigation project in Tamil Nadu was expanded from 251,000 acres to 366,000 acres during the late seventies. This expansion was approved despite the fact that 61,000 acres in the original command area had never been irrigated. After the expansion farmers received, on the average, enough water to irrigate one crop every two years as compared to water for a crop every 1-1/2 years before the expansion. Because of the limited and uncertain canal water supply, the area irrigated by wells increased significantly. However, little is known about the ground water supply and the recharge provided by the irrigation project (Palanisami 1980).

In another large south Indian irrigation system the pattern of water allocation from reservoir to fields had to be changed to accommodate an expanded command area. Due to the expanded command area and the resulting inadequacy of water, a "zonal system" of irrigation was introduced in 1959. The command area was divided into odd and even miles along the main canal. All distributaries along the odd numbered miles received a continuous supply of water for a rice crop during the wet season. The distributaries along the even numbered miles obtained water for dry crops on weekly intervals during the dry season. In the next year, the sequence changed so that the even numbered miles obtained water in the wet season while the odd numbered miles received water in the dry season. The "zonal system" was an attempt to serve as many farmers as possible given the political decision to have a command area larger than could be served, at one time, by the irrigation system (Palanisami 1981).

The allocation of water is a complex problem when the transfer of water to a new area involves a loss of income to farmers in the existing irrigated area. In this case, the following information should guide the decision makers:

1. The loss in income to farmers in the existing irrigated area.
2. The cost of delivery to the new area including water lost in delivery.
3. The net returns to irrigation in the new area.
4. The levels and distribution of income in both areas.
5. The environmental impacts of the increase in irrigated area.

At best, decision makers usually have a little information concerning net returns and the cost of delivery.

Another aspect of transmission which has been all but neglected is the economics of irrigation scheduling. In one of the few papers on the subject, non-adherence to the scheduling was found to be associated with lower yields and profitability (Taylor and Tantigate 1985). Farmers lost the most time relative to the posted schedule during transplanting and harvesting. In other words, actual time required was more than was allowed for in the schedule. The labor supply was inadequate for the two-week time specified in the posted schedule for each operation. The posted schedule calls for irrigation water to be supplied to all farmers simultaneously which is not possible. But to make phased scheduling possible would require investments in irrigation infrastructure, staff training, changing staff incentives, a larger tractor supply, irrigation extension programs for farmers, and farmer incentives to follow irrigation schedules. Thus scheduling of water deliveries is not a simple task particularly in large systems. It requires careful planning and information about local conditions from all groups of water users served by the system.

Water Source Allocation

A number of questions arise during the allocation of irrigation water at its source. One such question involves the allocation of water over time, both within a season and between seasons. Water in a reservoir or a ground water aquifer represents a source of income generation in the current period as well as in future years. Evaporation losses impose a penalty on water stored in reservoirs for future use, encouraging large, current releases as does the existence of a discount rate. In contrast, the diminishing productivity of water and the uncertainty of next year's water supply both encourage water storage.

Another question concerns the allocation of water among different uses. For example, if water is withdrawn for irrigation, what does this mean for other users? This appears to be a fairly common externality in parts of Asia such as the Philippines where upstream farmers use excessive quantities of water. The result is water shortages for downstream farmers. Return flows reduce this externality somewhat. The same externality exists in tank irrigation in south India where tanks are arranged in a series with the overflow from one tank going into the next tank. Farmers served by upper tanks use excessive water and double cropping, resulting in water shortages for the one crop grown under the lower tanks (Palanisami and Easter 1983). It will take action by the government irrigation agency to internalize this externality. The same problem exists when low valued irrigation water cannot be transferred to higher valued alternative uses, i.e., industrial and commercial uses (Kelso, et al. 1973).

Finally, what procedures can lead to an economically efficient joint allocation of ground water and surface water supplies (conjunctive use)? One such procedure has developed in the Kings River service area of central California (Maass and Anderson 1978). There, surface water prices are kept low as long as there is an adequate river flow which is usually the case until midsummer. When surface water supplies drop, the price for the surface water is raised above the marginal cost of pumping which encourages farmers to shift to ground water. Similar systems might be used in developing countries based on the equimarginal principle (the last unit of water in each use should have the same value).

INSTITUTIONAL AND ORGANIZATIONAL ARRANGEMENTS

Irrigation development and concern for management has gone through three stages in Asia. In the first phase the emphasis was on the capture and conveyance of water with the building of large dams and main canals. This was followed by a concern for agricultural water use and the agronomic aspects of irrigation which includes emphasizing on-farm water management. Finally, governments recognized the farmer as an active participant in irrigation and that

farmers' needs, as well as crops and soils, must be taken
into account in the system design, construction, and
operation. This directly involves institutional questions,
human management skills, and project implementation (Takase
1982; Levine 1980).

It is in this third stage where the importance of
institutional and organizational arrangements comes to the
fore.[2] What kinds of institutions will facilitate farmer
participation and high levels of production? Also what
institutions have farmers already developed to better utilize their irrigation water?

Although there are, at least, three levels of institutional and organizational arrangements involved, the most
important for direct farmer involvement are those dealing
with distribution of irrigation water and maintenance of the
irrigation system. Geographically, these institutions and
organizations are usually at the local or regional level.
Generally, they involve farmers, possibly in a water user
association. An irrigation department or bureau office in
charge of a particular sub-project is another example. The
success or failure of "management" is likely to be determined at the level where the farmer-user and the system
interact.

A second set of institutions and organizations are
those that directly affect distribution of costs and
benefits. These include both customary and legal institutions and organizations which deal with land tenure, crop
tenure, access to resources, division of production, access
to water, rights to water, and water pricing. This level of
institutions and organizations has considerable influence on
the attainment of management objectives in an irrigation
system and the eventual distribution of benefits. In fact,
if one is to influence the distribution of irrigation costs
and benefits, decisions concerning these institutions and
organizations have to be made at the design stage of the
project.

A third set of institutions and organizations is at the
national level. It consists both of organizations, such as
a ministry of irrigation or a national planning authority,
and of "rules" or ways of doing things. This includes such
things as how the central government decides to construct an
irrigation project, how the ministry of power and irrigation
decides to allocate water to irrigation rather than to power
generation and whether all signals come from the top down or
some come from the bottom up.

The study of institutional and organizational arrangements leads directly to questions of efficiency and equity
in the delivery of services, which may be the most critical

irrigation issue facing many countries. How to revitalize
institutions and organizations which have a negative effect
on productivity and how to develop new institutions or
organizations which improve irrigation efficiency and the
distribution of gains are crucial and unanswered questions
for most countries.

• Five general principles borrowed from Rawls (1971) have
been suggested for designing irrigation institutions:

1. Compatible liberty -- an equal right for all participants or the most extensive liberty compatible
   with similar liberty for others.
2. Knowledge and participation -- institutional
   systems widely understood by all participants.
3. Shared concept of justice -- general agreement on
   what is just and unjust.
4. Formal system of justice -- A justice system which
   is impartial and consistently administered.
5. Rational rules -- rules designed so that the self-
   interests of individuals lead people to act in ways
   which further desirable social ends (Bromley,
   et al. 1980).

Application of these principles, however, depends on
the basic "norms" of the society. Rawls' principles tend to
come out of the norm of northern Europe. But in this book,
we are dealing mainly with societies which have different
traditions and they may find Rawls' principles rather
strange. Thus one must be careful when judging or recom-
mending institutions for areas which have very different
traditions than those found in developed countries.

At best one may be able to suggest a set of questions
or criteria which should be satisfied concerning the institutional setting for irrigation development. For example,
is the disparity in land ownership and the underlying power
structure such that most of the benefits will go to the high
income groups? What changes in institutions or organizations are necessary if an irrigation project is to achieve
both equity and efficiency objectives? Do farmers have a
record of being able to work together to solve local problems? These and other questions concerning institutions and
organizations should be part of the overall evaluation of
project feasibility. Even if the benefit-cost ratio appears
satisfactory, the lack of appropriate institutional or
organizational arrangements may spell project failure.

National Water Institutions and Organizations

One important question with regard to institutions and organizations at the national level is: How should authority over water project planning and implementation be delegated? A number of authors argue that the most efficient form of administration is one in which all of the development activities within an irrigation project are coordinated by a single agency. In cases where separate departments exist whose authorities overlap, for example, a department of irrigation and a department of agriculture, conflicts arise and blame is placed on one for shortfalls perceived by the other. Delegation of responsibilities is a source of conflict between two such departments. This has led to recommendations that where both departments exist, one overseeing agricultural activities and one concerned with irrigation, they should be combined or one should be given overall responsibility. Yet such a merger can have serious consequences for existing government agencies and will be strongly resisted.

Taiwan has been able to develop an efficient irrigation system through a centralized planning of irrigation investment combined with decentralized management (Abel 1976). One of the keys to the early success of their irrigation management was the recognition by government that water was a scarce agricultural input. For irrigation to be effectively developed and used, efficient water use must have a high national priority.

If irrigation development activities are to be coordinated, the coordination should start at the national level. The existence of a national agency for overall coordination is crucial, especially for planning and evaluation of irrigation projects. In setting up such a unit, care must be taken to keep the planning and evaluation agency separate from the construction agencies. The experience in the United States with the Bureau of Reclamation and the U.S. Army Corps of Engineers is enough to highlight the problems created when a construction agency also does the planning and evaluation.[3] These are separate jobs with different incentives and should not be placed in the same agency (Easter and Waelti 1980).

Once efficient water use has been given high national priority the next step is to establish an agency with authority over water planning and evaluation. The agency will make decisions about the feasibility of large projects and the allocation of funds among projects and geographic areas of the country. The actual project proposals should come from the provincial or district level. The centralized agency usually does not have the data and information to develop projects for specific parts of the country. Project proposals should come from the regional or local level. Here the resource endowments, bottlenecks, and physical and social conditions are known and the government officials can directly interact with farmers.

Organizations for Water Distribution

It is widely agreed that effective organization and management of irrigation systems by informal or formal cooperative water user organizations (WUO) will increase the efficiency, equity, and productivity of irrigation projects. The existence of a WUO is a key asset in improving farmer cooperation in irrigation. In fact, a system could be developed to a stage where the government turns the water over to the WUO at some point in the system. It is likely to be difficult for farmers to take over much responsibility without an organization which can internalize the individual externalities involved in water allocation and canal main- tenance. The question is how to establish effective WUO to meet the project objectives and at the same time be adap- table to local conditions. In many cases, this means making use of informal WUO which farmers have already developed. There are many effective WUO which have been ignored by central governments (Poffenberger 1980).

In the irrigation associations of Taiwan much of the responsibility for decisions about water allocation and system maintenance is delegated to the users themselves. Although this institution was developed in a specific environment and is not widely applicable, the knowledge gained from the sequence of developments which took place in Taiwan may be useful in devising successful WUO elsewhere (Bottrall 1977).

Control and Ownership. One of the conditions under which these organizations developed in Taiwan was that of strict enforcement. Water user organizations were estab- lished by official decree and their rules were enforced by police power. Although this is a condition which may be undesirable to emulate, it does not rule out the possibility of using the Taiwan example as one possible pattern for WUO. It helps emphasize that, without strict control or strong leadership, successful WUO may be difficult to formally establish in areas which do not have a history of successful cooperatives (Duewel 1981).

A related major concern is how far control and owner- ship by a national or state agency should extend down the

irrigation system. At what point in time and space can the
farmers take charge of the water? In the case of large
irrigation systems constructed by the government, farmer
cooperation and control may be restricted to their own
immediate communities. The day-to-day management of the
main system is probably best in the hands of a technically
capable and impartial government or quasi-government agency.
Ideally, this agency should be responsive to farmers' needs.
In fact, farmer representatives should participate in the
development of each season's water allocation and in the
evaluation of the agency's day-to-day performance. The
farmer representatives should include a majority of tail-
enders and small-scale farmers (Bottrall 1981).

In smaller projects the level of farmer control should
be much higher. In fact, a system could be developed to a
stage where the government turns the water over to the WUO
at some point in the system. Coward in Chapter 13 shows
that when farmers control or own the irrigation system, they
take responsibility for and invest in the system. He argues
that ownership of irrigation facilities establishes, among
farmers, the property relationships which form the basis for
their collective action in using and maintaining the system.

Cooperation. As suggested above, a history of cooperation can replace the need for strict central control.

> The traditional moral obligation in the Japanese
> village community to cooperate in joint communal infra-
> structure maintenance has made it less costly to imple-
> ment rural development programs than in societies where
> such traditions do not prevail...Practices such as
> maintenance of village and agricultural roads and of
> irrigation and drainage ditches through joint acti-
> vities in which all families contributed labor were
> still practiced in well over half of the hamlets in
> Japan as recently as 1970 (Ishikawa 1981). The tradi-
> tional patterns of cooperation have represented an
> important cultural resource on which to erect modern
> forms of cooperative marketing and joint farming
> activities (Ruttan and Hayami 1984).

Chapter 11 includes an analysis of watercourses in
Pakistan which show that a history of cooperation had a
positive impact on the quality of maintenance. This supports the hypothesis that a group which has organized, and
is providing collective goods, has more at stake and the
members are more likely to understand the degenerative
effects of "freerider" behavior. Past cooperative activ-

ities can be expected to reduce the difficulties involved with establishing watercourse organizations (Sparling 1981).

Size. In smaller systems and in places where the farmers' management and technical capacities are well developed, the level of farmer cooperation in irrigation is much higher. Successful indigenous irrigation systems are established along the lines of an irrigation community which is not necessarily one and the same as the village community (Coward 1977).

The nature of groupings which farmers adopt in Philippine communal gravity systems and the ways in which they manage the irrigation has been found to vary with system size (De los Reyes 1980). The smaller the system, the more loosely organized the group managing it. Allocation procedures and system maintenance are greater tasks for larger schemes. Therefore, more complex methods are required to handle these tasks in larger irrigation projects.

Finance. The most frequently cited reason for the failure of Philippine communal associations was financial mismanagement (De los Reyes 1980). In northeast Thailand the lack of funds prevented WUO from playing a more important management role (Tubpun 1981). Two succesful lowland irrigation systems of central Java had a variety of sources which were used to finance irrigation. Membership fees, water charges, special levies on land owners, village funds, and revenues from village lands were all used to improve, maintain, and operate their irrigation systems. Both villages made major efforts to establish a sound financial footing for their irrigation (Duewel 1981). As discussed later in the chapter under water pricing, farmers served by communal irrigation systems are not averse to paying several different water charges. The whole question of methods for financing WUO and of their financial management needs to be addressed if WUO are to be effective on a wide scale.

Incentives. One of the necessary conditions for the formation of WUO to manage water collectively is water scarcity (Svendsen 1985). Water must be scarce in enough years so that farmers have a strong incentive to organize. This incentive will be weakened if the water supply can be increased with appeals for more water by local irrigators to government officials (Palanisami and Easter 1983).

Other incentives to organize may be necessary particularly if it is only downstream or tail- reach farmers who are faced with scarcity. These incentives could involve special assistance to farmers who have organized and made improvements in their irrigation system. Both the irrigation and agricultural departments should be involved in

providing incentives (Lowdermilk, et al. 1975). Finally, it
will be difficult to organize farmers unless the added
production which will result from improved management can be
marketed at reasonable prices.

Income Disparity and Leadership. A review of the
historical development of four farm level irrigation management systems in Indonesia found income distribution and
leadership as two important factors. The nature of village
values and leadership and the extent of economic and social
disparity within villages influenced the effectiveness of
farm level irrigation services. Local organizations in
communities with wide economic and social disparities were
less effective. It seems that in cases with wide disparities, there is a danger of conflicts of interest among
village leaders who seek to improve their personal welfare
at the expense of the community (Hutapea, et al. 1978).

A study of ten tanks in south India showed a direct
relationship between farm size variation and farmer cooperation in irrigation. The three tanks with the lowest farm
size variation had the highest level of cooperative management while the three with little or no cooperation had the
highest farm size variation (Palanisami and Easter 1983).

As will be discussed in Chapter 8, leadership was a
critical element in the effective use of water in three
small tanks in northeast Thailand. In fact, strong leadership in one tank made it the most productive tank in the
Khon Kaen area. In building organizations for the terminal
irrigation unit, identifying and keeping adequate leaders is
often a problem. For indigenous irrigation systems, traditional irrigation leaders serve relatively small groups of
water users, are selected by the local group which they
serve, and receive compensation directly from those they
serve (Coward 1977).

Boundaries and Location. Command areas often do not
coincide with village boundaries because of topographical
features. In cases where these boundaries do coincide,
irrigation systems are easier to manage and conflicts are
less likely. When possible, WUO should be established so
that their jurisdiction approaches, as nearly as possible,
that of both the village government and the command area
(Hutapea, et al. 1978). The question is how to do this and
what are the cost implications of such restructuring? In
many cases restructuring is not feasible and institutions
must be created which allow the WUO to function across
jurisdictional boundaries.

A related question is the location of the system relative to the village it serves, particularly if the project
is small. In Chapter 8 it is pointed out that the most

productive tank was located right next to the village. This allowed close supervision of the tank and enforcement of rules. Animals were prevented from damaging irrigation structures and fishing could be restricted to selected areas and times.

Technical Information. A major constraint to the efficient and equitable distribution of water is the absence of knowledge about irrigation technology. Effective information systems are needed which will permit the exchange of agronomic and water availability information between the WUO and the managers of the system. In most cases this requires an agricultural extension service and regular training sessions for farmers and agents about water use technology. Extension provides a way of combining some of the information disseminating efficiency of centralized control with the efficiency of decentralized decisions concerning special local situations. In addition, there must be some way of integrating and coordinating the activities of the agricultural extension service and those managing the irrigation system such as Easter (1977) found in Sambalpur, India. Without coordination, effective exchange of information will be hard to achieve.

Summary. The literature is quite consistent in identifying farmer involvement and decentralized decision making as two major water management issues. How do we get information and technology to the farmers and how can the farmer's management ability be used in distributing water? One of the preconditions for farmer cooperation and organization is water scarcity. Small units within large systems or small projects seem to be better able to develop cooperative irrigation. A past history of cooperation is also helpful as is a reasonably equal distribution of economic resources among irrigators. Village or group leaders and some continued source of finance are important to the success of a farmer organization.

Many of the factors which facilitate the organization of farmers relate to the assurance question, i.e., control, ownership, cooperation, and system size. Control and/or a history of cooperation provides farmers assurance that if they contribute to system maintenance, so will other farmers. Another example would be where strong leadership assures farmers that rules concerning water rotations or fishing will be followed by others. A key part of an effective WUO is to provide an institutional framework in which farmers are given assurance about the actions of other farmers.

Distribution of Benefits

The final level of institutional and organizational arrangements to be considered are those which directly affect the distribution of irrigation benefits such as the location of a farmer's fields along the irrigation watercourse, land ownership, water rights, and land tenure. A number of studies have found that farmers whose fields are furthest from the source of water frequently have the least secure water supplies. As the distance between water source and field increases, there is a greater cumulative effect of seepage and evaporation losses from delivery channels. There is also greater possibility for intervening irrigators to disturb intended water distribution as water flows from head-reaches to tail-reaches. The solutions suggested to alleviate this problem of location include strict water control, rotations, better maintenance practices, canal lining, land leveling, land reform, and measuring devices at the end of canals and ditches.

Decreases in water availability also occur along branch canals and distribution canals. The reasons are numerous: poor canal maintenance, a command area too large for the water available, and water stealing.

Conclusions drawn from the field study areas fully support evidence from elsewhere that serious deficiencies in water distribution practices are widespread in developing countries. In most cases a substantial proportion of overall inefficiency of water use could be attributed to shortcomings in main system management. Head-reach farmers were taking far more than their share of water on canals of area two and three, leaving tail-reach farmers with insufficient and unpredictable supplies (Bottrall 1981, p. 13).[4]

Radical changes in the structure of land ownership may have to accompany improvements in management and design if benefits of irrigation development are to reach the poorest farmers (Bottrall 1978). Case studies of areas which have experienced land reform are needed so that their influence on irrigation can be determined. Knowledge derived from such a study could be used to design and implement land reform programs before projects are constructed.

Another aspect of the distribution of benefits from irrigation is the impact on landless labor and input suppliers. For example, Adriano (1985) estimated the income distribution among four classes of Philippine earners: landlords, hired labor, farm operator, and input suppliers.

A comparison of income shares for rainfed and irrigated farms showed that hired labor had a decreased relative income share but an increased absolute income on irrigated farms. The input suppliers and farm operators had increased relative income shares while landowners had decreased relative shares. Also there was a decrease in family labor on the irrigated farms but an increase in hired labor.

The commonly cited direct beneficiaries -- small rice farmers and landless hired laborers -- are truly beneficiaries in terms of absolute income shares. The substantial absolute increase in labor's share of the income should not be overshadowed by the small decrease in labor's relative income (Adriano 1985, p. 159).

If equity is an important objective in irrigation, it requires deliberate attention. Three approaches have been suggested (Lazaro, et al. 1977). First, concentrate new irrigation in areas where farms are small and farmers are poor.

A strategy that emphasizes small-scale irrigation development would seem to contribute towards this end. Small-scale projects are usually found in rather remotely located areas where economic differences among farmers tend to be small and where economic development efforts usually receive low priority. Indonesia's program of small-scale sederhana irrigation may provide a contemporary illustration of such an approach...

Second, ensure that the views of disadvantaged irrigators receive recognition in irrigation decision-making ... Identifying precisely who the most disadvantaged are, and exploring ways of guaranteeing their rights in decisions on the design of further infrastructure or allocation, could contribute to ensuring greater equity in the distribution of water...

Third, analyze the distribution of benefits from alternative irrigation strategies. Relatively little emphasis seems to have been given to examining the effects of irrigation development on income distribution. Since such effects are of growing national concern in southeast Asia, their empirical examination would seem of high priority (Lazaro, et al. 1977, p. 11). [Underlined words added by authors.]

Although the research findings suggest that location, water rights, and land ownership can adversely or positively influence water distribution, additional analysis is needed to impress upon decision makers the importance of institutions and to show where changes are needed. Poorly managed systems will have farmers in the tail-reaches short of water. Irrigation projects with large differences in farm sizes will have an unequal distribution of benefits. Uncertain land or water rights will discourage farmers from making investments to improve their irrigation. Yet it is difficult to change institutions or organizations once the project is completed. The trick is to make the needed changes before water is delivered.

Water Pricing. Rules and procedures for water pricing will affect both the distribution of water and benefits. Charges for water can serve as instruments to resolve some of the conflicts related to the equitable distribution of irrigation services. In addition, water prices can help improve the efficiency of water distribution.

There are, at least, six general methods for levying water charges to cover the fixed and/or variable costs of irrigation (Seagraves and Easter 1983):

1. Direct charges based on measured volume of water.
2. Direct charges per share of the stream or canal flow, or per irrigation.
3. Direct charges per acre irrigated or potentially irrigated.
4. Indirect charges on crop outputs marketed or on inputs purchased such as fertilizer.
5. Development rebates or promotional water charges.
6. A general land or property tax.

Volumetric charges are only possible if water delivered to farmers can be measured. Charges based on shares received is best suited for rotating irrigations where water is delivered to the users along a canal in turns according to some prearranged schedule. Charges per acre are best fitted for continuous flow irrigation, where water flows continually in the main canal and farmers are free to take whatever quantity they need. This charge can either be the same for all farmers or varied by type of crop grown or by season. Indirect charges are used when ease of collection is an important objective. Development or promotional fees are used to encourage greater water utilization with lower fees at the start of a project. Finally, taxes or fees levied on all lands and property in the irrigated area are used when the objective is to distribute the cost of the project among all direct beneficiaries. The idea behind this tax is that irrigation increases economic activity throughout the areas and, therefore, everyone should pay for the benefits (Easter 1980). A more restricted land tax would be one just on the irrigated land. This is sometimes called a betterment levy and is based on the increase in land value due to irrigation.

Distribution systems for services such as water are often described as natural monopolies because larger volumes result in lower unit costs and it would be wasteful to have competing systems serving the same customers. Many economists argue that society should regulate the prices of such natural monopolies using marginal cost pricing. The water price should be set to equal the long- run marginal cost (the average total cost of the newest project) when the demand for water is expanding and the present facilities are fully utilized. A short-run marginal cost should be used if facilities are used below capacity. In this case the price should be equal to the short- run marginal costs of delivering water which includes only the operating and maintenance costs (Seagraves and Easter 1983).

Both national governments and international agencies are deeply concerned about policies for pricing irrigation water particularly in terms of repayment. Yet many problems exist in implementing a system of water charges. Official rates of irrigation assessments do no reflect actual payments. Water charges cannot be expected to provide incentives for more efficient water use unless they are based on the quantity of water used. Policies for financing irrigation projects need to account for the full range of irrigation beneficiaries from land owners to local businessmen. Water charges should be decided within the context of overall government agricultural development policy which may involve food subsidies or taxes on farmers (Lazaro, et al. 1977). Bowen and Young in Chapter 12 also point out that the transactions costs involved with different water pricing systems must be considered.

In project repayment a package approach should be considered for extracting funds from various beneficiaries. Direct taxes could be assessed against direct beneficiaries and production-related indirect beneficiaries, and indirect taxes against the general public who enjoy low cost irrigated agricultural commodities. The pricing system should also fit the conditions facing a particular country and project and should change with development. Indirect water charges coupled with close administrative control over water distribution may be best in the initial phase of a project when farmers are inexperienced in irrigation. As farmers gain more experience, the system could be converted to a system of fixed and variable water charges. In more highly industrialized countries, water prices can even be based on equilibrium prices (Doppler 1977).

Finally, farmers are more likely to pay charges or fees for specific purposes rather than for general purposes which suggests a strategy of local collection and utilization of fees.

In some communal irrigation systems, several different fees for specific purposes have been established. Although this adds complexity to the process of collecting and accounting for the funds for irrigation, the farmers involved apparently feel that the benefits associated with the greater incentives for payment outweigh these problems (Small 1982, p. 7).

Although there is much support for the use of some form of water charge to ensure the efficient and equitable distribution of water, such a charge is impractical without the necessary infrastructure to accompany it. Rules have to be made and prices estimated for water and irrigation services. An organization is required to determine and enforce these regulations and collect the charges. This organization will need information concerning the area and crops irrigated by farm.

The inability to collect water charges from higher income farmers has led many to argue against water charges of any kind in developing countries. Some type of volumetric measure of water delivered is also necessary if water pricing is to help improve water allocation, which requires devices that are often expensive and thus prohibitive in many schemes. A possible solution to this dilemma is to locate measuring devices at the head of each branch canal and to charge "branch canal water user associations" an aggregate fee for water delivered to that point (Easter 1975). This would necessitate strong leadership and effective organization in the form of a formal or informal WUO. They would be responsible for delivering the water in the branch canal and for collecting the fees from each user.

NOTES

1. <u>Warabandi</u> is spelled two different ways in this book. In the references to the irrigation systems of north

India it is spelled <u>Warabandi</u>. However, for the same types of systems in Pakistan it is spelled <u>Warabundi</u>. This difference in spelling probably relates back to the attempts of the British to translate the local language into English.

2. Institutions are broadly defined in this paper to include ways of doing things as well as legal and contractual arrangements for organizing activities and distributing property. Organizational arrangements involve how firms or government agencies do things. Institutions help define organizations through laws and administrative decisions which establish principles and guidelines for their formation and conduct. Institutions are collective conventions and rules which establish acceptable standards for individual and group behavior, reducing individual uncertainty concerning the action of others.

3. The Water Resources Council is an example of an agency established to coordinate water development across several powerful agencies involved in water development. Their record should help make the point that it is almost impossible to effectively coordinate water development spread over numerous agencies. The real solution is to include irrigation development as part of the responsibilities of a department or ministry of agriculture. But, as we all know, this requires some difficult political decisions.

4. There are several studies which have failed to find any yield differences between farmers in the head-reaches and in the tail-reaches of the canals (Taylor 1981; Tubpun 1981). Tubpun felt that differences in soil quality may have masked the locational differences. Taylor found that infrastructure intensity did not necessarily improve water distribution equity.

REFERENCES

Abel, Martin E. 1976. "Irrigation systems in Taiwan: Management of a decentralized public enterprise." <u>Water Resources Research</u> 12:341-48.

Adriano, Marietta S. 1985. "Impact of labor intensity and income distribution of the Sibalom Irrigation Project." In <u>Irrigation Management: Research from Southeast Asia</u>, (ed.) T. Wickham, pp. 141-59. A/D/C Workshop (1981), Kampangsaen, Thailand.

54

Bottrall, Anthony F. 1981. "Comparative study of the management and organization of irrigation projects." World Bank Staff Working Paper No. 458.

_____. 1977. "Evolution of irrigation associations in Taiwan." Agricultural Administration 4(4):245-50.

_____. 1978. "Technology and management in irrigated agriculture." O.D.I. Review 2:22-50.

Bromley, Daniel W., Donald C. Taylor, and Donald E. Parker. 1980. "Water reform and economic development: Institutional aspects of water management in the developing countries." Economic Development and Cultural Change 28(2):365-87.

Coward, E.W. 1977. "Irrigation management alternatives: Themes from indigenous irrigation systems." Agricultural Adminstration 4(3):223-37.

De los Reyes, Ramona P. 1980. "Managing communal gravity systems: Farmers' approaches and implications for program planning." Institute of Philippine Culture, Ateneo de Manila University, Quezon City.

Doppler, W. 1977. "Towards a general guidelines of irrigation water charging policy." Agricultural Administration 4(2):121-29.

Duewel, John. 1981. "Promoting participatory approaches to cultivating water users associations: Two case studies from Java." A/D/C Workshop, Bangkok.

Easter, K. William. 1980. "Capturing the economic surplus created by irrigation." Staff Paper P80-14, Department of Agricultural and Applied Economics, University of Minnesota.

_____. 1977. "Improving village irrigation systems: An example from India." Land Economics 53(1):56-66.

_____. 1975. "Field channels: A key to better Indian irrigation." Water Resources Research 11(3):389-92.

Easter, K. William, and John J. Waelti. 1980. The Application of Project Analysis to Natural Resource Decisions. WRRC Bulletin 103, Chapter 2. University of Minnesota.

Gopalakrishnayya, K. 1979. "An integrated approach to command area development programme." Indian Journal of Public Administration 25(1):74-85.

Hutapea, R., Prajarta Dirjasanyata, and N.G.S. Nordholt. 1978. "The organization of farm-level irrigation in Indonesia." In Irrigation Policy and Management in Southeast Asia, pp. 167-74. A/D/C, Bangkok.

Ishikawa, Shigeru. 1981. Essays on Technology, Employment and Institutions in Economic Development, pp. 325-47. Kinokuniya, Tokyo.

Kelso, Maurice M., William E. Martin, and Lawrence E. Mack. 1973. Water Supplies and Economic Growth in an Arid Environment. The University of Arizona Press, Tucson.

Lazaro, Rogelio, D.C. Taylor, and T.H. Wickham. 1977. Irrigation Systems in Southeast Asia: Policy and Management Issues. Teaching and Research Forum Seminar Report #6. A/D/C, Singapore.

Levine, Gilbert. 1980. "Irrigation development and strategy issues for the Asian region." Draft of Issues paper submitted to USAID. Cornell University.

Lowdermilk, M.K., Wayne Clyma, and Alan C. Early. 1975. Physical and Socioeconomic Dynamics of a Watercourse in Pakistan's Punjab: System Constraints and Farmers' Responses. Technical Report No. 42, Colorado State University, Fort Collins.

Maass, Arthur, and Raymond L. Anderson. 1978. ... and the Desert Shall Rejoice. The M.I.T. Press, Cambridge, Massachusetts.

Malhotra, S.P. 1981. The Warabandi System and Its Infrastructure. Publication Number 157, Central Board of Irrigation and Power, New Delhi, India.

Mirza, Ashaq H., David M. Freeman, and Jerry B. Eckert. 1974. Village Organization Factors Affecting Water Management Decision-Making Among Punjabi Farmers. Water Management Technical Report No. 35, Colorado State University, Fort Collins.

Palanisami, K., and K. William Easter. 1983. The Tanks of South India (A Potential for Future Expansion in Irrigation). Economic Report ER83-4, Department of Agricultural and Applied Economics, University of Minnesota. 137p.

Palanisami, K. 1981. "Problems of water distribution and management at outlet level: A case of Lower Bhawani Project, Coimbatore District." Workshop on Problems and Research Methods in Irrigation Systems Related to the Chak (Outlet) Requirements, Gandhian Institute of Studies. Rajghat-Varanasi, India.

_____. 1980. An Economic Evaluation of the Working of the Major Surface Irrigation Systems in Tamil Nadu: A Case of Parambikulam Aliyar Project. Research Report, Department of Agricultural Economics, Tamil Nadu Agricultural University, Coimbatore, India.

Poffenberger, Mark. 1980. "A feasibility study for a beneficiary evaluation of the Sederhana Irrigation Program." Counterpart Consultants, Inc. for USAID, Jakarta.

Rawls, John. 1971. A Theory of Justice. Harvard University Press, Cambridge, Massachusetts.

Reidinger, Richard B. 1974. "Institutional rationing of canal water in northern India: Conflict between traditional patterns and modern needs." Economic Development and Cultural Change 23:79-104.

Ruttan, Vernon W., and Yujiro Hayami. 1984. "Toward a theory of induced institutional innovation." Paper No. 200, Center for Economic Research, Department of Economics, University of Minnesota.

Seagraves, J.A., and K. William Easter. 1983. "Pricing for irrigation water in developing countries." Water Resources Bulletin 19(4):663-72.

Small, Leslie E. 1982. "Investment decisions for the development and utilization of irrigation resources in southeast Asia." Teaching and Research Forum Workshop Report #26, pp. 1-9. A/D/C, New York.

Sparling, Edward W. 1981. "Collective goods and conflict: An example of a positive feedback mechanism at work in rural Pakistan." Department of Economics, Colorado State University, Fort Collins.

Svendsen, Mark. 1985. "Group behavior of farmers in three types of Philippine irrigation systems." In Irrigation Management: Research from Southeast Asia, (ed.) T. Wickham, pp. 87-101. A/D/C Workshop (1981), Kampangsaen, Thailand.

Takase, Kunio. 1982. "Food production and Irrigation development in Asia." ADB Quarterly Review.

Taylor, D.C. 1981. The Economics of Malaysian Paddy Production and Irrigation. A/D/C, Bangkok, Thailand.

Taylor, D.C., and Kanaengnid Tantigate. 1985. "The economics of irrigation scheduling for the Kemubu agricultural development project in Malaysia." In Irrigation Management: Research from Southeast Asia, (ed.) T. Wickham, pp. 162-82. A/D/C Workshop (1981), Kampangsaen, Thailand.

Tubpun, Yuavares. 1981. "Economics of tank irrigation projects in northeastern Thailand." Ph.D. Thesis, Department of Agricultural and Applied Economics, University of Minnesota.

CHAPTER 4

IRRIGATION DEVELOPMENT NEEDS IN INDIA

R.K. Sivanappan and V. Rajagopalan

Indian farmers will have to produce 225 million tons of foodgrains to feed 935 million people by the turn of the present century. This will be an increase of 73 percent over the 1982 production of 130 million tons. The demand and supply projections are given in Tables 4.1 and 4.2. This would imply that production strategies, policies, and organizational changes would also have to be initiated which would support the efforts to produce that quantity of food. According to the National Commission on Agriculture, the major emphasis will be to achieve the following by 2000:

1. Increase the area under irrigation by 20.7 million ha over the 1970-1971 level.
2. Launch the Command Area Development Authority Program (CADA) on 22 million ha.
3. Introduce a massive program to improve dry farming methods on an additional area of 40 million ha.
4. Increase the use of fertilizers by 10.2 million tons of nutrients over the 1970-1971 level.
5. Expand the spread of the high yielding varieties (HYV) by 98.05 million ha over the 1970-1971 base.

Additional foodgrain production of 126 million tons is expected by 2000 from the above programs (Table 4.3). The area to be brought under irrigation will reach 42.7 million ha by 2000 from the first two sources (irrigation and CADA). This would be an increase in area under irrigation of 68 percent over the base period, 1970-1971.

TABLE 4.1
Demand projections for foodgrains in India: Aggregate consumer demand (in million tons)[a,b]

Crops	1971 (Base)	1985 Low	1985 High	2000 Low	2000 High
Rice	38.74	52.40	56.60	68.76	73.98
Wheat	20.85	29.60	33.39	41.04	45.89
Other cereals	24.40	30.93	30.73	37.79	37.53
Pulses	10.32	14.83	17.73	20.70	24.70
Total foodgrains	94.31	127.76	138.45	168.29	182.10
Total foodgrains and feedgrains[c]		130.30	162.90	205.30	225.10

[a]Based on the nutritional consideration, the total foodgrain demand consists of 84 percent demand for cereal and 16 percent demand for pulses.

[b]Population (million):
  1971 - 547
  1986 - 734
  2000 - 935

Low: Annual growth rate of per capita private consumption expenditure at 1 percent.
High: Annual growth rate of per capita private consumption expenditure at 2 percent.

[c]Besides foodgrains this total includes seed demand, feedgrain, and industrial use and wastage.

TABLE 4.2
Supply projections for foodgrains in India (in million tons)

Crops	1971/72 (Base)	1985	2000
Rice	41.9	61	80
Wheat	23.5	41	50
Other cereals	27.5	40	65
Pulses	11.5	22	35
Total foodgrains	104.4	164	230

IRRIGATION IN INDIA

Surface Water

There are eight major river systems in India with an average annual flow of 180 million ha meters of which 70 million ha meters are utilized. The percentage of utilization varied between rivers or groups of rivers, with the highest being 80 percent in the Indus Basin and the lowest being 12 percent for the Narmada and Tapi system.

There is significant scope for increasing the area under irrigation. The distribution of irrigation potential by state and source is presented in Table 4.4. Between the years 1970-1971 and 2025, the irrigated area could be increased from 38.5 million ha to 110 million ha, -- a jump of 186 percent. Of the 71.5 million ha increase, 64 percent would be surface water and 36 percent would be ground water irrigation.

TABLE 4.3
Projections of additional foodgrains produced by selected program sectors

Program Sectors	Additional Area Over The Base Period[a]		Additional Production Over The Base Period	
	1985	2000	1985	2000
	(million ha)		(million tons)	
Irrigation	15.0	20.7	7.5	10.4
Command area development programs	7.0	22.0	2.1	6.6
Dry farming methods	8.0	40.0	1.4	7.0
	(million tons)[b]			
Fertilizer use	4.9	10.2	49.0	102.0
Total added production over the base year			60.0	126.0

Source: Report of First National Commission on Agriculture, 1976, Vol. III.V.

[a]Base period 1970-1971.
[b]Million tons of nutrients.

Ground Water

There are several estimates of ground water potential prepared by various agencies. Estimates of a recent study are given in Table 4.5 which show only 29 percent of the potential was exploited by 1980. There are also wide interstate variations ranging from over-exploitation (105 percent) in Haryana to only a 4 percent utilization in

TABLE 4.4
Scope for development of irrigation in India (million ha)[a]

State	Years 2025	Years 1970/71	Balance	Surface Water	Ground Water
Uttar Pradesh	24.0	8.4	15.6	7.4	8.2
Bihar	13.1	2.7	10.4	7.0	3.4
Madhya Pradesh	9.1	1.5	7.6	5.2	2.4
Andhra Pradesh	10.2	4.2	6.0	4.5	1.5
Orissa	6.7	1.6	5.1	3.7	1.4
Maharashtra	6.5	1.7	4.8	3.9	0.9
Karnataka	5.9	1.4	4.5	3.2	1.3
West Bengal	5.5	1.5	4.0	1.5	2.5
Gujarat	5.0	1.3	3.7	3.2	0.5
Rajasthan	4.8	2.5	2.3	1.8	0.5
Kerala	2.6	0.6	2.0	1.7	0.3
Assam	2.5	0.6	1.9	1.2	0.7
Haryana	3.3	2.2	1.1	0.6	0.5
Punjab	5.0	4.2	0.8	0.2	0.6
Tamil Nadu	4.0	3.4	0.6	0.1	0.5
Jammu and Kashmir	0.7	0.3	0.4	0.2	0.2
All other states and union territories	1.1	0.4	0.7	0.6	0.1
Total	110.0	38.5	71.5	46.0	25.5

[a] The figures for 1970-1971 are taken from Indian Agriculture in Brief, 13th edition, published by the Ministry of Agriculture and Irrigation, New Delhi, India. Other figures have been derived from the data given in the Report of the Irrigation Commission (1972), the draft of India's fifth Five Year Plan, and information published or supplied by the states and central ministries.

TABLE 4.5
Ground water potential by state, 1980 (million ha meters)

State	Gross Recharge[a]	Recoverable Recharge (70 Percent of Column 2)	Existing Net Extraction	Ground Water Balance	State of Ground Water Development, 1980 (percent)
Andhra Pradesh	4.61	3.22	0.72	2.50	22
Assam	1.36	0.95	0.01	0.94	9
Bihar	2.91	2.03	0.74	1.29	36
Gujarat	1.63	1.14	0.48	0.66	42
Haryana	0.77	0.59	0.62	0.03(-)	105
Jammu and Kashmir	0.25	0.17	0.01	0.16	6
Karnataka	1.37	1.11	0.15	0.96	14
Kerala	1.05	0.75	0.03	0.70	4
Madhya Pradesh	8.20	5.74	0.42	5.32	7

Maharashtra	4.93	3.45	0.87	2.78	19
Punjab	1.40	0.98	0.89	0.09	91
Orissa	1.95	1.36	0.10	1.26	7
Rajasthan	1.43	1.00	0.37	0.63	37
Tamil Nadu	2.60	1.82	1.35	0.47	74
Uttar Pradesh	9.58	6.71	2.53	4.18	38
West Bengal	2.15	1.50	0.43	1.07	29
Total	46.00	32.20	9.54	22.66	29

Source: S.P. Sangal, Ground Water Resources and Development in India, December 1980.

[a]The revised figures of gross recharge in Column 2 are as reported by state ground water organizations (SGO) and are based upon the revised norms for ground water evaluation as recommended by the Over-exploitation Committee.

Kerala. The Punjab and Tamil Nadu are the only other states with high levels of exploitation.

The degree of exploitation of ground water in various states needs careful scrutiny. In some cases, detailed studies may have to be done at the block level. For instance, those blocks, where the ground water development is between 80 and 100 percent of the net availability, need well-designed studies and assessments of ground water to prevent its over-exploitation and to improve resource use efficiency.

Irrigation Investment

Irrigation development continues to register top priority with irrigation potential estimated at about 58 million ha at the end of 1979-1980. This accounts for roughly 50 percent of the gross ultimate potential of 110 million ha. Total investment in irrigation from the beginning of the planning era, 1951-1978, amounted to approximately Rs. 93 billion ($1 = Rs. 10) on major, medium, and minor projects. Expenditure on irrigation in future plans, in order to reach the ultimate target potential by the year 2000, will be substantial.

Total investment in major and medium projects during the period from 1950-1951 to 1977-1978 was Rs. 54.5 billion. The area under minor irrigation increased during this period by 14.4 million ha partly as a result of Rs. 20.0 billion in public sector outlays and Rs. 18.1 billion in institutional credit extended to cultivators by the land development banks, commercial banks, and cooperative banks with financing through the Agricultural Refinance Development Corporation. In addition, there was a sizable investment in minor irrigation by farmers themselves.

The sixth Five Year Plan (1980-1985) envisaged creation of an additional irrigation potential of 15 million ha. A public sector investment of Rs. 67 billion in major and medium projects will irrigate 6.5 million ha. The remaining 8.5 million ha comes from minor irrigation projects with a direct public sector investment of Rs. 14.1 billion, an investment by credit institutions of Rs. 22.0 billion, and a Rs. 10.0 billion investment by farmers themselves. The main emphasis is on higher utilization of the existing potential, speedy completion of ongoing projects, and efficient maintenance of the existing irrigation systems.

Potential for Improving Irrigation

In India, 45 percent of the total quantity of irrigation water is used for growing rice. Although the evapo-
transpiration of rice is 600 to 800 mm per season, the total
quantity of water used for growing rice varies from 1500 to
3000 mm. By adopting better irrigation management, it is
possible to save 30 percent of the water without affecting
the yield. For other crops such as cotton, sugarcane, vegetables, and other row crops different irrigation methods
such as border, furrow, and check basin are being adopted.
The new innovations of alternate furrow and skip furrow
irrigation are best for row crops and could save 30 to 50
percent of the irrigation water used in conventional
methods.

The advanced irrigation methods such as drip irrigation
and sprinkler irrigation have not yet developed in India due
to the high initial investment. There is a potential for
introducing drip irrigation into selected areas of India
where high-valued crops are grown. It is now being practiced only on government farms and agricultural university
farms on an experimental basis. The Government of India
(GOI) has appointed a National Committee on the Use of
Plastics in Agriculture (NCPA) in order to promote and
popularize drip irrigation among Indian farmers.

Command Area Development Authority (CADA)

Realizing that optimum development of the irrigation
potential requires careful and systematic administration of
water distribution and water management practices, the GOI
in 1973 called on the states to establish CADA. Their goal
was to modernize on-farm irrigation canals and other infrastructure such as markets and village-to-market roads and to
strengthen the organization of agricultural extension.
Forty-four CADA are now functioning in sixty major irrigation projects traversing a cultivable area of more than
13 million ha. The idea of command development area was
conceived as an integrated approach to optimizing irrigated
agricultural production. The components of CADA include:

1. Modernization and efficient operation of irrigation
   systems as well as development of drainage systems
   beyond 40 ha blocks.
2. Construction of irrigation and drainage channels
   including lining of channels.

3. Land shaping and land leveling with consolidation of holdings.
4. Exploitation of ground water through installation of wells.
5. Adoption of suitable cropping patterns.
6. Enforcement of appropriate irrigation rotation systems.
7. Timely supply of inputs to farmers.
8. Strengthening the existing extension training and demonstration organization.

Tubewell Corporation

The GOI has advised the states to form state tubewell corporations to assist in the development and utilization of ground water resources. These organizations will identify and exploit ground water potentials and augment ground water supplies. Tubewells and open wells will be constructed for agricultural and industrial purposes.

On-Farm Development (OFD)

There is a large potential for saving irrigation water and increasing the irrigated areas by using on-farm land development and water management practices. The OFD program practices include land consolidation, land reclamation, land leveling, soil conservation measures, irrigation water management measures, input supplies, and extension services. Water management measures include lining of channels, provision of control and regulation structures, equitable distribution of irrigation water among farmers, and the introduction of Warabandi or other rotational systems of irrigation in canal and tank irrigated command areas. The overall program focus is on increasing production efficiency, income generation, and levels of living.

Irrigation Project Administration

Irrigation development continues to be a state subject and public irrigation projects, except for a few very large interstate projects, are designed, constructed and managed by state public works and irrigation departments. The Central Water Commission was established to set standards, review and monitor plans, and implement projects involving the development of interstate rivers with the Ministry of Irrigation and Power.

Ground water development was managed by the Exploratory Tubewells Organization established in the Ministry of Agriculture in 1954 with USAID financing and technical assistance. This has now become the Central Groundwater Board which is responsible for macro-level hydrological investigation, deep exploratory drilling, and monitoring water table behavior.

IRRIGATION IN TAMIL NADU ₜ

Water resources have become limiting for agricultural development in Tamil Nadu. Nearly 90 percent of surface flow has been harnessed for development of irrigated agriculture. However, because of interstate dispute over sharing of water from the Cauvery River, the surface flow has been uncertain. The uncertainty in the minds of farmers concerning water deliveries has had a devastating impact on food production in the state. Even with difficult water management problems, there are favorable trends concerning the farmers' perceptions of water as a productive resource and the need for improved water management. The major trends are:

1. Willingness of farmers to take on-farm managment seriously and invest in additional irrigation structures.
2. Recognition of the need for conjunctive water use supported by state, cooperative, and commercial bank financing.
3. Changing attitudes towards flexible cropping and agricultural systems which optimize land and water productivity.
4. Readiness to cooperate in water management at the macro and micro levels in order to minimize water losses.

Tank irrigation in the state has been given new emphasis in areas of unstable rainfall where tanks provide an important source of supplementary irrigation. Yet most of the tanks are old and plagued by problems of inadequate maintenance, encroachment and inefficient water allocation. Thus, as will be discussed in the next two chapters, rehabilitation of thousands of tanks has the potential of increasing and stabilizing irrigation over a wide area of the state.

Tamil Nadu has a high level of ground water utilization and one of the largest number of pumpsets. Because of an early start in ground water exploitation, some of the hard rock areas found in Coimbatore and Salem are experiencing ground water 'mining' which has led to rising costs of pumping and consequent adjustments in farming systems. In alluvial areas which have recently been subject to water scarcity, tubewells have expanded rapidly providing both irrigation and drainage.

POLICY OPTIONS

Given the natural, human, and institution resource endowments and recognizing the progress made in research and development for agriculture and irrigation, it is clear that efforts to increase foodgrain production will have to encompass efforts to improve and expand irrigation. The critical task will be to match technologies with resources and to design appropriate management strategies and policies. The major focus should be on restructuring the existing irrigation systems to optimize resource use efficiency and to ensure equity in distribution of irrigation benefits. Historically, irrigation systems seem to have been conceived purely as engineering models for impounding water and controlling water flows. The major concern was reservoir and canal management whereas aspects of field level water management received very little attention. But these efforts have not solved many of the management problems associated with the main system.

The policy framework for efficient development and utilization of water resources should therefore include: (a) land and water policies, (b) research and development, and (c) training.

Land and Water Policies

Land and water policies are complex and involve cultural, social, and political issues. Development strategies involving land and water tend to be sub-optimal from an economic efficiency perspective because of social and political considerations. The general aspects of the policy should include the following:

1. Land and water management problems must be viewed as a whole and cannot be considered in isolation from each other. For example, land consolidation and land reform should be implemented before irrigation is provided for an area.

2. Top priority should be given to maintaining and replenishing ground water resources since over 40 percent of the irrigated area is from ground water.

3. Water conservation is another top priority and should be implemented to the maximum extent economically feasible. The prevention of soil erosion by water should form one corner stone of any water policy.

4. The rainfall should be used for raising crops where possible and irrigation should be used to make up water deficiencies when they exist.

5. Soils should be protected against flood damage and water-logging.

6. Conjunctive use of surface and ground water should be improved.

7. Cropping patterns must be developed and promoted which best fit the soil, climate, water availability, and other farming conditions.

8. On-farm irrigation management must have greater emphasis. Suitable on-farm irrigation development approaches must be devised.

9. Advanced methods of irrigation such as drip and sprinkler systems have to be introduced at appropriate locations. Underground pipelines and prefabricated channels should be used for conveyance of irrigation water where economically suitable.

10. A large number of demonstrations should be conducted on small and marginal farms to induce farmers to change to more profitable methods of cultivation.

11. The policy for regulating water fees should include consideration of the additional net benefit to cultivators and the operation and maintenance costs of the irrigation project. More specifically the fee could range from 20 to 50 percent of the additional net benefit or from 5 to 12 percent of the gross crop income.

12. In order to conserve water, the water charges should be imposed on a volume basis where feasible. When this is not possible, water fees should be levied on the basis of area cropped.

13. After construction and maintenance of field
    channels the most important priority is to
    establish and enforce field level water delivery
    schedules, particularly for those farmers in the
    tail-reaches.
14. The existing turn system of delivery in command
    areas induces the farmers to use more water than is
    needed. Also the administration of the turn system
    remains haphazard, which results in inefficient
    water use. New systems of scheduling such as
    Warabandi need to be tested and tried in many
    states of India.

Research and Development

Continuous research on and development of water
resources is essential for full utilization of these
resources. Furthermore, most important research findings
need to be transferred more quickly to the field by
extension agencies and problems encountered from the fields
brought back to scientists. This will require better
coordination and cooperation among scientists, extension
agencies, and farmers.

The major concern in irrigation research is the inadequate focus on social, economic, and political issues which
affect the basic tenets of efficiency and equality in
irrigation water allocation and management. As discussed in
the last chapter, case studies of institutions, their roles,
organizational patterns, and functional styles are needed to
help design policies and strategies for obtaining greater
farmer participation all along the irrigation chain from
dams to farm ditches.

Project evaluation and management strategies at various
levels should be closely coordinated among engineers,
irrigation bureaucrats, social scientists, and farmers.
Success of these strategies will depend on comprehensive
research and evaluation of many alternatives including the
likely farmer response.

Training

At present, appropriate technology and improved methods
of on-farm water management are not effectively reaching
most Indian farmers. Government officials and administrators and personnel from international donor agencies have
reached a consensus that there is a need for intensive

training to upgrade professional skills of personnel in the
Irrigation and Agriculture departments. Specifically, this
would include officers of the irrigation bureaucracy such as
chief engineers, superintending engineers, middle-level
officers, junior engineers, field-level workers, luscars,
and agricultural extension personnel. Ultimately, it is the
farmer who will need training in water management skills and
this must also be provided.

REFERENCES

Bottrall, Anthony F. 1981. "Improving canal management:
    The role of evaluation and action research." Water
    Supply and Management 5:67-69.
Government of India. 1981. Command Area Development
    Programme in India -- Achievements and Perspectives.
    Ministry of Irrigation, Government of India.
_____. 1976. Report of First National Commission on
    Agriculture. Ministry of Agriculture and Irrigation,
    New Delhi, India.
_____. 1972. Report of the Irrigation Commission.
    Vol. 1, Ministry of Irrigation and Power, New Delhi,
    India.
Lenton, Robert L. 1980. "Field experiments in irrigation
    development and management" (mimeograph). Ford
    Foundation, New Delhi, India.
Sangal, S.P. 1980. "Ground water resources and development
    in India" (mimeograph). Agriculture Refinance and
    Development Corporation, Bombay, India.
Sivanappan, R.K. 1984. "Land and water use in India."
    Land Use Policy 1(1).
_____. 1982. "Management of available water
    resources" (mimeograph).
_____. 1980. "Special issue on CAD programmes."
    Kurukshetra 26(24).
_____. 1980. "Water resources development in India"
    (mimeograph). American Embassy, New Delhi, India.

CHAPTER 5

ALTERNATIVES FOR IMPROVING SMALL-SCALE IRRIGATION SYSTEMS IN ALFISOL WATERSHEDS IN INDIA

M. von Oppen, K.V. Subba Rao, and T. Engelhardt

SOURCES OF IRRIGATION

India derives its irrigation water essentially from three sources, i.e., (1) tanks[1], (2) canals, and (3) wells. Each source was developed at different times in history in response to demands for irrigated land and to the availability of technologies for storing, transporting, and lifting water. In different regions these sources vary in importance depending upon conditions such as climate, topography, technology, hydrology, and local administration. Even in the last thirty years, very important changes in shares have occurred in the distribution of irrigation by source across India with well irrigation showing the major increase (Figure 5.1).

Tanks

Tanks constitute the oldest means of providing irrigation water through systematic storage of runoff water, controlled release and distribution by gravity. Many tanks are centuries if not millennia old. For instance, the bulk of present tank irrigated area in Tamil Nadu existed a century ago. At the all-India level, tank irrigation was still expanding in the early 1960s; however, since then the area irrigated from tanks has been stagnant and decreased in many areas (Figure 5.2). Not only did the area irrigated by tanks shrink but it also became less stable. An analysis using the moving coefficient of variation (MCV) (eight years) of tank irrigated area and of rainfall from 1958-1965 to 1968-1975 for districts in Andhra Pradesh and Tamil Nadu shows considerable decreases in the stability of the tank irrigated area. This was particularly true in all districts

73

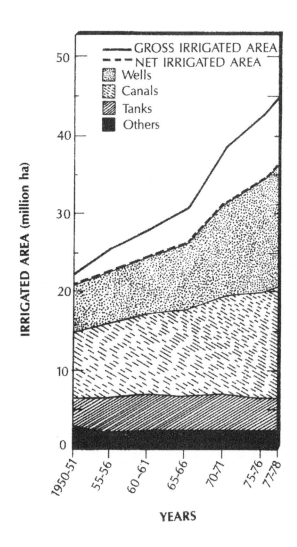

Figure 5.1 Area irrigated by source in India

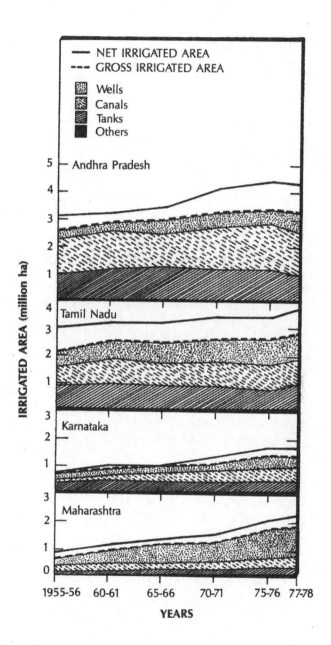

Figure 5.2 Irrigated area by source in selected Indian states

with a high proportion of tank irrigated area to total net irrigated area (von Oppen 1978). A good example is Warangal district in Andhra Pradesh state (Figure 5.3). Over the past two decades tank irrigation in India has degenerated not only in absolute area but also as a source of stability.

Canals

Large-scale canal irrigation began to develop about 100 years ago when more massive capital investments in irrigation became feasible. Under British rule these investments were based upon the economic interests in irrigated agriculture for export goods (Whitcombe 1971). After Independence, the interest was in irrigation to sustain self-sufficiency in food production (Abbie, et al. 1982). The construction of large-scale irrigation systems continues. However, enthusiasm for large-scale irrigation systems has been dampened by mounting costs as only the less favorable sites remain available, by disputes over water rights between neighboring states or neighboring countries, and by increasing long run problems (siltation, salinity, and delays in construction).

Wells

Until fairly recently, well irrigation was constrained by the source of power, with animal and human power being the major sources available for lifting the water. However, with advances in small engines, water lifting became simple and cheap. Consequently, the area under well irrigation expanded rapidly, especially after tubewells became popular in the 1960s. Since about 1973 the well irrigated area has surpassed the area irrigated by canals.

During the 1980s well irrigation is, again, running up against constraints. First, in many areas water availability is limited and ground water tables are falling as a result of well irrigation. Second, increasing shortfalls of diesel oil and electricity are limiting the power supply for well irrigation.

WAYS TO STABILIZE AND INCREASE WATER SUPPLY

In the following, two different possibilities are explored for improving tank and well irrigation on alfisol

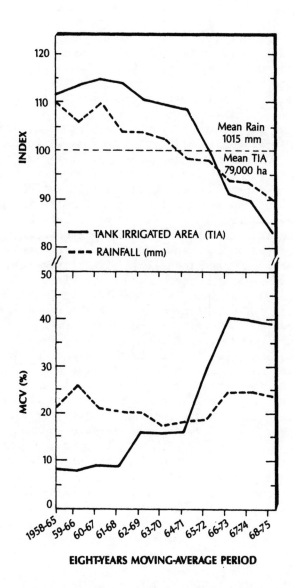

Figure 5.3 Indices (mean area and rainfall) = 100 and variability of rainfall and tank-irrigated area, Warangal District, India

watersheds.[2] These could be implemented individually or
jointly as the local conditions permit.

First, most tanks, even if they are in good condition
and receive runoff quite regularly, are not being managed
properly since there is no systematic release of water for
irrigation. The efficiency of water use of most tanks could
probably be increased by having a water controller who opens
and closes the sluice gate according to daily water requirements. A set of simple rules and a supervisory body would
have to be provided for necessary guidance to the water
controller.

Second, wherever an irrigation tank has a record of
poor performance because of factors such as siltation, lack
of runoff or unresolvable disputes over water rights and
encroachments, it might be preferable to abandon the tank,
and to use the fertile tank bottom for cultivation.[3] Where
hydrological and topographical features permit, irrigation
would be provided from wells. In order to retain within the
watershed the same amount or more of the runoff water
previously stored in the tank, water retaining structures
and soil management practices along with storage tanks in
the upper reaches of the catchment are required. As will be
explained below, such water management would increase ground
water recharge. Thus, it might provide the water supply for
a large number of low cost shallow wells serving a large
area with supplementary irrigation on a sustained basis.

In some cases where runoff is sufficient one could
envisage watershed management which incorporates both of the
above methods simultaneously. In other words an irrigation
tank with a water controller could be combined with runoff
collection for ground water recharge and well irrigation.
This would couple the advantages of erosion control to slow
down siltation of the tank with better water management for
well irrigation. The important features of these approaches
to improve water management are outlined below. Research
has provided some insights indicating the feasibility of
these methods. However, there is a need for more experimental tests in the field to confirm the validity of these
two approaches under varying conditions.

IMPROVEMENT OF WATER CONTROL IN EXISTING TANKS

Research on irrigation tanks in south India has shown
that tank irrigation can be profitable (Table 5.1).
However, the majority of irrigation tanks are performing
poorly and this is reflected in the overall decline of tank
irrigated area and growing instability (Figure 5.3).

TABLE 5.1
Benefit-cost ratios and internal rates of return (IRR) of
tank irrigation projects in selected districts of
Andhra Pradesh

District	Number of Tanks Studied	Benefit-Cost Ratio	IRR (%)
Medak	10	0.93	9.0
Mahabubnagar	10	1.08	11.1
Anantapur	3	1.23	13.6
Kurnool	2	0.58	4.3

Source: M. von Oppen and K.V. Subba Rao, 1980b.

Although some tanks may have a rudimentary form of water management through negotiation of a date on which to release water and procedures for allocating water, water is generally let out continuously once the sluice has been opened. Many of the water controllers who did exist in the past and who were in charge of operating the sluices have completely vanished. Better water management could be achieved by very simple measures such as: (1) reducing the outflow at night, since evaporation overnight is reduced and consequently water requirements are lower, (2) keeping the sluice closed on rainy days which assumes that rainfall will be sufficient to supply the water requirement, and (3) a combination of the two.

None of these measures would require any physical change in the tank. The structures at the water outlet would remain as they are as long as the sluice is still functioning. There would be no need for improved distribution channels nor for new cropping systems. Field to field paddy irrigation would continue.

To assess the impact of the second measure, i.e., water control on rainy days, a simulation model was built to compute the amount of water which could be saved. The model is

based on the following assumptions which represent a typical
situation in south India.[4]

1. A tank exists with the following features:
   catchment, 120 hectares; command area, 10 hectares
   with an option to expand to 12 hectares; length of
   bund (straight line) $1 = 100$ m; depth of bund (at
   maximum capacity) $a = 5$ m; length from bund to
   other end of tank (at maximum capacity) $b = 400$ m.
   This tank is rectangular and has a capacity of
   $(1)(a)(b/2)$ or $100,000$ m^3.

2. Evaporation 'EO' varies with exposed surface of
   water stored:

$$EO = c \sqrt{\frac{21b}{a}} \; WS$$

   where WS is the amount of water actually in the
   tank and c is daily normal evaporation on rainy or
   non-rainy days, varying from month to month.[5]

3. The catchment receives daily rainfall as recorded
   for 70 years at the Hyderabad station.

4. Runoff from the catchment is about 20 percent of
   rainfall, in alfisols, and the runoff occurs when
   rainfall is > 17 mm/day.[6]

5. Water requirement of the crop is 10 mm/day on non-
   rainy days and zero on rainy days.

6. The following two water control rules are applied:
   without control: the tank sluice is always open,
   and as soon as the tank has water it runs out at
   the speed of $1,000$ m^3/day in the existing tank and
   $1,200$ m^3/day in the larger tank; with control: the
   tank sluice is closed on all rainy days.

7. The following tank sizes are envisaged: existing
   tank: the water requirement for a 10 ha command
   area has to be met, i.e., $1,000$ m^3/day; larger
   tank: the water requirement for a 12 ha command
   area has to be met, i.e., $1,200$ m^3/day.

The simulations show that in the 10 ha command area
closing sluices on rainy days would reduce the number of
years, out of seventy, during which the tank runs dry before
harvest from forty-eight years to thirty-nine years, i.e.,
the probability of crop failure for this particular tank
would fall from 0.69 to 0.56 (Table 5.2).[7] If the command
area is increased by 20 percent to 12 ha, water control
would decrease the risk of crop failure from 0.73 to 0.59.

TABLE 5.2
Tank simulation model results, irrigation on alfisols using seventy years of daily
rainfall data (Hyderabad, 1901-1970)

	10 Ha Command Area 1000 m³ outlet		12 Ha Command Area 1200 m³ outlet	
	Without Water Controller	With Water Controller	Without Water Controller	With Water Controller
Number of years out of seventy that the tank runs dry at the end of forty-third week[b]	48	39	51	41
	(.69)[a]	(.56)	(.73)	(.59)
At the end of forty-third week the average water stored in the tank (m³)	23,800	33,000	22,200	29,600

Source: Own computations.

[a]Figures in parentheses indicate the probability of the tank going dry.

[b]The forty-third week is assumed to be the end of the first season for a rice crop which
takes about 120 days to mature.

In summary, water control of the kind described would permit irrigation of a 20 percent larger command area at a 17 percent lower risk of crop failure, (from 0.69 to 0.59). In addition, the water left in the tank at the end of the first season would be 24 percent above the amount under conditions of no water control in the existing tank.

Water control will, of course, not be free of cost. An organization to employ and supervise tank controllers has to be established. This organization has to be planned for individual states in India in such a way that it fits into the existing structure of the respective department responsible for tank irrigation.

Conditions prevailing in the states of Maharashtra, Andhra Pradesh, Karnataka, and Tamil Nadu were studied and the most feasible organization was projected (Venkataram 1980). The costs of the water control systems projected for each state were compared with the expected returns from a 20 percent larger tank irrigated area (Table 5.3). The returns to farmers exceed those to the state governments by multiples ranging from three to twenty since the farmers' average net returns from tank irrigated crops exceed the present water rates by the same multiples.

Two alternatives are envisaged for financing the schemes in the different states. First, a grant for a water regulator could be given by the governments for 20 percent of the salary while 80 percent would be borne by the farmers who also supervise the water regulators. Second, the farmers would pay the full amount of the water regulator's salary and the governments would provide supervision. The expenditures for farmers would, in both cases, be only a fraction of their returns from a 20 percent increase in command area. Also the expenditures by the governments would not exceed governments' returns from increased water fee collections.

This exercise is indicative of the feasibility of the scheme at the aggregate level. The scheme is feasible and economically highly profitable to farmers while being moderately remunerative to governments.

The implementation of the scheme at the village level may initially pose some problems. Those who now have access to the water would be concerned about water availability when the command area is extended. However, once the scheme is implemented the increased stability of water supplies for the first season and the 24 percent increase in water for the second season (which was not accounted for in terms of additional irrigated area) should help convince the reluc-

Expected returns and expenditures for improved water management alternatives in tank irrigated areas of selected states in India (in million rupees)

State	Expected Returns		Alternative Expected Expenditures				
			Grant for Water Regulator		Supervision and Water Regulation		
						Government[f]	
	Farmers[a]	Government[b]	Farmers[c]	Government[d]	Farmers[e]	Inspectors and Supervisors	Supervisors
Andhra Pradesh	140.0	6.8	24.0	6.0	30.0	6.24	4.80
Karnataka	65.6	5.2	19.2	4.8	24.0	3.12	2.40
Maharashtra	19.3	6.2	NA	NA	NA	NA	NA
Tamil Nadu	129.7	9.4	9.9	6.6	16.5	4.78	3.67

Source: B.R. Venkataram, 1980.

[a]From 20 percent additional irrigated area at average farmers' net returns.

[b]From 20 percent additional irrigated area at present water rates (changes).

[c]Farmers pay 80 percent of salary (Rs 100/month) for water regulators.

[d]Government pays 20 percent of salary (Rs 25/month) for water regulators.

[e]Farmers pay full salary (Rs 125/month) of water regulator.

[f]Government pays for special supervisory staff, either (a) inspectors (one per fifty tanks) and supervisors (one per twenty inspectors), or (b) supervisors (one per 100 tanks).

NA - Data not available.

tant farmers to collaborate. Nevertheless, further study in villages is required to decide how best and where to implement the scheme.

COMPOSITE WATER MANAGEMENT SYSTEM FOR WATERSHEDS

Even though the expected return from a water control system in an existing irrigation tank is attractive, one cannot reach the conclusion that it provides a best or even a feasible solution for all the watersheds and tanks. Historically there has been a non-linear relationship between population density and tank irrigation in large parts of India. Tanks tend to be established at population densities of fifty to sixty persons/sq km and higher population densities bring about more tanks up to a maximum of about 220 persons/sq km beyond which still more people cause tanks to decrease (von Oppen and Rao 1980a). This observation is based on the simple but powerful truth that with increasing population pressure the value of the land which a tank occupies increases. Consequently, the rationale of the use and maintenance of the land as an object of common property is increasingly being questioned by farmers and landless people. Private claims on the fertile tank land are followed by encroachments which in turn lead to lower water levels and decreased tank irrigation.

At the same time irrigation wells around the tank do provide water for irrigation. If tapped and recharged efficiently this ground water can irrigate all or more of the land formerly served by the tank, assuming favorable hydro-geologic characteristics.

If the gradual disappearance of tank irrigation has to be accepted as an inevitable consequence of population pressure, one should consider ways of facilitating this transition with the objective of reaching an optimal solution. The suggested approach aims at incorporating the entire watershed, i.e., the traditional catchment of a tank plus its submerged and command areas. For such an area a system is envisaged which combines erosion and runoff controlling land management (i.e., through vegetative cover, bunds, check dams, and small percolation tanks) with wells for irrigation. The well irrigation will be on a sustained basis only if the annual recharge of ground water is sufficient.

The system is an extension of another concept, commonly known as water harvesting, in which runoff water is collected in small ponds directly for gravity irrigation. However, through several years of experimentation it has been found that sustained water storage in small ponds especially on Alfisols is very difficult because of the leakage of these ponds (von Oppen 1974). Research at International Crops Research Institute for the Semi-Arid Tropics (ICRISAT) has shown that, despite efforts to seal such storage tanks (e.g., with polyethylene sheets), the leakage is about 20 to 30 mm/day. Thus, it makes sense to investigate the possibility of utilizing leakage for ground water recharge. Using small ponds as percolation tanks (and for gravity irrigation if water is available when needed) may be an economically feasible solution.

Assuming a given amount of rainfall (600 to 800 mm/year) under semi-arid tropical conditions, about 25 percent would disappear as runoff, 50 percent would be consumed in evaporation and transpiration, and 25 percent might go into deep percolation to become ground water. If only half of the runoff (12.5 percent) were kept in situ and added to ground water through percolation tanks and other means this would increase the ground water by 50 percent.[8]

On a watershed with 600 mm rain, 12.5 percent implies an additional 75 mm added to the ground water. Assuming that 20 percent of the watershed area has access to well irrigation for every acre of irrigated land, five times 75 mm, i.e., 375 mm of additional water would be made available. This would increase the 750 mm of ground water normally available to a total of 1,125 mm.

The advantage of such a composite watershed management system (combining runoff and erosion control with systematic ground water exploitation for irrigation) would be:

1. Reduced evaporation losses.
2. Higher reliability of ground water which can provide more efficient irrigation.
3. Higher ground water table which would reduce costs of pumping.
4. Improved irrigation efficiency since the cost of pumping induces farmers to be more judicious in the application of irrigation water than is the case for most gravity irrigation. The difficulties in administrative control of gravity water distribution would also be overcome by well irrigation.
5. A system of runoff control and water retention in the field will also help control erosion, thereby preserving soil fertility, which on Alfisols is a very serious problem (El-Swaify 1983).

On the cost side the following investments would be required:[9]

1. The costs of building and maintaining runoff control structures such as percolation tanks.
2. The costs of digging and maintaining wells.
3. The annual pumping costs for the wells.
4. The costs of administrative control for the allocation of water from runoff control structures, percolation tanks, and wells in an optimal configuration.

Research at ICRISAT was initiated in 1981 to assess the potential of this concept (Engelhardt 1983). This research was based on field surveys and a discrete stochastic linear programming model. The model developed allows the user to assess the impact of composite watershed management on semiarid tropical (SAT) agriculture, which is seriously constrained by the stochastic nature of its water supply. Parametric changes and sensitivity analysis of critical and unknown technical and economical parameters such as well density, factor costs, and product prices permits the identification of the natural and socioeconomic environment for promising implementation of the new concept.

The preliminary results from model runs can be summarized as follows:

1. The concept of composite watershed management as outlined above should have highest success in semiarid tropical regions with rainfall around 700 mm.
2. Only where a critical density of wells has been reached does it become economically sound to construct artificial ground water recharge structures such as percolation tanks. Depending on site specific conditions, results suggest that this density is around seven open dug wells per 100 ha for the region under study.
3. Percolation reservoirs in hard rock regions should be located on favorable hydro-geological formations. Construction of percolation reservoirs should be on top of fractures to guarantee the required technical performance. A seepage rate of 75 percent of the collected runoff should be achieved to give a reasonable internal rate of return of investment in such reservoirs.
4. The most important expected effect of the composite watershed management system is its impact on employment and production and, hence, on income for

the farming community. Sustained irrigation will tend to support more high value crops (i.e., paddy). An extensive watershed management program could, for example, double the output of rice in a region where ground water exploitation has reached its critical level.

However, it is necessary to point out that percolation reservoirs should not be the only element of the system. In addition, afforestation (or agroforestry using low water consumptive species), bunding, and other conservation activities are necessary as well as a review of the distorted input and output price relations caused by government interventions. For example, open and hidden subsidies on energy require special attention.

CONCLUSION

Water management holds one of the most important keys to improved productivity of agricultural land use in the semi-arid tropics. Tanks and wells are traditional sources for small scale irrigation in Indian agriculture. However, difficulties arise when tanks degenerate due to inefficient operation and maintenance and well irrigation becomes more expensive due to overexploitation of ground water and the higher energy costs.

The chapter proposes two concepts for improved watershed management on Alfisols: (1) improved tank management and tank water control, and (2) a system of runoff and erosion controlling land management practices for ground water recharge and well irrigation. Both concepts have been investigated to some extent at ICRISAT. The results achieved so far are promising and research in this direction will be intensified.

NOTES

1. An irrigation tank is a small reservoir constructed across the slope of a valley to catch and store runoff water. Generally, the tanks have a maximum depth of not more than 15 feet, although some have depths of 25 to 30 feet. Medium-sized tanks have the capacity of about 100 million cubic feet.

2. A watershed is understood here as comprising an area of several thousand hectares below a water dividing line, often the catchment area for one or several traditional irrigation tanks.

3. However, this can lead to some difficult equity problems since those who "own" the tank bottom land are usually not the same as those who receive tank irrigation. See the discussion of encroachment and conflict in Tank 10 in the next chapter for a different point of view.

4. A tank with a command area of 10 ha represents a relatively small tank which will give conservative estimates of the water control impact (see also footnotes 5 and 8).

5. Note that with increasing amounts of water stored, evaporation losses increase only by the square root, e.g., storing four times the amount of water implies only a doubling of the amount of evaporation losses.

6. The runoff percentage varies as it is computed from a regression equation which depends on rainfall, land condition, etc. (For details see Ryan and Pereira 1978.)

7. These probabilities of crop failure are relatively high because of the small tank size assumed. Larger tanks have relatively lower evaporation losses and, therefore, would benefit even more from water control involving water storage over longer periods.

8. These figures are first estimates to provide orders of magnitudes. The runoff and percolation data are likely to vary from region to region and detailed research is required for a correct quantification of the hydrological relationships.

9. The feasibility of underground water storage completely breaks down: (1) if geologic strata are salt-laden (e.g., northeast Thailand), and (2) if hydro-geology does not ensure self-containment of subsurface flow (El-Swaify, personal communication).

REFERENCES

Abbie, L., J.Q. Harrison, and J.W. Wall. 1982. "Economic return to investment in India." World Bank Staff Working Paper No. 536, Washington, D.C.

El-Swaify, S.A. 1983. "Conservation-effective farming systems for the semi-arid tropics." ICRISAT Farming Systems Research Program, Soil Physics and Conservation, India.

Engelhardt, T. 1983. "Economics of traditional small-
holder irrigation management in south India." Ph.D.
Thesis, University of Stuttgurt-Hohenheim.
Halcrow, Sir William, and partners in association with
Intermediate Technology Power Ltd. 1983. "Small-scale
solar-powered pumping systems: The technology, its
economics and advancement." (UNDP Project GLO/80/003,
Executed by the World Bank), Swindan and Reading.
Miranda, S.M., P. Pathak, and K.V. Srivastava. 1982.
"Runoff management on small agricultural watersheds:
the ICRISAT experience." The National Seminar on a
Decade of Dryland Agriculture Research in India and
Thrust in the Eighties, AICRPDA, India.
Ryan, J.G., and M. Pereira. 1978. "Derivation of empirical
models to predict runoff on small agricultral
watersheds in the semi-arid tropics." The International
Workshop on the Agro-climatological Research Needs of
the Semi-Arid Tropics, ICRISAT, India, pp. 128-41.
Venkataram, B.R. 1980. Administrative Feasibility of a
Tank Irrigation Authority. ICRISAT Economics Program
Consultancy Report, India.
von Oppen, M. 1974. "Determination of the optimum location
and capacity of a storage tank on a typical watershed."
ICRISAT Economics Program Occasional Paper 3, India.
_____. 1978. "Instability of area and production
under tank irrigation in selected districts of Andhra
Pradesh and Tamil Nadu." ICRISAT Economics Program
Occasional Paper 9, India.
von Oppen, M., and K.V. Subba Rao. 1980. Tank Irrigation
in Semi-Arid Tropical India. Part I: Historical
Development and Spatial Distribution. ICRISAT
Economics Program Progress Report 5, India.
_____. 1980. Tank Irrigation in Semi-Arid Tropical
India. Part II: Technical Features and Economic
Performance. ICRISAT Economics Program Progress
Report 8, India.
Whitcombe, E. 1971. Agrarian Conditions in Northern India,
Vol. I: The United Provinces Under British Rule 1860-
1900. New Delhi, India, Thompson Press.

CHAPTER 6

MANAGEMENT, PRODUCTION, AND REHABILITATION IN SOUTH INDIAN IRRIGATION TANKS

K. Palanisami and K. William Easter

As discussed in Chapter 5, many of the south Indian tanks are starting their second hundred years in a sad state of disrepair. Although tanks are found in all parts of India, they account for over 30 percent of the total irrigated area in Andhra Pradesh, Karnataka, and Tamil Nadu states of south India. There are about 39,200 tanks in Tamil Nadu state alone. Until recently, the government of India did not consider tank irrigation as an important source of irrigation. The major emphasis since 1950-1951 has been on ground water development and large-scale irrigation projects. This, coupled with poor tank management, pushed tank irrigation into the background. However, financial and physical constraints to further development of ground water and large projects have now brought tank irrigation back into consideration as a viable alternative for future expansion of irrigation, particularly in south India. Still, little effort has been made to study the feasibility of using tanks as an alternative for expanding the irrigated area and production.

To help fill this research gap, this chapter reports on the results of a study of tanks in Ramanathapuram District, Tamil Nadu. This district has over one-fourth of the Tamil Nadu tanks and 75 percent of the state's 10,000 Ex-zamin tanks.[1] The major focus is on identifying the major constraints to improving tank performance. This is done first by a detailed analysis of the water management and rice production in ten tanks during the 1981-1982 wet season and, second, by evaluating an additional forty-one tanks to determine what factors should govern the selection of tanks for rehabilitation (Table 6.1).

TABLE 6.1
Characteristics of the ten sample tanks, Tamil Nadu, India, 1982

Tank Number	Command Area	Percent Of Command Area Cultivated	1981/82 Rice Yield	Encroachment	Farm Size Variation[d]	Average Farm Size	Amount Spent On Water Management	Net Benefits[c] From Management Expenditures
	(acres)	(%)	(kgs/ac)	(%)	(%)	(acres)	(Rs/acre)	(Rs/acre)
1	990	84	1,390	--	31	2.0	9.8	70
2	910	99	1,670	--	66	3.1	0.3	--
3	1,590	97	1,460	20	51	2.5	0.2	--
4	1,170	85	1,100	10	24	1.3	4.7	43
5	190	58	1,590	--	86	2.0	0.4	--
6	230	21	1,490	--	67	2.0	0.5	--
7	390	88	1,110	25	72	1.9	2.2[a]	14
8	130	90	1,170	30	91	1.9	2.7[a]	15
9	90	93	1,450	15	33	1.1	7.4	73
10	90	88	1,270	40	104	2.3	1.8	b

[a] Amount spent was mainly for making representations to government for additional supplies.

[b] This tank had water rights from the Vaigai channel and the amount spent was just to divert the available water. Hence, the net benefits are from normal irrigation practices and are not the result of any special management investment.

[c] The value of additional irrigations due to management expenditures equals the cost of pumping water.

[d] ... of variation = (standard deviation ÷ mean) 100.

TANK MANAGEMENT

A random sample of 200 farmers was selected from those receiving irrigation from the ten tanks. Data were collected on water use, input use, water management strategies, crop yields, and constraints to tank management. Discussions were also held with the Public Works Department engineers and Revenue Department officials to determine their role in tank management.

The main source of water for primary tanks is rivers or reservoirs while for supplemental tanks it is rainfall.[2] In at least half of the past ten years, seven of the eight supplemental tanks did not receive adequate water and farmers had to augment supplies with well water. Water scarcity and the higher price of private well water provided an incentive for adoption of water distribution and management strategies both at the tank and farm level. Tank level strategies included unauthorized diversion of water being delivered to other tanks, pressure on irrigation officials to release reservoir water and expenditures on community wells and canal lining.

Some of the strategies adopted involved a direct substitution of management for scarce water. For example, strict rotation schedules were used so that farmers received tank water every four to six days rather than have a continuous flow. During periods of very limited tank water supplies, water deliveries were reduced to half of normal releases and an extra effort was made to clean the main canal and secondary channels.

The success of the management strategies adopted by the farmers is directly related to the strength of their cooperation. This is illustrated by the effects of water scarcity on farmer cooperation and the substitution of management inputs for scarce water. Only in the three tanks with water user organizations (WUO) were serious efforts made to substitute management for scarce water at the tank level. This occurred in Tanks 1, 4, and 9, where the amount spent per acre was Rs 9.8, 4.7, and 7.4, respectively. The net benefits per acre due to additional irrigations from improved management were high in these three tanks, ranging from Rs 43 to Rs 73 per acre.

In the case of Tanks 2, 3, 5, and 6, the management expenditures were routine and resulted in no direct benefits. Farmers at the two primary tanks, 2 and 3, did not face any water scarcity in 1981-1982. In the two new tanks, 5 and 6, the water was adequate for the reduced command areas. Only 58 and 21 percent, respectively, of the target command areas in these two tanks can be irrigated because of faulty technical design. The upper sluices are located below the land to be irrigated.

The other three tanks received direct benefits from water management by obtaining additional supplies from perennial sources. Farmers from Tanks 7 and 8 obtained water from the Pilavakal Dam, which collects runoff that originally fed these and other tanks. During the planning and construction periods, irrigation officials thought that water would be provided to thirty-seven tanks including Tanks 7 and 8. But no canal was provided to allocate the water from the Pilavakal Dam to each tank in the series. Thus water had to flow through one tank before it could be used in another tank. The end result was an overuse of water in the upper tanks such as Tank 2 and inadequate water for the lower tanks such as Tanks 7 and 8. Farmers served by Tanks 7 and 8 received additional water from the dam after they made numerous requests to the irrigation officials. They argued that prior to the dam construction their water supply was larger and more dependable.

Farmers should be able to refill Tank 10 whenever the tank water supplies are low. Yet even with frequent fillings, the tank supplies were not adequate. This is due to heavy encroachment (cropping) in the tank foreshore area (water storage area) and the unlawful release of tank water during the night by encroachers. This conflict of interest between tank irrigated farmers and encroachers prevented normal tank operations and caused water shortages.

One of the important factors besides water scarcity which encouraged farmer cooperation in the acquisition and distribution of the water was the homogeneity of farms. The smaller the variation in farm size, the better the cooperation among farmers on tank management issues. In Tanks 1, 4, and 9 the coefficients of farm size variation were by far the lowest (Table 6.1). These were the tanks where farmers were able to cooperate and make major water management expenditures which resulted in benefits significantly above costs. The tanks with the least amount of cooperation had the highest farm size variation. Tanks 2 and 3 had moderate farm size variation but did not need much cooperation due to abundant water supplies.

In addition to tank level management strategies, 120 farmers in Tanks 1, 4, 7, 8, 9, and 10 had to make farm level adjustments because of inadequate tank water supplies. About 73 percent of the farmers irrigated with tank water until it was gone and then supplemented it with well water. Another 5 percent supplemented with well water but lengthened the irrigation interval from the usual four to five days to seven to nine days because of the high cost of well water. Four percent of the farmers reduced the area under irrigation, although initially they planted their entire area in rice. They had to reduce the area planted by 30 to 50 percent and concentrate the water on part of their land. A few farmers, 7 percent, irrigated all their cropland by reducing the amount of water applied per acre. Finally, 11 percent of the farmers abandoned their fields once the tank water was exhausted due to their location relative to wells. Their fields were either too far from the wells or at a higher elevation.

The varying water supply has a direct impact on crop production. As the ultimate aim of improving tank water management is to increase crop production and farm income, it is important to estimate the impacts on crop production of varying water levels. If more water offers large increases in production and income, then a wider range of investments to improve tank irrigation becomes feasible.

Yield Response to Water

Rice yield response is estimated based on the sample of 200 farmers. A Cobb-Douglas production function, with paddy yield in kgs per acre as the dependent variable, is estimated using dummy variables for many of the water management issues.[3] An attempt is made to account for the quantity of water applied, the timeliness of the application, and the predictability of water supply. In addition, well water and tank water are separated into two variables. Because of intercorrelation between land, fertilizer and labor, a per acre production function is used. Finally, no restriction is imposed on the degree of returns to scale.

Most of the explanatory variables were statistically significant and the coefficients were relatively high for tank and well water (Table 6.2). The high adjusted R^2 indicates that the model explains most of the variation in yield. The only surprises are the low coefficient for fertilizer and the insignificance of WUO. A comparison of marginal value products (MVP) and costs of inputs indicate that both tank and well water were underused, fertilizer overused, and labor use was about at the optimum level (Table 6.3). This highlights the importance of water as the major constraint to increasing rice production and is consistent with our observations that farmers are applying more than the recommended levels of fertilizer.

TABLE 6.2
Regression of rice yield on inputs and tank
characteristics, 1982

Exogenous Variables	Regression Coefficients	T-value
Tank water	0.600	13.04***
Well water	0.374	13.85***
Fertilizer	0.010	3.33***
Casual labor	0.093	4.23***
Assets	0.032	1.23
Encroachment	-0.126	2.57***
Sluice location	-0.217	3.39***
Water user organizations	0.021	0.34
Channel structures	0.049	1.02
Rehabilitation	0.183	2.32**
Tank type	0.140	2.37**
Constant	-0.385	1.67*

$$\bar{R}^2 = 0.98 \qquad F = 947.26 \qquad N = 200$$

*Significant at 10 percent level.
**Significant at 5 percent level.
***Significant at 1 percent level.

What alternatives are available to increase tank water
supplies? The tank water supply can be increased by
reducing the encroachment in the tank foreshore area, by
reallocation of water among tanks and by diverting added
rainfall into tanks (water harvesting). However, some of
these alternatives will be difficult to implement because of
socio-political or physical constraints.

TABLE 6.3
The marginal value products and price or cost of inputs, 1982

Input	Unit	Marginal Value Product (MVP) (Rs)	Input Price or Cost (C) (Rs)	Ratio of MVP to C
Tank water	acre inch	30.36	1.94	15.65
Casual labor	man-day	4.45	5.67	0.79
Fertilizer use	rupee	0.04	1.06	0.04
Well water	acre inch	61.08	9.50[a]	6.43
		61.08	12.00[b]	5.09
		61.08	4.50[c]	13.47

[a]Price of water from electric-powered private wells.
[b]Price of water from diesel-powered private wells.
[c]Price of water from electric-powered community wells.

In contrast, a number of rehabilitation alternatives can be implemented fairly quickly in a limited number of tanks. Two types of measures, i.e., lining the main canal and community wells, have been introduced to increase the effective water supply in a few tanks. Both offer good real rates of return on investment (Table 6.4). The dilemma is to introduce the appropriate rehabilitation measures on a wide scale and to select the tanks best suited for such investments. A large variation in farm size, strong private groups of well owners, and encroachment in the tank fore-shore are factors which are likely to make rehabilitation difficult and unproductive (Palanisami and Easter 1983).

TANK REHABILITATION

To develop a criteria for selecting tanks to rehabili-tate the first step is to identify which factors influence tank performance. Since there are a large number of tanks the identification needs to be done without the benefit of a detailed study of each tank. A number of factors which influence tank performance have been tested in our analysis of ten tanks or suggested by other studies including farm size variation, WUO, the number of private wells, the depth of water in the tank, encroachment, tank type, tank size, location of tank, age of tank, rainfall, expenditure on tank maintenance, and water stored. The next step is to deter-mine which of the above factors are the most important in determining tank performance. To do this, one must select some measure of performance. Von Oppen and Rao (1980a) used actual area irrigated in their calculation of economic performance for tanks in semi-arid India. Lenton (1982) suggests four possible measures of irrigation performance: actual area irrigated, water delivery, crop yield, and vari-ation in the three measures over time. Given the data available and the fact that the main purpose of the analysis is to select tanks for rehabilitation, a five year average of the ratio of area irrigated to total command area is used as the measure of tank performance.

To test the effect of various factors on tank perfor-mance, forty-one tanks of varying size and type were selected at random in Ramanathapuram District of Tamil Nadu state during 1983. The ten tanks from the 1981-1982 tank study were also included to make the total fifty-one.[4] Data regarding the tank characteristics such as well numbers, capacity of tanks, expenditures on tanks, and location of tanks were collected from the Irrigation Department, the Revenue Department, and from a farmer survey. The relation-

TABLE 6.4
Internal rates of return (IRR) from tank rehabilitation,
1982

Project Life (Years)	Community Well	Canal Lining
	(percent)	
5	-9.7[a]	14.3
10	12.7	20.5
15	17.1	23.9

[a]Community wells under most conditions will be in use for
at least ten years. Thus, the negative return is not very
likely.

ship between the actual command area utilization and the
independent variables was analyzed using a linear regression
model since scatter diagrams suggested a linear relationship
between the dependent and independent variables.[5]

Six of the twelve variables were significant in
explaining differences in tank performance (Table 6.5). The
adjusted R^2 of 81 percent indicates that much of the variation in actual tank utilization is explained by the
variables considered. Depth of water, farm size variation,
encroachment, tank size, tank location, and private wells
are significant variables. The WUO variable is not significant which might be explained by the high intercorrelation
between WUO and encroachment, farm size variation, tank
location, and depth of water. The WUO has a high negative
correlation with encroachment and farm size variation but a
high positive correlation with depth of water and tank
location. The other six variables have positive signs, as
expected, but are not significant.

Farm size variation and encroachment are important in
determining farmer cooperation and water management but they
do so in the opposite direction. The shallow tanks are
generally those which have been silted up. Also, greater
tank depth indicates that the tanks will have shorter and

TABLE 6.5
Regression of tank utilization on factors influencing tank performance, 1983

Exogenous Variables	Final Model		Complete Model	
	Regression Coefficient	T-value	Regression Coefficient	T-value
Depth of water	.0415	3.15***	.04439	3.07***
Farm size variation	-.0021	2.72***	-.00208	2.19**
Encroachment	-.0069	5.35***	-.00664	4.38***
Tank type	--	--	.04957	1.17
Command area (tank size)	-.0001	2.56***	-.00007	2.29**
Location	.0560	2.13**	.06903	2.31**
Age of tank	--	--	.00366	0.15
Rainfall	--	--	.00002	0.85
Water user organizations	--	--	.01783	0.50

Expenditure/acre	—	—	.00004	0.89
Water stored/acre	—	—	.15091	0.79
Wells/acre	-.4161	1.85**	-.55634	2.17**
Constant	.9226	11.44***	.87633	8.74***
$\bar{R}^2$	0.82		0.81	
F	37.50***		18.06***	
N	48		48	

*Significant at 10 percent level.
**Significant at 5 percent level.
***Significant at 1 percent level.

higher levees. Normally shallow tanks have longer levees and require greater investment for repairs.[6] Larger tanks have longer canals and greater differences among upper and lower sluices. The lands under the upper sluices and at the end of long main canals usually do not get adequate water except in high rainfall years. In addition, as tank size increases, there is a higher probability of heterogenous farms. Favorable tank location normally means additional water supplies can be obtained from other tanks as well as from small streams and rivers. Finally, as the reliance on well water increases, the dependency on tank water and tank management decreases. This could result in poor tank water management and a decline in tank maintenance which would eventually mean a decline in water available for irrigation. Most of the farmers served by supplemental tanks obtain 30 to 50 percent of their irrigation water from wells.

Tank Selection

The magnitude of the variables influencing tank performance varies from tank to tank. For example, in one tank encroachment may be high and farm size variation low while in another both encroachment and farm size variation are high. Hence, different weights are given to each of the six variables according to their magnitude in each tank (Table 6.6). The cumulative value of each tank is then used to identify tanks for rehabilitation.[7]

Two alternative weights are assigned to each of the six significant variables. The weights for positive characteristics are given greater weight in the second alternative. For example, in Alternative I, favorable tank size (i.e., 0 to 100 acres) is given a weight of three, while in Alternative II, it has a weight of four. The cumulative value for each tank is determined by summing the weighted values of the six variables. The cumulative values are called the Tank Rehabilitation Index (TRI).

The TRI should give the highest number to those tanks best suited for rehabilitation. However, it is not clear which of the two weights gives the "best" ranking. To determine which weights provide the "best" priorities, nine out of the ten tanks from the 1981-1982 sample are ranked as follows based on what was learned during our detailed study of these tanks: 9, 4, 1, 3, 7, 5, 2, 8, 10.[8] The two alternative TRIs rank the ten tanks in much the same manner.[9] Alternative II puts the tanks in four distinct groups but does not differentiate between the tanks in each group. Alternative I has six different groups but still does not

TABLE 6.6
Tank performance variables with relative weights

Variables	Range of Variables	Alternative Weights	
		I	II
Tank size	0-100 acres	3	4
	101-400 acres	2	2
	> 400 acres	1	1
Tank location	Favorable	2	3
	Others	1	1
Wells per acre	0-0.5	3	4
	0.06-0.10	2	3
	> 0.10	1	1
Encroachment	0-10 percent	3	4
	11-25 percent	2	2
	> 25 percent	1	1
Depth of water	0-2.0 meters	1	1
	2.1-4.0 meters	2	2
	> 4.0 meters	3	4
Farm size variation	0-30 percent	3	4
	31-50 percent	2	2
	> 50 percent	1	1

differentiate between five tanks in two groups. However, this may be all one can expect from such a criteria. What is needed is some method to identify the best tanks for rehabilitation without doing a benefit-cost analysis of each. It does not matter whether Tank 9 or 4 is ranked first. The important thing is to identify them as high priority and not Tanks 8 and 10 (Table 6.7).

Tanks are now grouped into four priority ranges (high, intermediate, low, and very low) for rehabilitation. A comparison is then made between the two alternative weights and the ranking provided by the earlier 1982 study (Table 6.8). Tank 9 is ranked high priority because it is a small tank and farmers are cooperative and willing to make investment in water management. The two big tanks, 4 and 1, are also ranked high priority because both have effective WUO and invest in water management practices. Tanks 2, 3, 5, and 8 were listed as low priority because Tanks 2 and 3 are primary tanks and have adequate supplies in most years. There is no immediate need for rehabilitation but there may be possibilities for increased water use efficiency, provided the water saved by conservation can be diverted to other tanks. Tanks 7 and 8 are part of a system of tanks and the major problem is that of relaxing the barriers to obtaining water from a large upstream dam. Once this is done, then these tanks would be ready for rehabilitation. However, Tank 7 is ranked higher than Tank 8 because it is nearer the large dam and is more likely to receive water supplies in the future. Tank 5 is a new tank and its problems are related to poor design. Tank 10 is listed under very low priority due to the perennial conflicts among farmers. This tank has serious encroachment and the farmers do a poor job of irrigation with abundant tank water supplies. Permanent improvements are currently impossible because encroachers can block any efforts towards tank improvement.

The priorities found by using the two alternative TRIs are quite similar to that found in our more detailed analysis. Tank 3 ranks higher under Alternative II primarily because it was just recently improved and the effects are not picked up in our five-year average of area irrigated. The only other problem is that Tanks 4 and 7 are ranked lower under Alternative I while Tanks 1 and 8 are ranked lower under both alternatives. This points out that one must use the ranking system with some caution and that Alternative II is probably best. However, it cannot be expected to differentiate among tanks which have very similar characteristics.

TABLE 6.7
Tank rehabilitation index (TRI) for ten-tank sample

Alternative I		Alternative II	
TRI	Tank Number	TRI	Tank Number
8	10	9	8,10
9	8	10	--
10	2,5,7	11	2,5
11	3	12	--
12	1,4	13	1,3,7
13	--	14	--
14	9	15	--
		16	4,9

TABLE 6.8
Priority ranking of ten tanks for rehabilitation

Priority	1982 Study	Alternative I	Alternative II
High	9,4,1	9	9,4
Intermediate	7	4,1	1,3,7
Low	2,3,5,8	3,7,5,2	2,5
Very Low	10	10,8	8,10

The Public Works Department should use the criteria as a starting point for selecting tanks for rehabilitation. The high priority groups should be addressed first followed by those in the intermediate priority group. Many tanks in the low priority group would be difficult to improve, unless some major changes occur. Tanks in the very low priority group are probably beyond help unless some strong institutional assistance is provided to eliminate the social and/or physical constraints to development. This is true of Tank 10 and possibly Tank 8. Yet final decisions concerning whether or not to invest in a tank should not be made without on-site visits and more detailed study of the selected tanks.

The ranking of the forty-eight tanks is shown in Table 6.9. The PWD has ten to twelve tanks from which to select as high priority tanks for rehabilitation. In this selection it would appear that Tanks 20, 22, and 48 should be given highest priority because of their high TRIs while, of the ten tanks studied in detail, Tank 9 stands out as top priority.

CONCLUSION

Production in the tank irrigated areas is heavily constrained by water inadequacy. This is further complicated by encroachment, silting of tanks, and poor tank maintenance. Rehabilitation of these tanks to increase water supplies and production should be pursued on a large number of these tanks. Measures such as canal lining and community wells have already proven feasible on a small sample of tanks. The benefits from such improvement can be as high as the difference in crop output between primary and supplemental tanks.

The methodology suggested to select tanks for rehabilitation is a preliminary one. Further research is needed on the performance of different tanks under varying biophysical and socioeconomic conditions over time, particularly under varying rainfall levels. It is equally important to find ways to reduce or eliminate encroachment and foster cooperation among farmers.

TABLE 6.9
Tank priority for rehabilitation of forty-eight tanks in Tamil Nadu

Priority[a]	Alternative I	Total	Alternative II	Total
	- - - - - Tank Numbers - - - - -			
Very Low	8, 10, 12, 13, 14, 26, 34, 38, 39, 40, 44, 45, 49	13	8, 10, 12, 14, 26, 38, 44, 45, 49	9
Low	2, 3, 5, 7, 16, 17, 21, 23, 25, 28, 31, 32, 33, 36, 37	15	2, 5, 13, 16, 17, 21, 25, 31, 32, 34, 36, 39, 40	13
Intermediate	1, 4, 15, 18, 24, 27, 29, 30, 42, 43	10	1, 3, 7, 15, 18, 23, 24, 27, 28, 30, 33, 37, 42, 43	14
High	9, 11, 19, 20, 22, 35, 41, 46, 47, 48	10	4, 9, 11, 19, 20, 22, 29, 35, 41, 46, 47, 48	12

[a]The ranges in TRI used for the priority classification are the following:
Alternative I: TRI 7-9=very low; 10-11=low; 12-13=intermediate; and 14 and above=high.
Alternative II: TRI 7-9=very low; 10-12=low; 13-15=intermediate; and 16 and above=high.

NOTES

1. Ex-zamin tanks are the non-standardized tanks which, before independence, were controlled by the zamindars, and are likely to be the ones faced with the greatest management problems.

2. In this study a modified tank classification -- primary and supplemental tanks -- was adopted. Primary tanks are those which receive adequate supplies in most years for at least one rice crop and have a perennial source of supply such as a river. Supplemental tanks are those which did not receive adequate supplies in most years and farmers must use well water to obtain a crop of rice.

3. The following independent variables are included in the production function: tank water used in acre inches per acre; well water used in acre inches per acre; casual labor used in man-days per acre; fertilizer used in rupees per acre; asset value of the farmer in rupees; tank type, 0 if supplemental tank, 1 if primary tank; encroachment in the tank, 0 if no encroachment, 1 if encroachment; WUO, 1 if organizations are present, 0 if no organization; channel structures, 1 if structures are satisfactory, 0 if not satisfactory; sluice location, 1 for upper sluices, 0 for lower sluices; and tank rehabilitation measures, 0 if not rehabilitated, 1 if rehabilitated.

4. However, in the final analysis, only forty-eight tanks were included because three tanks behaved differently from the rest of the tanks. Tank 6 from the ten tank sample and two tanks from the forty-one tank sample were considered outliers and omitted from the analysis.

5. AU = f (RF, TS, TT, EN, TA, TL, DW, EX, WS, FV, WO, PW).

AU = average actual utilization measured as the ratio of the area irrigated to total tank command area for 1978-1982.

RF = average annual rainfall in mm for 1978-1982.

TS = size of tank command area in acres.

TT = tank type, 0 supplemental and 1 primary.

EN = tank encroachment as percent of foreshore area which is farmed.

TA = age of tank, 0 for tanks built in the past ten years and 1 for older tanks.

TL = tank location, 1 for tanks in favorable locations and 0 for others.

DW = depth of tank water in meters.

EX = expenditure on tanks in rupees per acre during 1970-1981.

WS = water stored per acre of command area in mcft.

FV – farm size variation in percent.
WO – water user organizations, 1 if organized and 0 if not.
PW – number of private wells per acre of command area.

6. Von Oppen and Rao (1980b) estimated that on average, the cost of the levees or dams constitute 57 percent of the total cost of tank construction.

7. Tank rehabilitation refers to a wide range of investments both in physical and human capital. The investment may be either above the outlet such as increasing the tank storage capacity or below the outlet such as reducing water losses in the canals. The investment may also be in helping organize farmers to allocate water or maintain the system. The specific type of investment will vary from tank to tank depending on the exact nature of the water problems.

8. Tank 6 was not included in the analysis due to its extreme variation in area irrigated because of faulty design of the sluices.

9. Our ranking was based on crop yields, net returns to water management, the presence of WUO, and the potential for yield increases, in addition to the six variables considered in the model. Our close observation of these nine tanks, as well as the opinion of the engineer from the Public Works Department, helped finalize the ranking.

REFERENCES

Lenton, Roberto L. 1982. "Management tools for improving performance." Paper presented at Special Course on Water Management in Irrigation Systems, Central Water Commission, New Delhi, India.

Palanisami, K., and K. William Easter. 1983. The Tanks of South India: A Potential for Future Expansion in Irrigation. Economic Report ER83-4, Department of Agricultural and Applied Economics, University of Minnesota, St. Paul.

von Oppen, M., and K.V. Subba Rao. 1980a. Tank Irrigation in Semi-Arid Tropics India. ICRISAT Economic Program Progress Report 9, Hyderabad, India.

_____. 1980b. Tank Irrigation in Semi-Arid Tropical India, Part II: Technical Features and Economic Performance. ICRISAT Economics Program Progress Report 8, Hyderabad, India.

CHAPTER 7

AGRICULTURAL INTENSIFICATION IN THAILAND: COMPLEMENTARY ROLE OF INFRASTRUCTURE AND AGRICULTURAL POLICY

Sam H. Johnson III

Many papers written about water resource development and water resource policy treat the subject in isolation. To a large extent, this is due to the complexity and widespread impacts of water resource systems, but it is also related to the fact that measuring and separating impacts of specific policies is difficult. However, if the agricultural sector is viewed as a system, it is clear infrastructure construction, management of this infrastructure, and other agricultural policies are an integral part of the system. Therefore, returns to investment in infrastructure to control water resources cannot be measured independently of policies existing in that sector.

Herdt (1980), a former economist from the International Rice Research Institute (IRRI), while acknowledging that water control is a major constraint to rice production and high rice yields in Asia, questions whether irrigation construction is not overstressed in development assistance. Irrigation projects attract development banks and aid agencies because they utilize large amounts of capital, result in highly visible infrastructure, and provide a service which nearly everyone agrees is a necessary requirement for agricultural development. Yet most irrigation schemes fail to reach expected levels of output and income. Agencies charged with operating completed irrigation projects have many problems including difficulty in operating sophisticated systems, shortage of funds for operation and maintenance, lack of community cooperation, and poorly trained staff with little incentive to operate the system more productively. Part of the reason may be, as argued by Herdt, that too many resources have been made available for irrigation infrastructure development too quickly. Another reason is that too little emphasis has been placed on management and on making certain that agricultural policies are complementary to intensified irrigation (Bottrall 1981). The purpose of this chapter is to illustrate the relationship between investment in irrigation infrastructure and other agricultural policies and their impacts on rice production. Data based on rice production functions from the Central Plain of Thailand demonstrate that irrigation infrastructure investment is a necessary, but not sufficient, condition for expanded agricultural production. Other agricultural policies must complement the irrigation investment in order to obtain positive production increases. Disaggregated data which differentiates between wet and dry season rice production offer new insights into the process of agricultural development. These insights are valuable as Thailand is the only country in Asia, and among six in the world, producing a net surplus of agricultural products for export continuously over the last thirty years.

RICE PRODUCTION

Rice is Thailand's leading earner of foreign exchange while the rice export premium provides an important source of government revenue. Rice is also the staple food in the diet of the 50 million Thai people and is the most important source of farm income. Over the last decade there has been diversification in employment in both rural and urban areas; yet 70 percent of the 22.3 million labor force continues to be engaged in agriculture. Given the importance of rice production, when rice exports dropped from around two million tons in 1964 and 1965 to less than one million tons in 1973, 1974, and 1975, the government of Thailand (GOT) realized that new programs were necessary to increase rice production. Since the establishment of IRRI in 1960, GOT has actively supported research on high yielding varieties (HYVs). Yet during the 1960s and early 1970s, while the green revolution in rice spread rapidly in other countries in Asia, the adoption of HYVs in Thailand was disappointing (Yotopoulos and Adulavidhaya 1979). Ineffective water control in the wet season and limited irrigation facilities in the dry season were identified as the primary environmental constraints. This led GOT to invest in the development of increasingly sophisticated irrigation schemes. As a result of irrigation investment in the Central Plain (estimated at $750 million), dry season rice production, which is almost exclusively HYVs, is providing an increasingly larger percentage of total rice production (Table 7.1).

TABLE 7.1
Paddy production in the central region of Thailand,
1962-1978 (million metric tons)

Year	Wet Season	Dry Season	Total Production	Percentage Of Total From Dry Season
1962	3.67	0.01	3.68	.3
1966	3.74	0.08	3.72	2.2
1970	3.38	0.26	3.64	7.1
1972	3.77	0.67	4.44	15.1
1974	3.99	0.80	4.79	16.7
1976	3.95	1.14	5.09	22.4
1978	4.12	1.93	6.05	31.9

Source: Government of Thailand, Ministry of Agriculture
and Cooperatives, Office of Agricultural Economics.

POLICY VARIABLES

Major policy variables influencing rice production in
Thailand are rice price, fertilizer price, land tenure, and
irrigation development. As a rice exporter, quality as well
as quantity is also of importance, hence, varietal type is
another important policy variable.

Rice Policy

The principal rice policy objective of GOT is to
control the volume of rice exports in order to make certain
that domestic supplies are adequate to maintain a desired
Bangkok consumer price level for rice. The second objective, maximizing foreign exchange earnings, comes into
consideration only after domestic supplies are assured.
Five mechanisms have been used to control the volume of rice

export and, hence, domestic rice prices, of which quotas, rice reserve requirements, and rice premium have proven to be the most effective (Pinthong and Siamwalla 1978).

The effects of rice export controls, particularly the rice premium, have been a subject of controversy in Thailand for many years and are likely to continue to be a major issue in the future. Proponents argue the premium is an important source of government revenue, that it has encouraged crop diversification, and that the burden is mainly borne by foreigners. Its critics claim that the tax burden is shifted directly back to the farmer (Welsch and Tongpan 1973). Wong's 1978 analysis of the past two decades suggests that the export premium may have generated a net gain in welfare for Thailand, although he did not consider foreign exchange losses as a social cost. However, he acknowledges that the rice premium represents a substantial burden on farmers which keeps prices low and lowers farmer incentives to improve yields by adopting modern production practices. In early 1978, for example, Thai farmers were receiving around $11 per hundred kg of paddy compared with $16.50 per hundred kg in nearby Malaysia and the Philippines for paddy of somewhat lower than average quality.

HYVs and Fertilizer Use

In addition to good water control, HYVs require an adequate nutrient supply. Thai farmers historically have used low levels of chemical fertilizer and even today, at 51 kg/ha, Thailand has one of the lowest per hectare fertilizer application rates in Asia (World Bank 1982). A number of reasons have been suggested to explain this low use rate. It appears to reflect a combination of many policy variables including fertilizer policy, rice price policy, availability of rice land, and rice quality.

Profitability of fertilizer application by Thai farmers is heavily dependent upon the rice variety used and the relative price of rice to fertilizer. In Asia, the rice-to-fertilizer price ratio varies widely from country to country, with ratio values close to 1.0 being rare and with modal values around 0.5 (Timmer and Falcon 1975). Thailand's policy of low domestic rice prices and protection for inefficient government fertilizer producers and distributors has resulted in one of the lowest rice-to-fertilizer price ratios in Asia. Only since 1977 has Thailand's ratio exceeded 0.5.

Land Tenure

Land tenancy and landlessness exist in Thailand at levels considerably lower than in many other developing countries. However, absentee landlordism is widespread in several provinces in the inner Central Plain. The percentage of farm families renting land (1978) varied from 33 percent in the Central Plain to not quite 10 percent in the northeast. Besides the Central Plain, only in the north is more than 10 percent of the land operated by tenants. About 60 percent of the landowners with more than 160 hectares in the Central Plain currently reside in Bangkok. The largest holders are the Crown Property Bureau, the Ministry of Finance, and members of several families long prominent in Bangkok circles (Fallon and Kanel 1978).

The above is misleading in that much of the land cultivated in Thailand is under unclear title. According to a study sponsored by the National Economic, Social, and Development Board, of the nearly 24 million ha of land under cultivation in Thailand, probably about 1.5 million ha, or 6 percent, are fully titled under the land code. Some 10.3 million ha (43 percent) are covered by a permanent possession right, and 1.2 million ha (5 percent) are covered by "preemption certificates" which are of questionable legal status. The remaining farmed area, about 11 million ha, or about 45 percent of the total agricultural area, has no legal status under the land code (TURA 1981). This lack of security constitutes an important obstacle to farm investments which are necessary for intensification of agriculture (World Bank 1982).

Irrigation Development

Major irrigation development in Thailand resulted from the signing of the Bowring Treaty between Siam (Thailand) and Great Britain in 1856 which necessitated the spread of rice production into areas where natural water conditions were less than favorable. This led to an increase in the frequency of severe crop failure. Between 1914 and 1949, a series of irrigation projects were completed which benefited over 650,000 ha. After World War II, using loan funds from the World Bank, three large dams were built in the Central Plain. Additional dams as well as an extensive Ditches and Dikes Program to improve distribution of irrigation water were started during the middle and late 1960s (Small 1973).

The majority of the above schemes had as their main objective the stabilization of wet season rice production.

Only with the integration of Sirikit and Bhumipol Dams, with
their vast storage potential, into the existing irrigation
system and the initiation of the Ditches and Dikes Program
did dry season production become feasible over large areas
of the Central Plain (Kaida 1978). Complementing these have
been investments by the GOT in intensification of existing
irrigation programs by land leveling, construction of
internal distribution systems, land consolidation, and
implementation of drainage schemes (Trung 1978). An
increasingly large percentage of rice is produced on lands
that are capable of more precise water control (Table 7.2).
This has resulted in more stability in the wet season and
increased production during the dry season.

Water Charges

The State Irrigation Act of 1942 actually authorizes
the collection of an irrigation tax, but no charges have
even been made under this act (RID 1949). Taylor (1978)
insists that farmers using water from an irrigation system
are able to produce and sell more agricultural products at a
lower price thus benefiting society as a whole, and hence,
should not pay a direct charge or should pay a reduced
charge for water. Since Thailand has never charged a direct
water tax on the resource used, one can argue that the GOT
has followed this policy. It is also possible to argue that
the rice premium, which holds domestic rice prices 10 to 30
percent below market prices, serves as a form of water tax
for those that raise irrigated rice. This tax is also
charged those who plant rainfed rice, and therefore, the
argument really only holds for the dry season when all rice
grown must be irrigated (Johnson 1979).
Bertrand (1980), in his study of agricultural input and
output pricing in Thailand, uses a procedure developed by
the Mekong Committee to estimate the real economic cost of
irrigation water. Bertrand admits that this cost does not
reflect the opportunity cost of using water in the existing
systems, but it does allow some account to be taken of irrigation project costs. Using this procedure Bertrand
estimates "economic" input costs of water for rice production in Thailand ranging from $38 to $234 per ha in the wet
season and $73 to $204 per ha in the dry season. In the
Central Plain where the existing irrigation systems are
older and more extensive, he estimates costs at around $40
per ha in the wet season and $91 per ha in the dry season.
This work shows that the zero cost of water from irrigation

TABLE 7.2
Production of paddy under improved irrigation systems,
Thailand (1976-1980)

Year	Production (1,000 metric tons)				
	Type I[a]	Type II[b]	Type III[c]	Type IV[d]	Total
1976/77	40	3,063	1,687	533	5,323
1977/78	59	3,146	1,485	797	5,487
1978/79	79	3,095	1,622	808	5,604
1979/80	138	3,012	1,678	1,066	5,894
1979/80[e]	(32.3)	(1,240.6)	(865.25)	(417.74)	

Source: Royal Irrigation Department, 1979.

[a]Type I, good distribution and drainage system with land consolidation.

[b]Type II, standard ditches and dikes with good distribution and drainage system.

[c]Type III, fair distribution and drainage system, but no ditches or dikes.

[d]Type IV, inadequate distribution and drainage system.

[e]Figures in parentheses refer to area for each type in 1,000 hectares.

facilities is an important subsidy to the agricultural sector. Using 1978 data, net returns to land, labor, and management for rice, without the costs of canal irrigation water, are estimated to be between 25 to 30 percent higher than they would be with water charges to cover the costs of irrigation water.

COMPLEMENTARY RELATIONSHIPS

Crop production in any agricultural system requires management of the factors of production to increase yield. When one factor essential to production is limiting, response to other inputs supplied may be zero or even negative. Water control is an important factor for increasing crop production. Keller, et al. (1981) suggests that lack of control of water and reliability of delivery are important missing factors limiting yields in Thailand as farmers are unwilling to make adequate investments without more reliable water supplies.

It is difficult to separate the benefits of effective water control from those of improved cultural techniques, cash inputs, increased economic incentives and other agricultural policies. However, observations made by the World Bank in the Central Plain suggest the yield relationships shown in Table 7.3.

Yields increase from 2 tons/ha under rainfed conditions to almost 5 tons/ha with intensive irrigation (Type IV) and high use of other inputs including new technology. Neither improved water control nor improved agricultural policy resulting in high input use can operate in isolation to increase output to optimum levels. Using the production function technique of Wickham, Barker, and Rosegrant (1978), it is possible to more explicitly define the yield relationship hypothesized by the World Bank. This provides a framework for categorization of the impacts of investment in irrigation and modern inputs in the following general functional form:

$$Y_w = a_1 + a_2N + a_3N^2 - a_4S - a_5SN$$

where: Y = yield in kg/ha, wet (w) or
dry (d) season.
N = elemental nitrogen in kg.
S = stress days in number of days.

From this equation it is possible to develop yield response functions for the Central Plain. Yield relationships for different discrete irrigation and fertilizer input conditions are presented in Table 7.4. From this table it is possible to see that irrigation development and intensification may affect rice yields in at least three ways: (1) yields may be improved as a direct effect of more favorable water conditions; (2) irrigation may increase yields indirectly by increasing the farmer's incentives to use, or

TABLE 7.3
Estimated average paddy yields in the central plain of Thailand under different
levels of inputs

Agricultural Services	Wet Season	Dry Season	Water Management
	- - - - t/ha - - - -		
Existing services	2.0	--	No effective irrigation
Existing services	2.5	3.0	Unimproved irrigation system (Types III and IV)
Improved services and improved cultural techniques	3.0	3.5	Unimproved irrigation system (Types III and IV)
Effective agricultural services	3.8	4.0	Improved system (Type II)
Improved techniques, higher cash inputs, and effective agricultural services	4.6	4.8	More intensive system (Type I)

Source: Keller, et al. 1981.

TABLE 7.4
Paddy yields at differing levels of modern inputs

Season And Case Number	Description Of Irrigation And Fertilizer Input Levels	Traditional Varieties (TVs) N^a (kg/ha)	Yield (t/ha)	Modern Varieties (MVs) N^a (kg/ha)	Yield (t/ha)	Increase In Yield Due To: Fertilizer	Irrigation	Variety
							– – (t/ha) – –	
WET SEASON								
1	Rainfed no N	0	1.51	--	--	--	--	--
2	Rainfed low N	10	1.71	--	--	.21	--	--
3	Irrigation Type IV low N	10	1.81	10	2.37	--	.10	.56
4	Irrigation Type III low N	10	1.96	10	2.63	--	.26	.67
5	Irrigation Type II low N	10	2.03	10	2.76	--	.13	.73
6	Irrigation Type II normal N	20	2.27	20	2.90	.14	--	.63
7	Irrigation Type IV high N	--	--	30	3.02	.12	--	--
8	Irrigation Type I normal N	--	--	30	3.37	--	.35	--
9	Irrigation Type I high N	--	--	40	3.59	.22	--	--
DRY SEASON								
10	Irrigation Type II normal N	--	--	40	3.54	--	--	--
11	Irrigation Type II high N	--	--	50	3.81	.27	--	--
12	Irrigation Type I normal N	--	--	40	3.79	--	.25	--
13	Irrigation Type I high N	--	--	50	4.08	.27	--	--

[a] Elemental nitrogen.

Dry season: MVs $Y = 2566.7 + 42.2 N - .13 N^2 - 88.8 S - .95 NS$

Wet season: TVs $Y = 1848.9 + 34.9 N - .21 N^2 - 52.8 S - 2.1 NS$

          MVs $Y = 2666.5 + 36.4 N - 0.05 N^2 - 24.1 S - 10.7 NS$

to increase the use of complementary inputs; and (3) irrigation may create the potential for an additional crop.

Various combinations of input levels in Table 7.4 illustrate the three types of effects which irrigation may have on yields. The direct effect of improved water conditions in the four types of irrigation systems found in the Central Plain is shown by the differences between Cases 2 and 3 with the introduction of irrigation; and by the differences between Cases 3, 4, 5, 7, and 8 with the improved irrigation and HYVs. Cases 10 and 12 illustrate the results of irrigation improvement in the dry season.

Yield increases resulting from the increased use of modern inputs are also exhibited in Table 7.4. The impact of nitrogen is shown by the difference in yields for the various levels (low, normal, and high) of nitrogen application. How irrigation affects the incentive to change from traditional varieties to modern varieties during the wet season is illustrated in the last column. In Thailand the incentive to switch to modern varieties is even greater in the dry season. This is primarily a function of water control and lack of flooding, but it also reflects higher potential returns from HYVs during the dry season.

From Table 7.4, it is possible to calculate yield increases attributable to irrigation from alternative sequences of input use. Significant incremental yield increases only result when farmers can shift to HYVs. In almost all of the rainfed areas and most of the Type IV and Type III irrigation areas, it is not possible to maintain a water depth less than 60 cm which is required for most HYVs. Therefore, it is only within well-drained areas of Type II and Type I irrigation areas where farmers have been consistently willing to shift to HYVs in the wet season. Shifting from a Type III to Type II system and then changing to a modern variety followed by the use of additional inputs results in a production increase of approximately 1 ton/ha. Further, improving the irrigation system to a Type I system and using additional inputs results in another increase of about .6 ton/ha. Use of modern varieties in the Type IV and Type III systems offers potential yield increases but it also increases the risk of crop loss due to flooding. Once farmers have secure irrigation and are raising a dry season crop, additional changes are not as dramatic. But since they start at much higher yields which are not as risky, additional changes have proven to be more appealing to these farmers in the Central Plain.

RICE AND FERTILIZER PRICE RELATIONSHIPS

A higher rice-to-fertilizer price ratio, other things being equal, would increase the rate of fertilizer utilization. The converse would happen with low rice-to-fertilizer price ratios. For example, a rice-to-fertilizer price ratio of 0.2 would require a ten to one yield response relationship to provide a benefit-cost ratio (B/C) of 2.0 between receipts and costs of fertilizer. Given the fact that other costs related to fertilizer application, such as greater labor used for weeding and harvest, are not considered in this B/C ratio, the value of two is usually considered as the lowest B/C ratio which would make fertilizer application profitable (Yotopoulos and Adulairdhaya 1979).

Using the production functions from Table 7.4, it is possible to calculate the B/C ratios for additional fertilizer application on wet and dry season rice. Based on 1978 prices the B/C ratios for wet and dry season rice in various types of irrigation systems are present in Table 7.5.

Data in Table 7.5 dramatically illustrates why farmers in Thailand use more fertilizer in the dry season relative to the wet season. Low B/C ratios in Type III systems during the wet season also explain why most of the fertilizer used in the Central Plain is concentrated in areas where water control is better (i.e., Type I and some Type II areas).

OTHER POLICY CONSIDERATIONS

Since rice uses large amounts of water, GOT has been trying to encourage crop diversification and discourage rice production during the dry season. The Tantigate (1978) study of conflict between rice and sugarcane farmers over water in the Central Plain demonstrated that water conflicts discouraged rice farmers from transplanting and cultivating a second crop in the dry season and also from using higher levels of modern inputs in the wet season. Rice yields on mixed ditches, e.g., those supporting both rice and sugarcane farmers, were 30 percent lower than rice yields on ditches used only by rice farmers. The conflict also adversely affected sugarcane production (sugarcane yields were 29 percent less on mixed ditches than ditches used solely by sugarcane farmers). Thus, crop diversification reduced returns to irrigation investments.

Failure of the GOT to collect water fees while providing a significant subsidy to irrigated rice farmers is continuing to impose an increasing burden on GOT tax

TABLE 7.5
Benefit-cost ratios for fertilizer use for wet and dry
season rice by irrigation system type

| | Irrigation System Type | | | |
	I	II	III	IV
WET SEASON[c]				
Modern variety[a]	2.64	1.54	.43	--
Modern variety[b]	4.06	2.37	.67	--
DRY SEASON[c]				
Modern variety[a]	4.12	3.93	--	--
Modern variety[b]	6.35	6.05	--	--

[a]Fertilizer applied 16-20-0 composite (N = $.96/kg).
[b]Fertilizer applied area (46-0-0) (N = $.64/kg).
[c]Rice price ($.10/kg).

revenues. Even though there has been a three to fourfold
increase in the Royal Irrigation Department's (RID) budget
between 1972 and 1981 (in current dollars), the budget for
operations and maintenance (O&M) as a percentage of total
construction budget has decreased from 7 percent to 2.6
percent. It is hard to determine an optimal annual allocation to O&M, but if the general engineering rule of thumb of
5 percent is used, then the 1981 O&M budget should roughly
be doubled (Keller, et al. 1981). With rapidly expanding
financial deficits and pressure from the World Bank to
control growth of expenditures in the public sector, it is
very unlikely that the GOT will adequatley fund O&M costs at
RID, or any other department for that matter. Only by collecting some of the surplus created by irrigation development and intensification can the RID realistically expect to
obtain an adequate O&M budget (Easter 1980).

While the impacts of unclear land tenure are difficult to measure they are significant. Land tenure problems are reflected in the costs of irrigation intensification, particularly in areas where land consolidation (which requires well-defined land ownership) and leveling are completed. In 1981 the costs of irrigation system intensification were running from $1,250 to $2,000 per ha (Keller, et al. 1981). In areas where yield increases after irrigation intensification average about .6 ton/ha and benefits average roughly $75/ha, the present value of the benefits (at 10 percent discounted over thirty years) is $875 per ha. Thus, the B/C ratio of wet season irrigation in these areas is only about 0.5. These figures are rough and vary from location to location, but in general, land consolidation and leveling are both the most expensive components and require the most time. In 1980 land consolidation cost $1,200 per ha. Unclear land titles have continued to be one of the major stumbling blocks to land consolidation. However, Seckler and Keller (1981) argue that in Thailand the "carrot" of land titles, if used, could be a strong incentive to bring about more farmer cooperation in land consolidation projects.

DISCUSSION AND CONCLUSION

The majority of Thailand's agricultural investments have been in water resources development. Without this investment Thailand would have lost much of its world market share of rice exports. Yet many of Thailand's agricultural policies have tended to retard, rather than encourage, increased agricultural production. Original land policy, which encouraged the opening and cultivation of new land, led to extensive rather than intensive agricultural production practices. Now with an end to the land frontier in the Central Plain, these land policies are restricting the transition from traditional to more modern agriculture. In particular, the lack of clear land title is a significant constraint on individual investment by farmers. Maintaining domestic rice prices 20 to 30 percent below world prices while holding domestic fertilizer prices above the world market price has also discouraged farmers from shifting toward more modern practices. This is especially true in the higher risk irrigated areas where there is a lack of water security and the danger of flooding. Finally, the failure to collect water fees has led to a situation where, despite massive investment by GOT, the irrigation systems are not properly funded and, hence, are inadequately operated and maintained.

Economic returns to irrigation investment are dependent both upon water policy and other agricultural policies. In the not unusual situation where policies are uncoordinated, returns to irrigation investment are lower than they should be. This situation is often further complicated by poor operation and maintenance of the irrigation systems leading to reduced project life with resulting B/C ratios far below 1.0. Increasing these ratios requires more then just improved water policy. It involves improved and better coordinated input, land tenure, and output purchase policies.

REFERENCES

Bertrand, Trent. 1980. "Thailand: Case study of agricultural input and output pricing." Staff Working Paper No. 385, World Bank, Washington, D.C.

Bottrall, Anthony F. 1981. "Comparative study of the staff management and organization of irrigation projects." Working Paper No. 458, World Bank, Washington, D.C.

Easter, K. William. 1980. "Capturing the economic surplus created by irrigation." Staff Paper P80-14, Department of Agricultural and Applied Economics, University of Minnesota, St. Paul.

Fallon, Edward, and Don Kanel. 1978. "Report on land tenure conditions and land reform in Thailand." Land Tenure Center, University of Wisconsin, Madison.

Herdt, Robert W. 1980. "Studies in water management economics at IRRI." Report of a Planning Workshop on Irrigation Water Management. International Rice Research Institute, Los Banos, Laguna, Philippines, pp. 115-38.

Johnson, Sam H. III. 1979. "Major policy issues in the development of irrigation in Thailand." Paper presented at the Annual Conference of the Agricultural Economics Society of Thailand, Kasetsart University, Bangkok, Thailand, December 13-14.

Kaida, Yoshihiro. 1978. "Irrigation and drainage: Present and future." In Thailand: A Rice-Growing Society, (ed.) Yoneo Ishi, pp. 205-45. University Press of Hawaii, Honolulu, Hawaii.

126

Keller, Jack, et al. 1981. Thailand/USAID Irrigation
Development Options and Investment Strategies for the
1980s. WMS Report 5, Water Management Synthesis
Project, Utah State University, Logan, Utah.

Pinthong, Chirmsak, and Ammar Siamwalla. 1978.
"Preliminary background notes on food and nutrition
policy in Thailand." Discussion Paper, Thammasat
University, Bangkok, Thailand.

Royal Irrigation Department (RID). 1949. Report on
Irrigation Drainage and Water Communication Project of
the Chao Phya River Plain. Report by M.L.X. Kambhu,
Director-General, Bangkok, Thailand.

_____. 1979. Report on the Production of Rice in
Irrigation Project Areas, 1977-78, 1978-79. Bangkok,
Thailand.

Seckler, David, and Jack Keller. 1981. "Regional
agricultural development authorities." Appendix A of
Thailand/USAID Irrigation Development Options and
Investment Strategies for the 1980s, pp. A/1-A/8. WMS
Report 5, Water Management Synthesis Project, Utah
State University, Logan, Utah.

Small, Leslie E. 1973. "Historical development of the
Greater Chao Phya Water Control Project: An economic
perspective." Journal of the Siam Society 61(1):1-24.

Tantigate, Kanaengnid. 1978. "Conflict between rice and
sugarcane farmers over irrigation water: A case study
in Thailand." In Irrigation Policy and Management in
Southeast Asia, pp. 175-83. International Rice
Research Institute, Los Banos, Laguna, Philipppines.

Taylor, D.C. 1978. "Financing irrigation services in the
Pekalen Sampean Irrigation Project, East Java,
Indonesia." In Irrigation Policy and Management in
Southeast Asia, pp. 111-22. International Rice
Research Institute, Los Banos, Laguna, Philipppines.

Thai Universities Research Association (TURA). 1981. Land
Use and Development Policy (in Thai). TURA Institute,
Bangkok, Thailand.

Timmer, C. Peter, and Walter P. Falcon. 1975. "The
political economy of rice production and trade in
Asia." In Agriculture in Development Theory, (ed.)
L.G. Reynolds, pp. 373-408. Yale University Press,
New Haven, Connecticut.

Trung, Ngo Quoc. 1978. "Economic analysis of irrigation
development in deltaic regions of Asia: The case of
central Thailand." In Irrigation Policy and Management
in Southeast Asia, pp. 155-64. International Rice
Research Institute, Los Banos, Laguna, Philippines.

Welsch, D.E., and S. Tongpan. 1973. "Background to the introduction of high yielding varieties of rice in Thailand." In Technical Change in Asian Agriculture, (ed.) R.T. Shand, pp. 124-43. Australian National University Press, Canberra, Australia.

Wickham, T.H., R. Barker, and M.V. Rosegrant. 1978. "Complementaritied Among Irrigation, Fertilizer, and Modern Rice Varieties." In Economic Consequences of the New Rice Technology, pp. 221-32. International Rice Research Institute, Los Banos, Philippines.

Wong, Chung Ming. 1978. "A model for evaluating the effects of Thai government taxation of rice exports on trade and welfare." American Journal of Agricultural Economics 60(1):65-73.

World Bank, East Asia and Pacific Regional Office. 1982. Thailand: Program and Policy Priorities for an Agricultural Economy in Transition. World Bank, Washington, D.C.

Yotopoulos, Pan A., and K. Adulavidhaya. 1979. "The Green Revolution in Thailand." In Readings in Asian Farm Management, (eds.) T.B. Thiam and Shao-er Ong, pp. 241-58. Singapore University Press, Singapore.

CHAPTER 8

THE ECONOMICS OF SMALL TANK IRRIGATION IN NORTHEAST THAILAND

Yuavares Tubpun

Tank irrigation was considered by the Royal Irrigation Department (RID) and many foreign missions as the most appropriate answer to the severe water shortage problem in the northeast region of Thailand. During 1951-1955, 104 tanks were built in the region. About 86 percent of the tanks were concentrated in the size ranging from 0.1-5.0 million cubic meter (mm^3). During 1955-1975, only sixty-one tanks were constructed, of which thirty have capacity larger than 5 mm^3. In other words, size concentration had moved towards the larger sized tanks (Tubpun 1981).

DEVELOPMENT OF SMALL TANKS

In 1975, the Thai government brought the tank irrigation issue to the forefront again by announcing the policy to spread small irrigation tanks throughout the northeast region as soon as possible. The investment strategy was to have each proposed project finished within a year and to cost not more than 2 million Baht. The 2 million Baht budget put a limit on the tank size, i.e., tanks of 1 mm^3 capacity or less. According to RID classification, a reservoir of 1 mm^3 or less is designed primarily for domestic water supply. Therefore, tanks of this size are considered as village ponds rather than irrigation tanks.

In the northeast alone during 1975-1981, RID (1982) reported that there were approximately 1,000 small tanks completed, with a combined total storage capacity of approximately 260 mm^3. Although meeting basic household needs was the main purpose of these tanks, the same source reported about 448,000 rai were irrigated out of the approximately 600,000 rai of planned irrigable area.[1]

These small tanks were built in response to requests from villagers through their tambol councils. After a brief survey of the appropriateness of the construction site, a meeting is held in the village to ask for the consent of the villagers, especially those villagers who will have part or all of their land flooded. Since there is no compensation for the flooded land in these projects, the villagers have to work out among themselves the means of compensating farmers for the flooded land. If there is any objection, there will be no construction. For example, in one of our study tanks farmers who lost part of their land were given first priority to work on the tank construction and earned money wages.

Once the tank is built it belongs to the village where the tank is located and is the responsibility of the village water user organization (WUO). There will be no RID personnel located at the tank sites. The WUO is responsible for operation, administration, and maintenance. The RID will provide help only for major repairs which the WUO is unable to deal with themselves, such as the damage caused by severe floods. However, the villagers still have to provide their labor to repair the damages. Therefore, the performance and project life depend on the leadership and the cooperation among members of the WUO.

PROBLEM STATEMENT AND OBJECTIVES

Hundreds of tanks have been built since 1975 under the small tank program with the main purpose of providing the villagers with their basic water needs. Ex-ante economic evaluation of the tanks was not done for several reasons. First, each individual project was considered too small to justify spending time and budget trying to predict performance. Second, lack of baseline data and other information necessary for an ex-ante evaluation discouraged such studies. Third, measuring benefits of domestic water uses and assigning values is not a simple task.

Even though each individual project is small, large numbers of them exist and there are more to come. Therefore, this study was conducted in order to meet the following objectives: (1) to evaluate the ex-post economic costs and benefits of the small tanks; and (2) to develop simple evaluation techniques which require a minimum amount of data for other project evaluations.

SAMPLING PROCEDURES AND DATA COLLECTION

Three tanks in Khon Kaen Province were selected for study: Tha Malai, Nong Num Kliang, and Ban Tham Khae (Figure 8.1). These three tanks were all built as the result of the small tank policy announced in 1975. The criteria used in selecting these three tanks for the study was simple. The tanks should have been constructed about the same period and should be, at least, three years old so that farmers have had time to develop some water use. In addition, each of the three tanks should have a different level of performance.

For comparison, three nearby villages without tanks were also selected, one for each tank village. The control villages were limited to being less than 5 km from the tank villages in order to minimize the difference in socio-economic and agroclimatic factors. The three "without tank" villages are: Ban Kok Lam, Ban Non Lan, and Ban Nong Nok Khian.

For each pair of villages three groups of farmers were interviewed: (1) farmers in the tank village who are members of the WUO; (2) farmers in the tank village who are not members of the WUO; and (3) farmers in the corresponding non-tank village.

The chairman or secretary of the WUO provided a list of members from which the first group was selected. For the second and third groups lists of households were provided by the village headman of each village. In each group samples were selected using a table of random numbers. However, some of the selected farmers were not available and the next number in the random table was selected as a substitute.

The field survey was conducted during March 25-April 4, 1983. A total of 128 farm households were interviewed. A sample of fifteen households in each group was considered manageable and adequate for statistical reliability.

Prior to the field survey, during December 1982-April 1983, data were collected through observations and interviews at the tank sites. Two enumerators were at each tank site one day a week to observe and interview those who came to draw water for home use and livestock. They were asked why they had come to the tank, how often they came, and where they had come from. This information is used to help evaluate the benefits from domestic water uses during the dry season. Besides the primary data collection, supplemental information was obtained from the local and Bangkok RID offices.

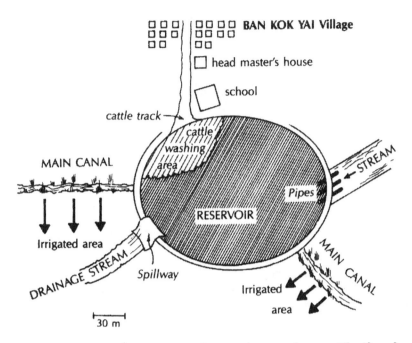

Figure 8.1   The Tha Malai tank, northeast Thailand

DESCRIPTION OF STUDY TANKS

Tha Malai tank (1) belongs to Ban Kok Yai village
(Figure 8.1). It is located 25 km southwest of Khon Kaen
and is only 2 km from the main road. This small, high
performance tank was developed in 1978 from an old weir
which had been used for irrigation and domestic water supply
(Table 8.1). A WUO was officially formed in the following
year. The WUO consists of sixty-three members out of
approximately 185 households in the village.
After the tank was completed in 1978, the members of
the Tha Malai WUO dug two unlined irrigation canals of a
combined length of 850 meters with technical advice from
RID. The tank has the capacity to irrigate about 1,000 rai
of paddy during the wet season and approximately 350 rai of
dry season crops.
In the wet season all of the irrigated land is under
paddy (glutinous rice) while in the dry season sweet corn is
the major irrigated crop. Although a lesser area is irrigated during the dry season than in the wet season, more

TABLE 8.1
Characteristics of the three study tanks

Item	Tha Malai (1)	Nong Num Kliang (2)	Ban Tham Khae (3)
Year constructed	1978	1979	1978
Capacity (m^3)	110,000	300,000	860,000
Catchment area (km^2)	9.5	2.9	7.1
Area planned to be irrigated (rai)			
Wet season	1,000	210	500
Dry Season	350	50	--
Actual irrigated area 1982-1983 (rai)			
Wet season	722	176	0
Dry season	340	50	10

Source: Royal Irrigation Department (RID), Thailand, 1982.

farmers benefit. Only about 340 rai of land which are adjacent to the head-end of the canal were irrigated in the dry season. The owners of this land share part of their land with their friends and relatives for dry season cultivation. Before paddy is ready for harvesting their relatives and friends in the village will come and tell them that they would like to grow some sweet corn on their land. The farmers will assign each of them two to three parcels of land (ranging from .25 rai to 2 rai for each person) for dry season cropping while saving some for themselves. During the wet season paddy harvest the relatives and friends will help harvest the paddy which includes transporting the paddy to the farmers' houses. The assigned parcels of land will then be farmed rent free.[2] The only condition which must be

met is that the land has to be cleared by the time the
farmers are ready to plant paddy rice in the next rainy
season. By this sharing process more households can benefit
from irrigation in the dry season than is possible in the
wet season.

Besides the strong leadership and farmer coordination,
one factor which has facilitated good management is location
of the tank itself. The tank is located adjacent to the
village. Any misuse of the tank or breaking of rules can be
easily seen. The WUO has agreed on a set of rules for using
the tank. For example, fishing is prohibited in part of the
tank. Those who violate these rules will be punished by
having to dig a certain length of canal. Buffaloes are not
allowed to walk on the earth dam in order to keep the dam in
good condition. If animals are found walking on the dam the
owners are fined. These rules would be difficult to enforce
if the tank was located away from the village.

In some years the WUO will declare a fishing day,
usually before the Thai New Year, April 13. Villagers from
Tha Malai and nearby villages must pay fees based on the
type and size of fishing equipment used. The fees collected
belong to the village. The WUO committee and the village
headman will call a village meeting to decide how to use the
money.

Nong Kum Kliang tank (2) is located in Ban Num Kliang
village which is about 13 km north of Khon Kaen on a hard
surface road. It was completed in 1979 and a WUO was formed
in the same year. In March 1983, the WUO included eighteen
households out of sixty-six households in the village.

The tank irrigated about 210 rai of paddy in the wet
season. Approximately 50 rai of groundnut and other crops
were irrigated during the 1983 dry season. They have a land
sharing system similar to the Tha Malai tank. The WUO has
also arranged for fishing days in some years.

Even though this tank contains about three times as
much water as the Tha Malai tank, it can irrigate only one-
fifth as much as Tha Malai in both the wet and dry seasons.
A major reason for the lower level of production appears to
be weaker leadership. In addition the tank is located away
from the village which makes it more difficult to manage and
police.

Ban Tham Khae tank (3) is about 60 km southwest of Khon
Kaen and was completed in 1978. A WUO was not formed until
the end of 1981 and has done very little since then. There
are no irrigation canals and, hence, no irrigation benefits
during the wet season. In the dry season, a combination of
crops is grown such as sweet corn, string beans, and chili
pepper. To irrigate these dry season crops farmers have to

carry water from the tank to their plots by bucket. Very little land can be irrigated by this method and most of it is for home consumption.

Utilization of this tank is low. Animals seem to be the major user of the tank for drinking and soaking. Household consumption in any form is low compared to the other two tanks due to a snail problem. Fishing is also difficult due to the same problem.

PROJECT EVALUATION

Two approaches are used to measure the benefits from the three tank projects. First, benefits are estimated using market based approaches to value agricultural and fish products, and time saved. Second, benefit estimates are obtained through farmer interviews. The interviewed farmers were asked hypothetical questions concerning their maximum willingness to pay and the minimum compensation they would require to forego the tank project. The benefits from these two approaches are compared before the market based benefits are used to calculate economic returns.

<u>Market Based Benefits</u>

Two major categories of benefits from the tanks are defined as follows: (1) Agricultural benefits: increases in production from tank water used to irrigate the paddy nursery bed and supplement the rainfall for wet season rice will be referred to as wet season benefits (WB) while production from the dry season crops will be called dry season benefits (DB). (2) Domestic benefits: use of tank water for household consumption will be called household benefits (HB), use of tank water by livestock will be referred to as livestock benefits (LB), and use of tanks for fish culture will be identified as fish benefits (FB). Therefore, total discounted benefits are:

$$B_t = WB_t + DB_t + HB_t + LB_t + FB_t$$

Wet season benefits from paddy production is measured by calculating the value of the yield difference between the irrigated and the nonirrigated farms.

$$WB_t = (Y_{IR_t} - Y_{NR_t})\ P_t \cdot A_{w_t}$$

where P_t - farm price of paddy in year t.

Y_{IR_t} - average yield per rai from irrigated farms.

Y_{NR_t} - average yield per rai from non-irrigated farms.

A_{w_t} - wet season irrigated area.

t - 0, 1, 2,..., n years where n is project life.

No crop production, except upland crops such as cassava, is possible during the dry season in the northeast without irrigation. These upland crops are usually not grown on the paddy land. Therefore, irrigation benefits from dry season cropping on paddy land is measured by the net income earned from the crops grown, i.e.,

$$DB_t - (Id_t) \, Ad_t$$

where Id_t - net income per rai from dry season cropping.

Ad_t - area under dry seaon cultivation in each year t.

The primary household water consumption benefit is the value of tank convenience or time saved over using another water source. Although in a number of areas this benefit is quite significant, in the three tanks studied it was fairly small. For simplicity, the value of water for household uses is taken as 0.50 Baht per family per day in Tank 1 and Tank 2 and 0.25 Baht per family per day in Tank 3 during the six months of dry season.[3]

Without tanks, during the dry season, villagers have to drive their animals (especially water buffalo) to some natural pond for the animals to soak and drink. The time spent doing this can be saved with a tank. Each day on the average, there were 88, 116, and 295 head of cattle and water buffalo driven to tanks 1, 2, and 3, respectively.[4] The value of this water for livestock (LB) is the time saved in taking animals to an alternative source of water. It is estimated at 0.25 Baht per head per day for six months during the dry season.

Fish production in the tanks has provided additional protein for the villagers within and outside the tank village. The estimate of FB was based on the data obtained during the observations at the tank sites. Due to our failure to disaggregate the volume of fish caught by type of fish, the low price of 5 Baht per kg was used to obtain a conservative estimate of the value of fish caught.

Benefits Measured by Hypothetical Approach

During the field survey two hypothetical questions were asked. First, the head of each household was asked to express the whole family's maximum willingness to pay to have the tank built or to save the tank from being lost. Second, the respondents were asked to estimate the minimum amount of compensation their family would be willing to accept for giving up the tank.

The answers to both questions provide estimates of the tank benefits perceived by the villagers. The reliability of the answers depends on the way the questions were asked. It is difficult to properly present the hypothetical questions. However, the survey results are in a reasonable range except at tank 2 which was the first tank at which farmers were surveyed. The value of compensation requested by members of the WUO served by this tank was too high as was the willingness to pay by non-members. This was probably because the interviewers did not make the questions clear. Consequently, adjustments in the data are made based on the results from the other two sites.

As shown in Table 8.2, the average maximum willingness to pay for the tanks ranged from a high of 2,813 Baht per family for the WUO members of tank 1 to a low of 2,100 Baht per family for members of tank 3. The results are in a comparable range. Furthermore, the difference in results reflects the differences in performance of the tanks. Among the three, tank 1 is the best, tank 3 is the worst, and tank 2 is somewhere in between.

The average minimum compensation requested by tank 1 WUO members is 14,428 Baht per family, which is about five times higher than their average willingness to pay. The amount requested by WUO members of tank 3 is lower than in tank 1 and also five times higher than their willingness to pay. For tank 2, the average compensation should be somewhere in between the first two tanks. The very high compensation value, i.e., eleven times higher than their willingness to pay, appears to be too high. This unexpectedly high value probably occurred because the interviewers failed to emphasize that the compensation should represent the minimum amount. Therefore, based on the results from the other two sites, the figures are adjusted to be about five and seven times higher than their willingness to pay,

TABLE 8.2
Willingness to pay and compensation requested for the three tanks in
northeast Thailand, 1983

	Tanks		
	1	2	3
Willingness to Pay	- - - (Baht) - - -		
Maximum per family			
Member of WUO	2,813	2,758	2,100
Non-member of WUO	872	1,490	433
Total per village			
Members of WUO	185,658	49,644	84,000
Non-members of WUO	45,344	71,520	23,38:
TOTAL	231,002	121,164	107,38:
Compensation Requested			
Minimum per family			
Member of WUO	14,428	30,417	10,65.
Non-member of WUO	6,143	12,727	2,97!
Total per village			
Members of WUO	952,248	547,506	426,12
Non-members of WUO	319,436	610,896	160,86
TOTAL	1,271,684	1,158,402	586,98
Per Family: Compensation Requested Divided by Willingness to Pay	- - - (Ratio) - - -		
Member of WUO	5.13	11.02	5.07
Non-member of WUO	7.04	8.54	6.88
Adjusted Compensation Requested	- - - (Baht) - - -		
Minimum per family			
Member of WUO	nr	14,065	nr
Non-member of WUO		10,430	
Total per village			
Members of WUO	952,248	253,170	426,1
Non-members of WUO	319,436	500,640	160,8
TOTAL	1,271,684	753,810	586,9

nr = not required.

i.e., 14,068 and 10,430 Baht per family. Yet these figures may still be high given that the non-members' adjusted compensation is still higher in tank 2 than in tank 1.

The willingness to pay and the compensation requested are lower for the non-members of WUO than for the corresponding members in all three cases. Those who are members are more likely to receive direct benefits from the projects, especially agricultural benefits. However, the non-members benefit from domestic water uses and some might also receive agricultural benefit.

For each tank, total willingness to pay for members and non-members together is estimated by multiplying the average willingness to pay per family by the corresponding number of families in each group. A similar method is used for deriving the total compensation. The estimated total (compensation or willingness to pay) for non-members is likely to be underestimated because the number of families used included only families in the village where the tank is located. Households in nearby villages will also benefit from the tank, primarily in terms of domestic uses and water for livestock.

The willingness to pay and compensating values are, with one exception, well below the market based benefit estimates even with a ten year time horizon (Table 8.3). This suggests that the survey may not have obtained an accurate estimate of the value of tanks based on the one time payment question. A more appropriate procedure may have been to determine the annual payment villagers would have been willing to make over the life of the project. In the case of the compensating test, the question should have been what annual payment would they require to give up the tank? There is also a concern that the heads of households may not provide an accurate estimate of the entire family's willingness to pay.

Project Costs

Total project costs (TC) include construction costs (CC), costs of digging the unlined canal (UC), and operation and maintenance costs (MC). Thus, the total project costs when appropriately discounted are:

$$TC_t = CC_t + UC_t + MC_t$$

As with most irrigation projects, construction costs are the big item in all three tanks (Table 8.4). The zero costs for

TABLE 8.3
Market based benefit estimates for the three tanks

	Tanks		
	1	2	3

Annual Benefits

Wet season crops	249,812	60,896	n.i.
Dry season crops	1,196,448[a]	32,610	6,780
Livestock benefits	3,960	5,220	13,275
Household consumption	8,280[b]	5,840	5,940
Fish production	26,100	52,650	36,000
TOTAL	1,484,600	157,316	61,995
PVB (10% and 10 years)[c]	8,202,869	966,639	380,932
PVB (7% and 10 years)	9,487,433	1,104,922	435,427

n.i. = no irrigation.

[a]During 1980-1984 the benefits varied as the area planted in the dry season expanded. The estimated benefits are:

1980	186,945 Baht
1981	992,508 Baht
1982	1,444,575 Baht
1983	1,155,660 Baht
1984	1,196,448 Baht

After 1984 dry season benefits are assumed to remain constant at 1.2 million Baht for the life of the project.

[b]After another tank was completed near the village, only half of the village households used water from tank 1 for human consumption.

[c]The present value of benefits (PVB) is calculated based on the dry season benefits shown in footnote a. Other benefits are assumed to remain constant for the ten years.

TABLE 8.4
Project costs in 1978 prices

	Tanks		
	1	2	3
INITIAL COST	- - - (Baht) - - -		
Construction Cost (CC)	1,335,500	1,559,129[a]	1,516,000
Cash cost	1,275,500	1,379,129	1,000,000
Opportunity cost of flooded land[b]	60,000	180,000	516,000
Cost of Digging the Canals (UC)[c]	58,482	14,256	--
ANNUAL COST			
Operation and Maintenance Cost (MC)[d]	13,340	13,934	--[e]

[a] The actual current cost was 1,701,780 Baht in 1979. It was adjusted to 1978 price by wholesale price index for construction material.

[b] Using the AIT estimate for the typical 100,000 m^3 reservoir, 30 rai will be flooded for every 100,000 m^3 capacity at a cost of 2,000 Baht per rai (AIT 1978).

[c] It was estimated at 81 Baht per rai of irrigated land (Tubpun 1981).

[d] Estimated as 1 percent of cash construction cost and of the cost of digging canals.

[e] So far, there have been no operation and/or maintenance expenditures.

digging canals and for operation and maintenance in tank 3
are consistent with zero levels of wet season irrigation.

Economic Life and Discount Rate

According to RID, the physical structures associated
with a tank (earth dam and spillway) should last for thirty
years if properly maintained. However, in some of our study
tanks such as Tha Malai tank, the rate of siltation is quite
high. If nothing is done to reduce the siltation rate the
Tha Malai tank will not last longer than fifteen years.
Asian Institute of Technology (AIT 1978) used a project life
of twenty years in their evaluation of the typical tank.
Therefore, the three alternative time horizons of fifteen,
twenty, and thirty years are used to show the sensitivity of
the final outcomes to length of project life.

Since all the prices and costs are expressed in constant 1978 prices, the discount rates employed do not
include inflation. To be consistent with the previous tank
study, 7 percent and 10 percent discount rates were employed
(Tubpun 1981). The lower rate is the rate of interest on
government bonds and represents the social rate of discount.
The higher rate is the lowest lending rate charged by commercial banks and represents an opportunity cost of capital.

Economic Returns

The evaluation results, based on market related
benefits, are presented in terms of benefit-cost ratios
(B/C) and net present values (NPV) (Table 8.5). Tha Malai
is the only project which passed the economic efficiency
test. It yields benefits over costs ranging from 7 million
Baht to more than 14 million Baht. Benefits derived from
this tank are about six to ten times higher than costs.

There are various factors which contribute to these
impressively high returns. First, the location is convenient for tank policing and management. Second, the village
has strong leadership. Third, the WUO has succeeded in
organizing its members to dig and maintain the irrigation
canals in good condition. Fourth, rules were set by the WUO
and are actively and consistently enforced. With the tank
in good condition and proper water management, the WUO members can fully utilize water available in the tank in both
the wet and dry seasons. Finally, the profitability of
sweet corn has provided the necessary incentive for WUO
members to practice dry season cropping.

TABLE 8.5
Economic returns for the three tanks (NPV in million Baht)

Project Life		Tanks		
		1	2	3[a]
		7% Discount Rate		
15 years	B/C	7.09	0.73	0.32
	NPV	9.10	-0.45	-1.03
20 years	B/C	8.52	0.87	0.38
	NPV	11.40	-0.22	-0.93
30 years	B/C	10.21	1.03	0.46
	NPV	14.20	0.57	-0.81
		10% Discount Rate		
15 years	B/C	5.92	0.61	0.26
	NPV	7.26	-0.65	-1.12
20 years	B/C	6.87	0.70	0.30
	NPV	8.73	-0.50	-1.05
30 years	B/C	7.81	0.79	0.35
	NPV	10.22	-0.36	-0.99

[a]There were no wet season benefits.

For tank 2, benefits derived from wet season and dry season irrigation were only about one-half of the project cost, i.e., it cannot pass any standard investment test for irrigation alone. Even if benefits from domestic uses are included, the total benefits are not high enough to make benefits larger than costs except when the project life is thirty years and the discount rate is 7 percent. Its poor performance compared to tank 1 is due mainly to the smaller area irrigated. In spite of three times more storage capacity the area irrigated by tank 2 is only about one-fifth of that under tank 1 not to mention double cropping during the dry season in tank 1. Furthermore, the net return per rai from groundnut was lower than from sweet corn.

The last tank studied, tank 3, is the least productive. The WUO has not been active. The benefits are derived from a small area of bucket-irrigated land during the dry season and water for household and livestock use and fish production. The value of these benefits was estimated to be only about one-fourth to one-third of the project cost.

CONCLUSION AND RECOMMENDATIONS

At least three major conclusions can be drawn from this study. First, fish production has the potential of being a major benefit from the small tanks. Next to irrigation, fish production was by far the most important source of project benefit. In fact in tank 3 fish production accounted for over one-half of the benefits while in tank 2 it contributed one-third of the benefits. Second, benefits from household and livestock water use alone did not meet the economic efficiency criterion for any of the three tanks studied. Even the addition of fish benefits is not enough to raise benefits above costs. This suggests that the government goal of constructing these very small tanks just for storing and providing water for household and animal consumption, with irrigation benefits as a by-product, should be reconsidered. Water supply for household use might be provided cheaper by other means such as wells or rainwater catchment jars. If ground water or other sources are not adequate to provide a year-round water supply, then small tanks may be the only means available. In that case, to be able to pass the economic efficiency test, irrigation should be one of the main objectives even for tanks as small as 100,000 m³ storage capacity. However, having irrigation as a main goal in designing and constructing a tank is a necessary but not sufficient condition for economic justification of the investment. The sufficient condition is that the irrigation water has to be effectively utilized.

This leads to the third general conclusion, that to gain full benefit from irrigation four factors are necessary: (1) leadership, (2) cooperation, (3) good tank location, and (4) market and price incentives. No single one of the four factors can be said to be the most important. The general impression is, however, that in the presence of strong leadership the other conditions can be achieved or their absence compensated for by leadership. Certainly, in the three tanks studied, leadership made the difference. A strong leader can encourage cooperation among the members of the WUO. Examples of cooperation include land owners who give up land for the reservoir site or for canals. An additional example involves land owners in the command area willing to "loan" or rent their land to others for dry season crops.

Location was important for tank 1 in preventing damage to the structure by animals and in enforcing fishing rules. The lack of a convenient location for personal supervision around the clock seemed to be a drawback for tank 2 and tank 3. Markets which provided strong price incentives were crucial in making dry season irrigaton highly profitable for farmers served by tank 1.

If all four conditions are not present then the government should seriously consider not constructing a tank at that location. What can be done if the four factors are not present and the decision to build a tank or tanks has already been made? First, a leadership training program could be initiated. Second, special educational efforts could be made to show villagers the value of cooperation. Third, marketing information could be provided by a government agency such as the Office of Agricultural Economics. This would require special studies of markets and prices for dry season crops in the northeast. Fourth, RID should work closely with the villagers to select a favorable site. Finally, very small tanks could be constructed which had just enough water for household and animal use. This would at least minimize costs.

NOTES

1. 6.25 rai equal one hectare.
2. Even though rents were not charged explicitly, implicit rent can be estimated based on the wage paid for labor to harvest and transport paddy. If dry season crops proved to be highly profitable, demand for irrigated land during the dry season might increase up to the level that explicit rent is paid. Rent, whether implicit or explicit, is another possible measure for dry season irrigation benefits.
3. The values for household water use and livestock use are based on an AIT study done in 1978.
4. These averages are based on data collected during observations at the tank sites.

REFERENCES

Asian Institute of Technology (AIT). 1978. <u>Water for the Northeast: A Strategy for the Development of Small-Scale Water Resources, Vol. 1: Main Report</u>. Bangkok, Thailand.
Royal Irrigation Department (RID), Ministry of Agriculture and Cooperatives. 1982. Table showing water resource development in Thailand completed to the end of fiscal year 1980 and under construction in 1981 (in Thai). Bangkok, Thailand.
Tubpun, Yuavares. 1981. "Economics of tank irrigation projects in northeastern Thailand." Ph.D. thesis, Department of Agricultural and Applied Economics, University of Minnesota, St. Paul, Minnesota.

CHAPTER 9

AN EVALUATION OF RIVER PUMP AND TANK IRRIGATION SYSTEMS IN NORTHEAST THAILAND

Adul Apinantara and Jerachone Sriswasdilek

The northeast region is the poorest among the regions in Thailand. Approximately 80 percent of the population is in the agricultural sector. The major portion of farm land is devoted to rice production and yields are the lowest in the nation. Rainfall is more uncertain than in the other regions of Thailand. Water supply is the foremost constraint to crop production especially in the dry season. It is insufficient to meet crop production requirements in many years and during the dry season water is not even adequate to meet the demand for human and livestock consumption.

IRRIGATION INVESTMENT

Because of this situation the Thai government has invested in several large-scale irrigation projects in the northeast. But it is estimated that the large projects currently operating, plus all of those potential projects which are economically feasible, if developed, could provide water for only 8 to 9 percent of farm families in the northeast[1] (AIT 1978, p. 11-14). A second source of water for irrigation in the northeast is pumping from reliable rivers (Figure 9.1). Assuming 10 rai of wet season irrigated rice per farm family, full development of all pumping potential would serve about another 10 percent of the farm families in the northeast (AIT 1978, p. 14-17).

Therefore, the other 80 percent would have to depend solely on rainfed crop production in the wet season and an undependable supply of water for household and livestock needs in the dry season. A program of developing small-scale water projects to meet these needs has been underway for over two decades. These small projects include:

147

Figure 9.1   **River pump system, northeast Thailand**

natural or dug ponds, weirs and topographical alterations to
nearby watershed areas, shallow or deep wells, river pumping
systems, and, as discussed in Chapter 8, small reservoirs
called "tanks." The purpose of the small-scale projects is
to meet the "basic requirements" of the population, defined
as the basic subsistence requirements for domestic water
needs (household and livestock), for minimal supplementary
irrigation (chiefly the rice nursery for wet season
transplanting), and for minimal dry season irrigation of
garden plots (AIT 1978, p. 7).

PROBLEM STATEMENT AND OBJECTIVES

One of the serious problems associated with these projects is the lack of effective and efficient utilization of
water. Associated with this inefficient utilization is the
absence of viable water user organizations (WUO). Another

serious problem is the magnitude of investment involved in developing irrigation projects. Therefore, it is important to carefully analyze these investments and their implementation.

The chapter objectives are to compare the effect of different types of small-scale irrigation on: (1) crop production and farm income, (2) water allocation and project maintenance, (3) the level of farmer participation in WUO, and (4) the economic efficiency of project investments.

SAMPLING PROCEDURE

Two river pump and four tank irrigation projects were selected for this study. They are: (1) Ta Sa Bang pump representing high performance pumps (pump 1), (2) Nong Bua Dee Mee pump representing low performance pumps (pump 2), (3) Huai Sai tank representing high performance, small tanks (tank 1), (4) Huai Yang tank representing low performance, small tanks (tank 2), (5) Huai Aeng tank representing high performance, large tanks(tank 3), and (6) Huai Kho tank representing low performance, large tanks (tank 4). The descriptions of these six projects are given in Table 9.1.

A sample of 177 farm households was randomly drawn from the six projects. The head of each household was interviewed during October-November 1981. The data were obtained concerning their 1980-1981 crop production and the management of their irrigation projects.

SYSTEM MANAGEMENT

Water Allocation. Maintenance. and Water Fees

During the wet season, a majority of the farmers reported that water was allocated according to established delivery schedules for tanks 1, 2, and 3. In contrast, only about 20 to 30 percent of farmers under the two pumps and tank 4 were able to obtain water by schedules. In the pump projects, the schedule gave the priority to the farmers who asked for water first, but in tank projects the priority was given to the farmers who were at the head of the canal. No farmers in pump projects broke the schedule. For tanks 1, 2, and 4 only 20 to 25 percent of the farmers reported breaks in the schedule but in tank 3 over 52 percent said there were interruptions.

TABLE 9.1
Background information on the six irrigation projects, northeast Thailand, 1980–1981

Characteristics	Pumps		Tanks			
	Ta Sa Bang 1	Nong Bua Dee Mee 2	Huai Sai 1	Huai Yang 2	Huai Aeng 3	Huai Kho 4
Province	Roi Et	Khon Kaen	Khon Kaen	Khon Kaen	Roi Et	Mahasarakham
Construction period	1976–1979	1977–1979	1963–1964	1951	1963	1968–1977
Storage capacity (mcm)	--	--	2.4	3.0	21.9	31.4
Surface area[a] (rai)	--	--	710	662[b]	4,575	7,000
Irrigable area (rai)	3,000	3,000	1,100	3,700	19,000	21,000
Pumping capacity (m^3/sec)	0.3	0.3	--	--	--	--

Source: National Energy Authority (mimeo).
Royal Irrigation Department, 1982. Table showing water resources development in Thailand completed to the end of 1980 and under construction in 1981 (large- and medium-scale projects).

[a]1 hectare = 6.25 rai.
[b]Estimated based on storage capacity.

No farmers under tank 2 used irrigation water during
the dry season except for home gardens. As in the wet
season, not more than a third of the farmers served by pump
2 and tank 4 received water by schedule. Dry season delivery schedules were adopted by half of the farmers served by
pump 1 and tanks 1 and 3. Again, two groups of farmers,
those who asked for water first under the pump projects and
those who were at the head of the canal in the tanks,
obtained water first. Most of the farmers in all projects
reported no breaks in the schedules (14 percent report
interruptions in tank 1 and 9 percent in tank 3).

For the pumps, the delivery schedules were set by the
project officials in both cropping seasons. However, in the
tanks, project officials, the WUO, the village head, and
informal groups of farmers set schedules. During the wet
season the project officials and the WUO set schedules in
tanks 1 and 2. For tanks 3 and 4 informal groups of farmers
and project officials set schedules with a little help from
the village head in tank 3. The major difference in the dry
season was that only informal farmer groups set schedules in
tank 4.

Only in the case of pump 2 did a majority of farmers
pay water fees during the wet season. The average water fee
actually paid in the two pump-served areas was 78 and 52
Baht per hour or 77 and 63 Baht per rai. This is much
higher than the 1 to 2 Baht per rai paid by tank irrigated
farmers. Almost all farmers in tank 3 and all farmers in
tanks 1, 2, and 4 did not pay water fees in the dry season.
The majority of farmers served by pump 2 and all of those
under pump 1 paid water fees. The average water fee paid
ranged from 60 to 112 Baht per hour or from 62 to 76 Baht
per rai for the pump projects and 2 Baht per rai for tank 3.

In the wet season, the majority (over 60 percent) of
farmers in pump projects did not contribute labor for canal
and ditch maintenance while the majority (over 70 percent)
of farmers in tank projects did. The average labor contributed was 0.6 man-days per family for the pump projects and
2.5 man-days per family for tank projects. None of the
farmers in pump projects and less than 10 percent of the
farmers in tank projects contributed money for canal and
ditch maintenance. The amount of money contributed was
minimal, approximately 2 Baht per family.

No farmers in any project contributed money for canal
and ditch maintenance in the dry season. The proportion of
farmers who contributed labor for canal and ditch maintenance was quite low. It ranged from only 3 percent for
tank 2 to 59 percent in tank 1. The average labor contributed was less than 1 man-day per family.

Conflict

The respondents were asked to rate the level of problems and conflicts among themselves in using irrigation water. Three-fourths of the respondents reported conflict low and one-fourth rated it medium. No respondents reported a "high" level of conflict (Table 9.2). All the respondents in the two pump projects reported very low levels of problems and conflicts in using irrigation water. The most severe problem reported by farmers was "stealing of water," particularly for tank irrigated farmers in the wet season.

The findings tended to imply that the farmers did not have serious problems and conflicts over water. However, it was observed that they have had problems and conflicts particularly during the transplanting of rice in the tank irrigation areas. As should be expected, problems and conflicts were highly correlated with water scarcity which tends to occur during transplanting.

Factors Affecting Farmer Participation

The four tank projects had some form of WUO but the two pump projects did not. The respondents had a good knowledge of the purpose of establishing WUO as over three-fourths (77 percent) of them mentioned that a WUO was established for "system operation and maintenance" (Table 9.3). Most of the farmers (84 percent) felt that they received a high level of benefit from being members of WUO and almost the same number (87 percent) were satisfied with crop yields they obtained from irrigation. More than four-fifths (85 percent) of the respondents had a high opinion of the group work on irrigation. The finding seems to show that the farmers knew about the irrigation system and that cooperation was needed for it to be successful.

The respondents rated the level of benefit from cleaning and repairing irrigation channels as follows: great, 54 percent; some, 30 percent; little, 3 percent and none, 13 percent. When asked about the sanction for non-participation in cleaning and repairing the channels, a great majority (92 percent) of the respondents said "none." Of this number, all respondents in the two pump projects said no sanction at all. About three-fourths (71 percent) of the respondents reported no rules or regulations for restricting water use. Farmers appear to resist setting restrictions because they would lead to disputes or violence among farmers. It would also be difficult to effectively enforce the rules.

TABLE 9.2

Response to question about the level of problems and conflict among farmers in using water

	Project Area										
	Pumps			Tanks							Total Tanks
				Low Performance			High Performance				
	1	2	Total	2	4	Total	1	3	Total		
Respondents (No.):	20	24	44	35	40	75	17	41	58		133
Level of Water Problems				- - - (percent) - - -							
Low	100	100	100	71	70	71	76	56	62		67
Medium	--	--	--	29	30	29	24	44	38		33
High	--	--	--	--	--	--	--	--	--		--
TOTAL	100	100	100	100	100	100	100	100	100		100

TABLE 9.3
Response to questions about WUO, yield, group work, maintenance, and irrigation official-farmer interaction

Questions	Pumps	Tanks		Total Tanks	Overall Total
		Low Tanks	High Tanks		
Respondents (No.):	44	75	58	133	177
		— — — (percent) — — —			
Purpose for establishing WUO					
System operation and maintenance	66	81	81	81	77
Water distribution	7	11	9	10	9
Others	16	4	9	6	9
No response/don't know	11	4	2	3	5
Level of benefit from being WUO member					
Low	7	19	21	20	16
High	93	81	79	80	84
Level of satisfaction with yield from irrigation					
Highly dissatisfied	--	--	--	--	--
Dissatisfied	5	9	5	8	7
Uncertain	9	7	2	4	6
Satisfied	50	61	53	59	56
Highly satisfied	36	23	38	29	31

Level of satisfaction with group work for irrigation activities					
Low	20	13	12	13	15
High	80	87	88	87	85
Level of benefit from cleaning and repairing irrigation channels					
A little	2	5	—	3	3
Some	25	37	26	32	30
Great	52	49	60	54	54
Sanction for non-participation in cleaning and repairing channels					
No	100	89	90	90	92
Yes	—	11	10	10	8
Rules for restricting excessive water use					
No	70	72	69	71	71
Yes	30	28	31	29	29
Frequency of approach to farmer by irrigation officer					
Low	2	15	9	12	10
Medium	25	37	38	38	34
High	73	48	53	50	56
Frequency of approach to irrigation officer by farmers					
Low	27	59	21	42	37
High	73	41	79	58	63

The respondents were asked to indicate the frequency with which the irrigation officers approached or contacted the farmers. More than one-half (56 percent) considered the frequency of irrigation officer contact with farmers as high; 34 percent, medium; and only 10 percent, low. When asked about the respondents' activities in approaching the irrigation officer, 63 percent of the respondents considered it high and 37 percent low. The findings tended to indicate that irrigation official-farmer interaction was fairly frequent.

Water Utilization

The water utilization measured by cropping intensity was more than 90 percent in all the projects in the wet season. The degree of water utilization during the dry season, however, was relatively low and varied considerably among the six projects. The dry season cropping intensity index was highest (39 percent) in tank 1 and lowest (0.2 percent) in tank 2 (Table 9.4). Among the other four projects, this index ranged from 4 to 24 percent. The farmers reported that adequacy of irrigation water was the most important factor affecting cropping intensity. Yet this appears to be more a problem of location and timing than adequacy of water in the river or tank. In the case of the pumps, a number of farmers did not get enough water because they did not pay their water fees. Insufficient labor also was a crucial factor causing the low dry season index.

Crop Production and Income

During the wet season rice was the main crop in all six projects, occupying over 90 percent of irrigated area. The yield of rice was quite low in pump projects, approximately 260 kilograms per rai. Among the tank projects, yields ranged from 298 to 527 kg per rai. Rice production cost did not vary much among the six projects. Therefore, net income from rice production in pump projects was much lower than that in tank projects. For example, it was 143 and 874 Baht per rai in pump 1 and tank 1, respectively (Table 9.5).[2]

The main crop during the dry season differed from project to project. Rice, corn, and peanuts were planted under pump 1, but all three crops had negative net returns due to low yields and high labor use. If the imputed cost

Cropping intensity index in the six projects, northeast Thailand, 1980–1981

	Pumps		Tanks			
Performance and Size	High	Low	Small High	Small Low	Large High	Large Low
Crop	1	2	1	2	3	4
			--- (percent) ---			
Wet Season Cropping Intensity Index						
Rice	93	92	98	90	91	98
Dry Season Cropping Intensity Index						
Rice	21	4	98	--	1	--
Corn	1	2	7	--	5	1
Peanut	2	1	7	--	1	2
Soybean	--	--	2	--	--	--
Watermelon	--	--	18	--	2	0.2
Melon	--	--	2	--	--	--
Kenaf	--	--	--	--	0.1	--
Tobacco	--	--	--	--	0.1	--
Vegetables	--	0.4	3	0.2	1	1
TOTAL, Dry Season	24	7.4	39	0.2	10.2	4.2

TABLE 9.5

Net return from crop production in six projects and in non-irrigated areas in Khon Kaen and Roi Et provinces, northeast Thailand, 1980-1981

| | Net Return (Baht/rai) | | | | | | | |
| | Pumps | | Tanks | | | | Non-Irrigated | |
Crop	1	2	1	2	3	4	Khon Kaen	Roi Et
WET SEASON								
Rice	143	259	874	515	378	439	98	170
DRY SEASON								
Rice	-83	-650	--	--	118	--	--	--
Corn	-1,566	542	445	--	1,421	-259	--	--
Peanut	-384	968	1,378	--	828	391	--	--
Soybean	--	--	-300	--	--	--	--	--
Watermelon	--	--	908	--	1,501	1,845	--	--
Melon	--	--	1,647	--	--	--	--	--
Kenaf	--	--	--	--	-40	--	--	--
Tobacco	--	--	--	--	-1,061	--	--	--
Vegetables	--	-468	-1,127	-1,014	-519	619	--	--

of family labor is not included in the production costs, all crops would show positive net returns.

For pump 2 rice, corn, and peanuts were irrigated in the dry season. Rice yielded negative net returns while positive net returns were obtained from corn and peanut production. The negative returns from rice production were primarily due to very low yields resulting from severe pest damage. The small quantity of vegetable production in this project was for home consumption and large amounts of family labor were used in its production.

Quite a variety of crops were planted in tank 1 during the dry season. Vegetable production resulted in negative net returns due to a high family labor input. Soybeans, which are not well adapted to northeast Thailand, had very low yields and a negative net return. The other four crops had positive net returns.

Farmers served by tank 2 planted only vegetables for home consumption. Again, the use of large amounts of family labor resulted in negative net returns when the imputed cost of family labor is included.

Most, if not all, of the tobacco and vegetables irri- gated by tank 3 were for home consumption with high family labor inputs. A large amount of family labor was also used in kenaf production. Thus, all three crops yielded negative net returns. Small areas were also planted to rice, corn, peanuts, and watermelons. Labor use in these crops was lower which resulted in high positive net returns.

A small area of watermelons and vegetables were irri- gated from tank 4 during the dry season. Watermelon produc- tion in this project yielded a relatively high net return. Even though a large amount of labor was used in vegetable production, it also produced a positive net return due to high yields. Corn production was not profitable because of low yields and high labor use. Peanut production had a positive net return, although it was much lower than that obtained under pump 2 and tanks 1 and 3.

IRRIGATION PRODUCTIVITY[3]

Model

A number of factors appear to be important in deter- mining irrigated rice production in the wet season. To estimate which factors are the most important in the six projects a regression model was estimated for wet season rice production. The independent variables in this model include physical factors of production, project location variables, several socioeconomic characteristics, and a number of irrigation management conditions. A squared term was also included for fertilizer, the most significant physical production factor.

The physical production factors include seed, fertilizer, insecticide, herbicide, and labor (all in per rai units).[4] Dummy variables (0 or 1) are used to account for flood damage that occurred on some farms and to account for differences between project sites due to differences in soil, weather, and management. Socioeconomic variables include credit use for agriculture, farm assets (both in Baht per rai units), and farmer's education (0 if the farmer had less than four years of formal education, and 1 otherwise). Finally, the irrigation management variables are:

1. The distance from farmer's field to the main canal (in meters).
2. The number of irrigations during the season.
3. The location of farmer's field in the system (0 for farms at the head-reaches of the system and 1 for farms at the tail-reaches).
4. Water user organization (WUO) membership of the farmer (0 for non-membership, 1 for membership).
5. The type of irrigation system at that project site (0 - tank and 1 - pump).

The above dummy variables cause shifts in the intercept of the production function. Also included in the model were a series of dummy variables that measured the interaction between project location and selected production and management variables. These slope dummies are of the form:

$$X_{ji} - P_i X_j$$

where P_i - 1 for project i and 0 otherwise (see J. Johnston (1972) for a thorough discussion on the use of dummy variables). Slope dummies were included for fertilizer (both linear and squared terms), distance from the field to the canal, flood damage, WUO membership, and location of fields in the irrigation system.

The final model contains only those variables significant at the 15 percent level according to the F-test (Table 9.6). An exception was made to the 15 percent decision rule in the case where slope dummies were used. If a slope dummy was significant, then the reference variable associated with that dummy was retained, regardless of its significance.

TABLE 9.6
Regression results for irrigated farms in northeast Thailand, 1980-1981

Variable	Symbol	Coefficient	Standard Error	Regression Significance[a]	$B_i + C_i$[b]
Labor	X_1	-0.009	0.006	.116	--
Seed	X_2	5.226	1.910	.007	--
	X_3	1.230	0.578	.035	--
	T_1X_3	-2.696	1.350	.048	-1.466
	T_2X_3	2.975	1.114	.009	4.205
	T_3X_3	-3.239	0.707	.000	-2.009
Fertilizer	X_3^2	-0.035	0.023	.137	--
	$T_1X_3^2$	0.091	0.051	.078	0.056
	$T_2X_3^2$	-0.156	0.073	.035	-0.191
	$T_3X_3^2$	0.111	0.025	.000	0.076
Herbicide	X_4	1.586	0.706	.026	--
	X_5	16.536	12.910	.203	--
	P_1X_5	-37.864	13.999	.008	-21.328
Flood Damage	P_2X_5	-38.500	15.612	.015	-21.964
	T_3X_5	-20.282	14.170	.155	-3.746
	T_4X_5	-37.329	15.191	.015	-20.793
Distance From Canal To Field	X_6	-0.001	0.001	.392	--
	T_4X_6	0.017	0.004	.000	0.015
Number of Irrigations	X_7	0.063	0.032	.055	--
	X_8	8.156	3.990	.043	--
Field Location Along Canal	P_1X_8	-20.309	6.773	.003	-12.153
	T_1X_8	-23.846	8.122	.004	-15.690
	T_2X_8	-15.129	6.041	.014	-6.973
	T_4X_8	-14.460	5.680	.012	-6.304
Tank 1 Dummy	T_1	28.034	5.992	.000	--
Tank 3 Dummy	T_3	12.140	4.997	.000	--
Constant	A	24.737	3.544	.000	--

[a]Probability of a Type-1 error.

[b]The sum of the reference variable coefficient (B_i) and the slope dummy coefficient (C_i) gives the specific location effect.

This only occurred for two variables; distance from the canal to the farmer's field and flood damage.

Results

All of the production variables except insecticides are retained by the final model. None of the socioeconomic variables were significant (assets, credit, and education). Of the irrigation management variables, the number of irrigation applications, the distance from the field to the canal, and the location of the field in the system are significant, but system type (whether tank or pump) and WUO membership are not. Coefficients for slope dummy variables were also added to the coefficients of the reference variable to determine the overall effect. These are reported in the "$B_i + C_i$" column. The R^2 is 0.75, i.e., 75 percent of the variation in rice yield is explained by the variables in the final regression estimation.

The Production Variables. The results suggest that seed and herbicides had significant positive effects on yield on the sample farms but that insecticides did not. Fertilizer variables contributed substantially to explaining differences in yield. But the sign of the fertilizer coefficients tended to vary between projects. There was a positive yield response to fertilizer applications but the value of the coefficients for the linear and quadratic terms varied considerably among locations. The amount of fertilizer application was substantially higher at the high performance, large tank, Huai Aeng, suggesting that a more dependable water supply encourages more fertilizer use.

The labor coefficient was negative and was less significant than other variables. Rice production in northeast Thailand relies on an intensive labor input during two specific periods, transplanting and harvesting, and relatively low labor input during the rest of the production period. This may result in surplus family labor being available through much of the wet season, particularly for small farms, leading to inefficient labor use. It is also possible that measurement problems caused a downward bias in the coefficient (see footnote 4).

Flood damage coefficients were all negative except for the reference variable, which was positive. The coeffieicnt for the reference variable is likely to be a statistical aberration since there was only one farm in tanks 1 and 2 which suffered any flood damage. Overall, flood damage significantly reduced yields, especially at the pump sites which are located on a major river.

Irrigation Management Variables. A particular focus of this analysis is the relationship between crop production and irrigation. Both the field location along the canal and the distance from the field to the canal were evaluated for their effect on crop production (as proxies for irrigation performance). It was hypothesized that, because of inadequate water management, farmers further from the canal would have greater difficulty getting adequate water supplies and thus experience lower yields.

Regression results only partially support this hypothesis. Distance between the field and the canal was not significant except for tank 4 and in that case the coefficient was positive. Thus, field distance had no adverse effects on yields. Location along the canal, however, was negatively related to production at most sites. Only the reference variable encompassing pumps 2 and tank 3 retained a positive coefficient. Yet both were insignificant and only one farm from pump 2 was reported to be a tail-reach farm, which tended to distort this result.

The values of these two variables appear to indicate that while water is not evenly distributed along a canal system, once it reaches a point on the canal it is evenly distributed laterally from that point. Distributing water along a canal tends to be the responsibility of the entire group (poor performance) whereas lateral distribution from the canal tends to be an individual or small group responsibility (adequate performance). It is in the interest of tail-reach farmers to have a smooth water flow throughout the system (so water reaches the very last field). But no such incentive exists for head-reach farmers. Within a large group, such as those served by a canal, it is difficult to pressure head-reach farmers into taking only their fair share. In addition, the head-reach farmers tend not to contribute to tail-reach canal maintenance and may actually take measures to block the water flow to lower ends of the system. In small groups, such as those served by a lateral, it is much easier to monitor the performance of one's neighbors and make sure they are not exploiting your altruistic behavior. Thus, in small groups, the objective of fairness seems to dominate as there is some assurance that everyone will only take their share.

The number of times irrigation water was applied had a significant positive affect on yields. Farmers at tanks tended to apply water more frequently than farmers at pump projects. This is quite consistent with the difference in water charges. The pump irrigated farmers paid per hour of pumping while tank farmers paid a fixed per rai charge.

Thus, only the farmers served by pumps had an economic incentive to limit irrigation.

PROJECT EVALUATION

Measuring Benefits and Costs

Benefits for the pump projects were derived only from wet and dry season crop production benefits (WB and DB). In contrast, tank projects provide three additional benefits: (1) fish production benefits (FB), (2) household consumption benefits (HB), and (3) livestock water benefits (LB). Just as in Chapter 8, there are five basic sources of tank benefits.

$$B_t - WB_t + DB_t + HB_t + LB_t + FB_t$$

Annual net benefits for the six projects are presented in Table 9.7. The values used to calculate benefits and costs are shown in Table 9.8.

The wet season benefits are calculated by subtracting the net returns per rai (Y_{NI}) for non-irrigated rice production from the net returns per rai (Y_I) obtained in the project-irrigated rice area. The difference is then multiplied by the area of rice irrigated (A) in each project.

$$WB_t - (Y_I - Y_{NI})A$$

Since no crops were grown during the dry season before the irrigation projects, dry season benefits are just the sum of gross returns ($Q_i P_i$) from each crop (i) minus the production costs (X_i) times the area of that crop irrigated.

$$DB_t - \sum_{i-1}^{n} (Q_i P_i - X_i)A_i$$

The water stored in the tank for irrigation purposes is complementary to fish production but the water released for irrigation is competitive as it reduces the area for fish production. The fish yield in the tank is calculated as a function of the reservoir surface area, i.e., yield is reduced as the area is reduced (Tubpun, et al. 1982).[5] One study suggests that 4,680 Baht per hectare (about 749 Baht per rai) of surface area is an average return to expect from a small reservoir which does not receive a continuous flow

TABLE 9.7
Annual net benefits from the six irrigation projects,
northeast Thailand, 1980-1981

	Net Crop Production Benefits		
Project	Wet Season	Dry Season	Total
	- - - (thousand Baht) - - -		
Pump 1	-75	-114	-189
Pump 2	437	-35	402
Tank 1	840	305	1,145
Tank 2	1,382	-6	1,376
Tank 3	3,579	2,256	5,835
Tank 4	7,004	254	7,258

	Non-Crop Benefits		
Project	Fish	Household	Livestock
	- - - (thousand Baht) - - -		
Tank 1	290	13	9
Tank 2	270	39	29
Tank 3	1,870	171	128
Tank 4	2,860	184	137

TABLE 9.8
Summary of values used in the project evaluation

Variable	Values
1. Rice farm price	2.7 and 3.0 Baht/kg
2. Fishery benefit	1,166 Baht/rai of surface area
3. Household benefit	212.5 Baht/family/year
4. Livestock benefit	158.0 Baht/family/year
5. Pump maintenance cost	3.5 percent of construction cost per year starting from year 3
6. Electric cost	
a. Wet season rice	15.4 Baht/rai
b. Dry season rice	65 Baht/rai
c. Dry season other crops	50 Baht/rai
7. Field channel cost	106.6 Baht/rai of irrigated land
8. Discount rate	
a. Social rate of discount	11 percent
b. Opportunity cost of capital	15 percent
9. Economic life of the projects	30 years
10. All values based on 1980 prices	
11. Average tank surface area	35 percent of maximum surface area

of fresh water (Kloke and Potaros 1975). Since there is no evidence of intensive or commercial fish production in the study tanks, the estimate of 749 Baht per rai of surface area appears to be more appropriate than a 2,000 Baht estimate from the Kalasin demonstration pond (AIT 1978). Adjusting the 1975 estimate of 749 Baht per rai by agricultural wholesale price index, the fishery benefit becomes 1,166 Baht per rai of surface area at 1980 prices.

Tanks also provide water for household consumption and livestock, especially in northeast Thailand where natural ponds, small streams, and wells usually dry up during the long dry seasons. One study estimated that without tanks one family has to spend 8.5 man-days per year to get water for household uses (Tubpun, et al. 1982). With the average wage rate of 25 Baht per man-day obtained in the survey, a household consumption benefit of 212.5 Baht per family per year is obtained from the tanks. Livestock water benefits are based on the opportunity cost of school age children required to drive livestock to water. This is estimated to be 120 Baht per family per year at 1978 prices or 158 Baht at 1980 prices (Tubpun, et al. 1982).

Total pump project costs include construction (CC), system maintenance (MC), electricity (EC), and farmer maintenance expenses (FC), which encompasses labor with the imputed cost of family labor. The electricity costs are assumed to include the cost of operating the pumps.

$$TC_p = CC_t + MC_t + EC_t + FC_t$$

Total tank project costs include the same costs, except for electricity, and contains the additional costs required for tank operation (OC) and for constructing field channels (IC).

$$TC_T = CC_t + MC_t + FC_t + OC_t + IC_t$$

Economic Returns

When a rice price of 2.70 Baht per kg and an 11 percent discount rate are used and all benefits are included, the four tank projects pass the economic efficiency tests (Table 9.9).[6] In contrast, the two pump projects fail to pass the test and even have negative internal rates of return (IRR). If only crop benefits are considered, tank 4 also does not pass the efficiency test unless the social rate of discount is only 6 percent.

When the discount rate is increased to 15 percent, the discounted benefits are less then discounted costs for

TABLE 9.9
Economic returns for the six irrigation projects, northeast Thailand

RICE PRICE = 2.70 Baht/kg

Projects	IRR (percent)	11% Discount Rate NPV[a] (mill. Baht)	11% Discount Rate B/C Ratio	15% Discount Rate NPV (mill. Baht)	15% Discount Rate B/C Ratio
All Benefits					
Pump 1	negative	-10.35	-0.21	-8.94	-0.19
Pump 2	negative	-6.65	0.37	-6.55	0.32
Tank 1	23.1	6.08	1.76	3.13	1.40
Tank 2	36.9	9.72	2.42	6.34	1.96
Tank 3	41.3	45.27	2.42	29.79	1.97
Tank 4	13.5	9.90	1.11	-4.15	0.95
Only Crop Benefits					
Tank 1	16.9	3.08	1.39	0.78	1.10
Tank 2	27.4	6.45	1.95	3.78	1.57
Tank 3	25.3	24.37	1.76	13.48	1.44
Tank 4	6.2	-20.77	0.77	-28.15	0.66

RICE PRICE = 3.00 Baht/kg

All Benefits

Pump 1	negative	-9.31	-0.09	-8.13	-0.08
Pump 2	negative	-6.53	0.38	-6.46	0.33
Tank 1	25.0	6.91	1.87	3.79	1.48
Tank 2	40.1	10.72	2.57	7.12	2.08
Tank 3	45.5	49.85	2.56	33.37	2.09
Tank 4	14.6	14.06	1.15	-0.89	0.99

Only Crop Benefits

Tank 1	18.6	3.91	1.49	1.44	1.18
Tank 2	30.1	7.44	2.09	4.56	1.69
Tank 3	28.4	28.95	1.91	17.02	1.56
Tank 4	7.1	-16.61	0.82	-24.89	0.70

[a]NPV = net present value.

tank 4 even when all benefits are included. With this
discount rate, the performance of the other five projects
does not change significantly.

A sensitivity test was done by raising the rice price
to 3.00 Baht per kg but this did not significantly improve
the benefit-cost (B/C) ratios for the pump projects.
Discounted benefits in the pump projects were still less
than costs. The B/C ratio was, again, greater than one for
tank 4 only when all benefits were considered and an 11
percent discount rate was used.

The results from the project analysis is different from
what was expected by many government officials. Most
thought the pump projects would have higher rates of return
than the tank projects. There are, at least, four reasons
why this did not occur and why the pump project results must
be interpreted with care. First, during the 1980-1981 wet
season there was extensive flooding in northeast Thailand
which caused crop damage and reduced yield particularly for
the pump projects which are located next to the river.
Although yields were adjusted for flood damage, the wet
season rice yields for the pump projects were still low
relative to the other projects. Second, 1980-1981 was only
the second year of operation for the pump projects and the
farmers had not fully adjusted to the irrigated conditions.
Thus, yields will likely go up as the adjustment takes
place. Third, the pump projects had higher costs than the
tank projects because of the high cost of operation and
maintenance, and the cost of the elaborate delivery systems.
Finally the pump projects did not generate significant
benefits for uses other than crop production such as fish
production or livestock water.

To determine if the low yields might be the major cause
for the low return from the pump projects, yields and production costs are adjusted and the B/C ratios are recal-
culated. First, for pump 1, dry season corn and peanut
yields are raised to 70 percent of the average of the other
projects, and labor costs for dry season corn and peanut
production are lowered to the average of the other projects.
Then the analysis is rerun and the results labeled pump 1
(1) in Table 9.10.

Second, wet season rice yield for pump 1 is raised to
298 kilograms per rai, which is the lowest yield among the
four tank projects. The results are shown in Table 9.10 as
pump 1 (2). Third, changes in yields and costs in pump 1
(1) and pump 1 (2) are added together and are shown as pump
1 (3). Fourth, the rice yield for pump 2 is also raised to
298 kilograms per rai, and the analysis rerun with the
results shown as pump 2 (1). None of the four adjustments

TABLE 9.10

The economic returns for the two pump projects in northeast Thailand under alternative yields, labor costs, and rice price assumptions

Projects	IRR (percent)	11% Discount Rate		15% Discount Rate	
		NPV (mill. Baht)	B/C Ratio	NPV (mill. Baht)	B/C Ratio
RICE PRICE = 2.70 Baht/kg					
Pump 1 (1)[a]	negative	-9.68	-0.14	-8.42	-0.12
Pump 1 (2)[b]	negative	-7.11	0.17	-6.41	0.15
Pump 1 (3)[c]	negative	-6.44	0.24	-5.88	0.22
Pump 2 (1)[b]	negative	-4.50	0.57	-4.87	0.49
RICE PRICE = 3.00 Baht/kg					
Pump 1 (1)[a]	negative	-8.64	-0.01	-7.60	-0.01
Pump 1 (2)[b]	negative	-5.70	0.33	-5.30	0.29
Pump 1 (3)[c]	negative	-5.03	0.41	-4.77	0.36
Pump 2 (1)[b]	negative	-4.25	0.60	-4.67	0.51

[a]Dry season corn and peanut yields and labor costs for dry season corn and peanut production were adjusted.

[b]Wet season rice yield was adjusted.

[c]Combined adjustment from footnotes a and b.

described above made any differences in the earlier
conclusions, namely that the pump projects fail to pass the
economic efficiency tests, and that the tank projects
generally appear to be better investments than the pumps.

A final word of caution is in order regarding the
results. The estimated acreage of irrigated crops could be
high for several of the projects, particularly the large
tanks. This may explain why the internal rate of return for
tank 3 is so high.

CONCLUSION

The six irrigation projects are not faced with major
conflicts which would prevent the productive use of water.
However, flooding and location on the canal have been
important factors effecting yields. Flooding was
particularly bad around pump 1 while farmers located near
the end of the canal had difficulty obtaining water when
they needed it. Still, organization of the water
distribution has not prevented the tank projects from
generating benefits greater than project costs. Delivery
schedules were adopted by a majority of farmers to allocate
irrigation water.

In contrast, the pump projects appear to be in an
adjustment phase and are producing low levels of project
benefits due to low yields and high labor costs. The cost
of irrigation in the pump projects is also high relative to
the tank projects. They are newer projects and have had
greater investments in canal lining and control structures.

The analysis of wet season irrigated rice production
supports the idea that small groups of farmers are more
effective in allocating water than a large WUO. This suggests that the WUO, for the whole command area, needs to be
divided into sub-units possibly by the area served from a
farm ditch or turn-out. The sub-units should be responsible
for control of water, water distribution, and maintenance
within the sub-unit. The sub-unit leader will represent the
members on the WUO management committee for the whole
command area both in the pump and tank systems.

The WUO should meet regularly and as often as
necessary, especially before each cropping season. Responsibilities, rules, regulations, and authority of the WUO
officers and sub-unit leaders should be specifically determined, including sanctions for violaters of the rules. When
the members have agreed on a set of rules and regulations,
the sub-units should be given major responsibility for
implementation.

NOTES

1. Assumes irrigation of 20 rai in wet season per family from new projects where 1 rai = 0.16 hectare.
2. $1.00 = 22.90 Baht in 1984.
3. This section is from a paper done by Keith Fuglie as a graduate assistant at the University of Minnesota.
4. Definition of variables used in regression model:

Yield. The dependent variable was paddy rice output measured in tang (1 tang = 15 kg).

Labor. This was measured as family, hired, and exchange labor days per rai spent in rice production. Male and female adult labor was weighted equally but child labor was multiplied by a factor of 0.75. This parallels the wage rates for hired farm labor. Since flood damage occurred between transplanting and harvesting, time spent during the first period was multiplied by the correction factor whereas harvest time was not. But even so, the measurement of this variable is quite suspect, for two reasons: (1) It is difficult for farmers to recall accurately time spent in each operation (the data may reflect labor availability rather than actual labor used), and (2) except for the discounting of child labor, all labor was assumed to be of constant quality. In the first case, the labor coefficient estimate would likely be biased downward but still be positive. In the second case, the coefficient could be biased either upward or downward (Griliches 1975). These explanations demonstrate how measurement errors can bias the coefficient. It is unlikely that the real coefficient, and thus the marginal product of labor, would be either zero or negative.

Seed. Seed (measured in tang per rai) was broadcast on nursery beds and then the seedlings were transplanted to each field. Seed was discounted by the flood damage factor.

Fertilizer. Nitrogen fertilizer applications were measured in kg per rai. This variable was not discounted for flood damage since it was not clear when applications took place (i.e., before or after flooding). Probably there was more than one application, with the bulk being applied after flood damage.

Herbicide. Chemical herbicide use was measured in Baht per rai. Application probably took place during the initial cultivation. Therefore it was discounted for flood damage.

Insecticide. Again measured in Baht per rai, insecticide use tended to be applied selectively, on fields already infested with stembore and blast. The fact that they are often used on already damaged fields can lead to a specification error. This error tends to bias the coefficient downward, even to a negative value.

5. Johnson (1979) found that if the surface area at the start is 5 hectares and is gradually reduced due to evaporation, seepage, and withdrawal for irrigation use, there may be no more than 2 hectares of surface area by the end of the year. This means that the minimum reservoir surface area will be no more than 40 percent of the maximum reservoir surface area. To be safe, 35 percent of the maximum reservoir surface area is used to compute fishery benefits.

6. The negative B/C ratio for pump 1 is the result of large negative returns from dry season crops. Thus, a negative B/C ratio is obtained when the negative total benefits are divided by positive project costs. This is an unusual situation that will not continue over the long run. If the benefits from dry season irrigation continue to be negative, farmers will stop irrigating in the dry season.

REFERENCES

Apinantara, Adul. 1983. "Socio-economic and organizational factors affecting water user associations and effectiveness of water utilization in northeast Thailand." Water Management and Policy Workshop Paper, Khon Kaen, Thailand, 27 p.

Apinantara, Adul, and Jerachone Sriswasdilek. 1983. "A socio-economic and organizational analysis of two pump and four tank irrigation projects in northeast Thailand." Water Management and Policy Workshop Paper, Khon Kaen, Thailand, 20 p.

Asian Institute of Technology (AIT). 1978. Water for the Northeast: A Strategy for the Development of Small-Scale Water Resources, Vol. 1: Main Report. Bangkok, Thailand.

Fuglie, Keith. 1984. "Off-farm labor supply and the value of irrigation water in northeast Thailand." Plan B Project Paper, University of Minnesota, St. Paul, Minnesota.

Griliches, Zvi. 1960. "Measuring inputs in agriculture." Journal of Farm Economics 42:1411-29.

_____. 1975. "Specification bias in estimation of production functions." Journal of Farm Economics 57:8-20.

Johnson, Sam H. 1979. "Economic possibilities of small reservoirs for irrigation: Northeast Thailand." Seminar on Natural Resource Management in Developing Countries, University Pertinian Malaysia, Serdang, Selangor, Malaysia.

Johnson, Sam H., and Terd Charoenwatana. 1981. "Economics of rainfed cropping systems: Northeast Thailand." Water Resources Research 17:462-468.

Johnston, J. 1972. Econometric Methods. 2nd ed. McGraw-Hill.

Kloake, C.W., and M. Potaros. 1975. "Aquaculture as integral part of the agricultural system: A case study in northeast Thailand." Occasional Paper 1975/4, Indo-Pacific Fisheries Council.

Peterson, Willis. 1981. "The market as an experiment: Problems of data generation." Staff Paper P81-17, University of Minnesota.

Royal Irrigation Department (RID), Ministry of Agriculture and Cooperatives. 1982. Table showing water resource development in Thailand, completed to the end of 1980 and under construction in 1981 (large-scale project and medium-scale project), Bangkok, Thailand.

Sriswasdilek, Jerachone. 1983. "An economic analysis of two pump and four tank irrigation projects in northeast Thailand." Water Management and Policy Workshop Paper, Khon Kaen, Thailand, 75 p.

Tubpun, Yuavares, K. William Easter, and Delane Welsch. 1982. Tank Irrigation in Northeastern Thailand: The Returns and Their Distribution. Economic Report ER82-6, Department of Agricultural and Applied Economics, University of Minnesota.

CHAPTER 10

THE ASIAN DEVELOPMENT BANK APPROACH
TO RESEARCH DESIGN FOR IRRIGATION PROJECTS[1]

Dimyati Nagnju

Since its establishment in 1966, the Asian Development
Bank (the Bank) has been active in providing loans and technical assistance for irrigation in its developing member
countries (DMCs) in the Asia-Pacific region. As of December
1982, the Bank has financed seventy-two irrigation projects[2]
in twelve DMCs totaling about $1,519 million. This is about
13 percent of the total Bank investment of $11.5 billion or
44 percent of agriculture and rural development sector
lending. During the same period, the Bank also provided a
sizable quantity of technical assistance amounting to $32.6
million for project preparation and advisory/operational
purposes.

The Bank's emphasis on lending for projects in the
irrigation sub-sector has been based on the high priority
given to increased food production, and the strong linkage
between adequate water control and successful crop intensification, particularly activities related to the promotion
of high-yielding varieties and improved technology.
Furthermore, irrigation projects have been recognized as
having employment generation potential which is crucial in
rural areas where unemployment or underemployment is
widespread. However, it is also recognized that some
completed irrigation projects have failed to generate the
expected project benefits despite high investment in
irrigation infrastructure. Recent experience indicates that
the expected benefits from large irrigation projects can
only be achieved if all mutually complementary development
needs of the service area can be satisfied in the orderly
implementation of a comprehensive and well-coordinated
development program. The development needs include
sufficient and timely water supply, proper facilities for
on-farm water control and management, locally adaptable
knowledge for improving soils and crop production, effective

177

organization of farmers, adequate marketing facilities, and timely supplies of rural credit and other farm inputs (Figure 1.3).

The Bank has always been concerned with the performance of irrigation projects in view of high costs of irrigation construction, operation, and maintenance. During project formulation and project implementation, every effort is made to ensure that the expected project benefits are achieved on the completion of the irrigation projects. The Bank's approach, to ensure that irrigation projects achieve the expected project benefits, operates at two levels. First, at the national level, the Bank and the host government participate in agricultural policy dialogues designed to significantly improve crop production and farmers' incomes. Some of the assurances given by the government to the Bank on agricultural policy are included in the loan covenants of the respective projects. Second, at the project level, the project staff must implement measures to improve the agencies' coordination, to train farmers in on-farm water management and improved production practices, and to monitor and evaluate project performance. This chapter discusses the Bank's research approach in Bank financed irrigation projects, at the project level, with a view to ensuring that the estimated project benefits are achieved.

SMALL-SCALE PILOT SCHEMES

At a regional workshop on irrigation water management held by the Bank in Manila in January 1973, it was decided that in order to achieve the full benefits from large irrigation projects, three steps would be essential: (1) establish an experimental farm for location-specific research, (2) establish a pilot scheme for demonstration of, and training in, water management and modern farming techniques on an operational scale, and (3) establish a pioneer project as a model of a full-scale irrigation development for actual farm management, including its economics and institutional arrangements.[3]

As a result of this workshop, most of the Bank financed projects in the late 1960s and throughout the 1970s contained a provision for construction and operation of an experimental and pilot scheme covering an area of about 50 to 150 ha to implement the first two steps of irrigation development, i.e., crop research and training of farmers.[4] The pilot scheme is generally constructed two years after the start of the project or soon after the project office is established in the project area. The site of the pilot scheme is carefully chosen so that it is accessible to most farmer beneficiaries, representative of the soils in the project area, and located near the water source from which water can be pumped for irrigation while the main irrigation system is being constructed.

The pilot scheme is operated by the farmers under the supervision of project staff with assistance from the appropriate agricultural department. The objectives of the pilot scheme are four-fold:

1. To teach farmers how to grow crops under irrigation.
2. To demonstrate improved varieties and technology to farmers including on-farm water management practices.
3. To multiply seed of high-yielding varieties.
4. To do applied research which will be used in the formulation of an appropriate package of production practices suitable to the conditions in the project area.

The research conducted in the pilot scheme generally deals with agronomic practices such as rates and method of fertilizer application, plant spacing, time of planting, planting methods, weed control, insect control, and varietal trials. In some cases the project staff also engages in basic research to determine percolation rates and evapo-transpiration rates, the results of which are used in estimating irrigation requirements on different soil types in the project area. One of the best examples of this type of pilot scheme is the 140 ha pilot scheme located at the Angat River project in the Philippines which was established under Bank assisted technical assistance for the water management project in 1968. From this experience, the National Irrigation Administration has extended similar pilot schemes in all new irrigation projects in the country to build up the competence of farmers and project staff in irrigation management.

Yet the limitations of the pilot scheme became evident when several Bank financed irrigation projects completed in late 1970s did not achieve the pre-project level of estimated benefits. The major limitations of the small-scale pilot schemes are as follows: (1) It is not possible to apply the water management practices developed in the pilot scheme to the whole project area because the pilot area is too small and the socioeconomic conditions in the pilot schemes are different from those in the project area, and (2) the results of the pilot studies are not always applicable to solving the problems related to operation and maintenance of the project. As a result, the pilot scheme has produced only technical information on crop production. It failed to provide full-fledged socioeconomic and institutional information to the project staff on how to operate and maintain the project after its completion.

LARGE-SCALE PILOT SCHEMES

To overcome the deficiencies of the small-scale pilot scheme approach, the Bank has begun experimenting with a much larger pilot scheme which would represent the actual socioeconomic and institutional conditions of the entire project. The optimum size of the larger pilot scheme has not been determined, but it is probably on the order of 10 percent of the net service area of the project. A pilot scheme larger than 10 percent of the service area would be too cumbersome and costly to manage effectively.

Nong Wai Pioneer Agricultural Project

The Bank chose the Nong Wai Pioneer Agricultural Project (NWPAP) as a site for the first large-scale pilot scheme (Figure 10.1). The NWPAP is the Bank's first irrigation project in Thailand, approved in December 1974, and was designed as a pioneer project in the Lower Mekong Basin to achieve and demonstrate rapid integrated agriculture in northeast Thailand. The NWPAP consisted of the rehabilitation and improvement of the existing main irrigation and drainage system constructed in the mid-1960s, the implementation of land consolidation in the entire irrigable area of about 11,000 ha, and the strengthening of agricultural support services. Agricultural development was slow during the first five years of project implementation (1975-1980). Despite the establishment of a multipurpose Nong Wai Agricultural Cooperative Society, Ltd. (NACS) in 1976, the promotion of improved varieties and technology by the Department of Agricultural Extension (DAE) and the completion of on-farm development in 55 percent of the project area by 1980, the cropping intensity increased only slightly from 79 percent in 1975 to 98 percent in 1980 (Table 10.1). Most farmers continued to grow low-yielding, traditional paddy varieties using low input levels and unimproved technology. As a result they were in debt and could not repay their loans to NACS.

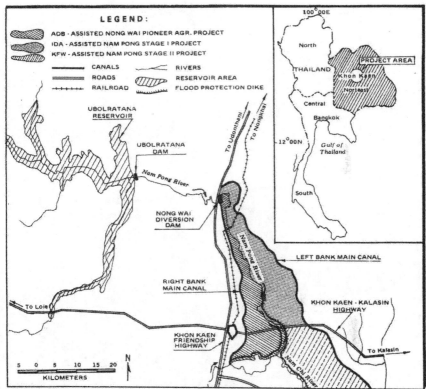

Figure 10.1   Nong Wai pioneer agriculture project

Nong Wai Irrigation Management Project

To facilitate the construction of a large pilot scheme in NWPAP and to assist the government in accelerating agricultural development, the Bank provided the first post-construction advisory technical assistance for the Nong Wai Irrigation Management Project (NWIMP). The technical assistance was approved by the Bank in December 1980. The rationale for NWIMP was based on the insufficient institutional capabilities of the government agencies in the NWPAP area which had resulted in unsatisfactory project benefits during 1975-1980. This deficiency, if not corrected, would have had adverse effects on the economic viability of NWPAP.

TABLE 10.1
Cropped area, yields, and production in NWPAP area from 1975 to 1983

Year	Season	Paddy Area (ha)	Paddy Yield (mt/ha)	Paddy Production (mt)	Peanuts (ha)	Sweet Corn (ha)	Vegetables (ha)	Total Area Cultivated (ha)	Cropping Intensity (percent)
1975	Wet	8,501	2.10	17,852	--	--	--	8,501	79
1976	Dry	3	--	--	--	--	--	3	79
	Wet	8,501	2.14	18,192	--	--	--	8,501	
1977	Dry	38	2.31	88	103	30	435	606	85
	Wet	8,501	2.81	23,888	--	--	--	8,501	
1978	Dry	558	2.60	1,451	94	26	147	825	90
	Wet[a]	8,843	flood	--	--	--	--	8,843	
1979	Dry	1,810	2.54	4,597	124	53	255	2,242	106
	Wet	9,172	2.66	24,398	--	--	--	9,172	
1980	Dry[b]	1,572	2.80	4,402	98	21	159	1,850	98
	Wet[a]	8,693	2.80	24,340	--	--	--	8,693	
1981	Dry	2,337	3.13	7,315	289	60	330	3,016	122
	Wet	10,132	3.00	30,396	--	--	--	10,132	
1982	Dry[b]	2,260	3.31	7,481	24	4	72	2,360	122
	Wet	10,760	3.13	33,679	--	--	--	10,760	
1983	Dry[c]	6,494	3.60	23,378	--	81	--	184	6,759	163

[a] 1978 and 1980 wet season crops partly or wholly destroyed by floods.

[b] 1980 and 1982 dry season cropping area limited by water shortages due to drought.

[c] 1983 cropping intensity assumes that all of 10,760 ha net irrigable area will be cropped in wet season.

The technical assistance was, therefore, aimed at strengthening the concerned government agencies so that they could help improve NWPAP's performance. The technical assistance included the following components:

1. Establish a systematic water management program in an area of about 928 ha (about 10 percent of the net service area) at the center of the NWPAP area and prepare an operational manual.
2. Intensify agricultural extension services in the NWPAP area.
3. Strengthen the NACS.
4. Train farmers and project staff in the project area and abroad.
5. Strengthen the project benefit monitoring and evaluation.

The Royal Irrigation Department (RID) served as the principal executing agency for the NWIMP. In addition, Cooperative Promotion Department, DAE, and the Department of Land Development were also involved in implementing NWIMP. The cost of the technical assistance was estimated at $450,000 of which the Bank provided a grant of $360,000 while the government of Thailand (GOT) covered the remaining costs.

Technical Assistance

The technical assistance for NWIMP was approved by the Bank after the GOT gave written assurances that it would provide adequate agricultural support services as stipulated in the loan covenants of NWPAP. These assurances were crucial since the slow progress of agricultural development in the NWPAP area was partly attributed to insufficient extension agents. When the technical assistance was approved in December 1980, the GOT was committed to increase the ratio between the number of extension agents and the number of farmers from 1:1,200 to at least 1:500.

The technical assistance began in October 1981 and was terminated in June 1983. It provided three consultants in the fields of irrigation management, agricultural extension/agronomy, and rural institutions/cooperatives. A total of forty man-months of consultant services were provided under NWIMP. The GOT provided full-time counterpart staff for each of the consultants to ensure a technology transfer between the consultants and the project staff. The counterpart staff also helped the consultants in overcoming their communication problem with non-English speaking Thai farmers and GOT officers.

The consultants used a standardized approach in their assignment to improve the project's performance. During the first two months the consultants identified various constraints in irrigation management, agricultural extension, and cooperative services in the project area. Thereafter, the consultants proposed several alternative solutions to overcome the constraints. In the case of water management, the consultants tested the proposals in the pilot area of 928 ha to find out whether the proposed practices were appropriate and effective before they were recommended to the operations and maintenance (O&M) staff and the farmers. In the case of agricultural extension and cooperative services, the consultants prepared detailed procedures on how to overcome the constraints. They then closely supervised the DAE and NACS staff while they implemented the recommended procedures.

The technical assistance was continued for twenty months. During this period the consultants' major achievements were to:[5]

1. Develop improved water management practices which are applicable to the whole project area. The improved practices included rotation irrigation and a Feedback Information System, which is designed to monitor weekly water demands and the progress of land preparation and planting. This information is used by the Chief of O&M to regulate the release of water from the Nong Wai diversion dam (Figure 10.2).

2. Reorient the extension service to meet the challenge of servicing a modern and intensive irrigated farming system which will replace the standard training and visit approach used in the past by DAE.

3. Improve credit services and repayment rate of NACS through better planning, programming, appraisal, and monitoring of short-term and medium-term loans.

4. Establish and activate 164 water user groups covering the whole project area.

5. Complete integrated training of a large number of project staff and farmers (Table 10.2). Some of the project staff were trained in India and the Philippines.

6. Develop a simpler, cheaper, and more effective project benefit monitoring system applicable to NWPAP.

185

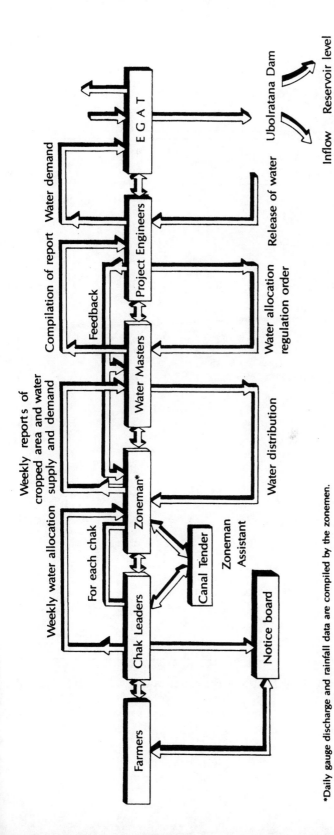

Figure 10.2   Schematic diagram for feedback information system (FIS)

*Daily gauge discharge and rainfall data are compiled by the zonemen.

TABLE 10.2
Accomplishments of training programs under the project

Type of Training	Groups	Total Trained
	- - - (numbers) - - -	
A. FARMERS' TRAINING		
1. Irrigated crop production	60	1,500
2. Cooperative work	10	1,250
3. Water management	--	500
4. Leadership course		
-- Extension	2	66
-- Cooperative	1	91
5. Farmers' foremen	10	200
6. Integrated course	2	100
B. PROJECT STAFF'S TRAINING		
1. O&M staff	1	10
2. Extension agents	11	66
3. Cooperative officers	1	13
4. PBME officers[a]	1	10
5. Overseas training		
-- India	1	2
-- Philippines	1	7

[a] PMBE = project benefit, monitoring, and evaluation.

7. Prepare a comprehensive operational manual for the use of the NWPAP staff in achieving the agricultural development plan targets during the five-year agricultural development phase (1983-1987).

Results from Technical Assistance

The technical assistance for NWIMP has been considered instrumental in bringing NWPAP to the take-off stage of agricultural development. Other factors have also contributed, such as the creation of a project-level Dry Season Cropping Committee by the Ministry of Agriculture and Cooperatives, the implementation of the World Bank assisted National Agricultural Extension Project, and the implementation of flood protection measures. Before NWIMP, the Bank was deeply concerned about the slow pace of agricultural development in the NWPAP area. At the conclusion of NWIMP in June 1983, there were several indications that NWPAP was finally taking off. During the period 1981-1983, cropping intensity increased from 98 percent to 163 percent, paddy production went up from 29,000 to 56,000 metric tons (mt), average paddy yield in the wet season exceeded the appraisal target of 3.0 mt/ha, the average paddy yield in the dry season reached 80 percent of the appraisal target of 4.0 mt/ha, and the average farm income rose from $340 to $855 per family (Table 10.3). It is now expected that the project will be able to substantially achieve the agricultural development targets upon its full development in 1987 or even earlier.

Overall, the Bank's approach of providing post-construction technical assistance was justified. The specific experience from NWIMP indicates that such tehnical assistance is extremely beneficial and cost-effective. However, success of this type of technical assistance will depend on the active participation and cooperation of the concerned government agencies and the farmers, and the ability of the consultants to work as a team and establish good working relationships with the project staff.

CONCLUSION AND RECOMMENDATIONS

A large, integrated pilot scheme appears to be more effective than a small-scale pilot scheme since it can cover various aspects of irrigation management, agricultural extension, agricultural cooperatives, and input-output moni-

TABLE 10.3
Summary of the progress of agricultural development from 1974 (at the time of appraisal) to 1980 (prior to technical assistance to NWIMP) to 1983 (at the completion of NWPAP and NWIMP)

	1974	1980	1983	Appraisal Targets (1985)	Revised Targets (1987)
PROJECT BENEFITS					
Paddy Area (ha):					
Wet season	8,501	8,693	10,760	11,470	10,760
Dry season	—	1,572	6,494	11,040	7,586
Upland Crop Area (ha):					
Dry season	—	278	265	930	1,050
Cropping Intensity (percent)	79	98	163	200	180
Paddy Yield (mt/ha):					
Wet season	2.1	2.8	3.1	3.0	3.5
Dry season	—	2.8	3.6	4.0	4.0
Paddy Production (mt):					
Wet season	17,852	24,340	33,356	34,410	37,660
Dry season	—	4,402	23,378	44,160	30,344
Total	17,852	28,742	56,734	78,570	68,004
Net Service Area (ha)	8,501	8,693	10,760	11,470	10,760
Farm Income (Baht) (in constant 1983 prices)	8,922	7,957	20,348	27,360	22,247

OPERATION AND MAINTENANCE

Project Engineer	1	1	1	1
Assistant Project Engineer	0.3	0.3	0.3	0.3
Water Masters	n.a.	2	3	3
Zonemen	n.a.	8	15	15
Other Staff	n.a.	89	89	85
Water User Organizations	2	82	166	166
Budget Allocation (million Baht)	n.a.	n.a.	7.0	7.5

AGRICULTURAL EXTENSION

No. Subject Matter Specialists (for the Province)	1	1	3	4
No. Extension Agents (Kaset Tambon)	3.0	3.5	13	11
Ratio Between No. Extension Agents and Farmers	1:1,500	1:1,200	1:400	1:500
No. Contact Farmers	None	647	647	550

AGRICULTURAL COOPERATIVES

Multipurpose Cooperatives	4	1	1	1
Total Membership (percent of total farmers)	63	39	44	72
Credit Assistance (million Baht)	7.0	3.5	5.1	12.0
Repayment Rate (percent)	n.a.	36	44	70-75
Marketing of Paddy (mt)	n.a.	231	436	2,000
Fertilizer Sale (mt)	99	130	267	500

n.a. = not available.

toring. However, the success of the program depends on the
following three factors:

1. Adequate irrigation water. A large-scale irrigated
   pilot farm can be operated only when at least 20 to
   30 percent of the service area has been irrigated.
2. Adequate funds and staff. The operation of a
   large-scale pilot farm requires sizable quantities
   of funds and a number of staff. Unless these are
   made available on a timely basis it is unlikely
   that it can be operated effectively.
3. A teamwork approach. A team of experts consisting
   of at least one irrigation engineer, one agronomist, and one credit specialist are required to
   work on the pilot farm for a period of at least one
   year and preferably two or three years. The staff
   of the agencies involved in the project's operation
   and maintenance and agricultural development should
   be made available as counterpart to the experts on
   a full-time basis so that technology transfer to
   project staff can be facilitated through on-the-job
   training.

The experience of the NWPAP area, although limited,
suggests that the Bank should provide post-construction
advisory technical assistance to other ongoing Bank assisted
projects which have problems similar to NWPAP. Some modifications in the approach may have to be made to suit local
conditions. For new irrigation projects, it may be more
desirable to build in consulting services for irrigation
management, agronomy, and agricultural economics during the
project formulation stage to ensure that the expected project benefits are achieved shortly after project completion.

NOTES

1. The views expressed in this paper do not necessarily represent the views of the Asian Development Bank.
2. This number includes integrated agricultural
development projects which involve irrigation and drainage
as a major component.
3. Asian Development Bank. 1973. Regional Workshop
on Irrigation Water Management, 325 pp.
4. In DMCs, except Thailand, the third step (establishment of a pioneer project) has not been adopted.

5. The details of the technical assistance are described in the publications entitled "The Proceedings of the Nong Wai Irrigation Management Seminar" and the "Operational Manual for the Nong Wai Pioneer Agriculture Project." These publications can be obtained from the Asian Development Bank free of charge.

CHAPTER 11

PRIVATE TUBEWELL AND CANAL WATER TRADE
ON PAKISTAN PUNJAB WATERCOURSES

Raymond Z.H. Renfro and Edward W. Sparling

Pakistan's irrigation system is one of the world's largest -- serving over thirty million cultivated acres on approximately three million farms. Historically the system, along with that of north India, was designed to spread seasonally high river flows over wide land areas. Population growth, urbanization, and most recently, new high yielding grains have drastically increased the value of water supplies. In this chapter we examine certain efforts of Pakistan's farmers to cope with this pressure through transactions between farmers involving irrigation water supplies. Of particular interest is the relationship between sale of water from farmer-owned tubewells and the trading of canal water supplies.

During 1981, Renfro studied water transactions on twenty watercourses in the Faisalabad district of Pakistan's Punjab Province. Analysis of Renfro's data suggests that there is a strong relationship between tubewell use and canal water trading. We conclude, as does Malhotra (1980), that farmers using the Warabundi system have little incentive to trade canal water unless there is supplemental water from private tubewells. Availability of private tubewells appears to be a strong incentive for trading in canal water.

Canal water trading necessitates an informal reciprocity relationship which, in turn, requires trading partners to develop trust among themselves. Renfro's data provides some support for this argument. The number of collective projects operating on a given watercourse is positively correlated with the extent of private tubewell use in that watercourse.

An interesting corollary to the private tubewell/ cooperation hypothesis is that watercourses with more private tubewells, and, therefore, more intra-watercourse cooperation, are more attractive candidates for government

subsidized watercourse improvement projects. If watercourses are selected for improvement based on the likelihood
that farmers will organize to maintain their improved watercourse, it follows that improved watercourses will be more
likely to have private tubewells than the average watercourse. Unfortunately, watercourses with more tubewells
than neighboring watercourses stand to benefit less from any
addition to their effective water supplies because their
water supplies are already augmented by tubewell water.
This may explain why Renfro and others (e.g., Shaner and
Landgren 1983) have had difficulty in quantifying effects of
Pakistan's watercourse improvement program.

It is tempting to draw the conclusion that private
tubewell investment is doubly desirable because the direct
benefits of tubewell use are augmented by an increased pro-
pensity of farmers to cooperate with their neighbors. There
are, however, undesirable side effects from private tubewell
investment, particularly with respect to income distribution. It appears that while purchasers of tubewell water
benefit from private tubewells, owners of private tubewells
benefit far more.

A BRIEF OVERVIEW

Water transactions described in this chapter are local
in nature and nearly always between farmers who share a
common outlet from their watercourse. A brief description
of the Warabundi system will make it clear why trading tends
to be geographically limited.

Pakistan's 80,000 watercourses represent the last links
in a hierarchy of dams, diversion works, and canals which
move water from the Indus River system to farmers' fields.
Below the watercourse outlet there are field channels which
may be shared by a few farmers using the same watercourse
outlet. Typically, the watercourse serves between twenty
and 100 farmers on 200 to 1,000 acres. Watercourses may be
dichotomized as perennial or non-perennial according to
whether they receive water year-round (perennial) or just
between April and October (non-perennial). All twenty
watercourses in Renfro's study were perennial.

Except in periods of especially low flow, water enters
each watercourse continuously and (in principle) at a constant rate which is calculated to be proportionate to the
number of acres served by the watercourse. Water is allocated to individual farmers through a rotation system in
which each farmer receives the entire flow of the watercourse for a period of time based on the proportion of the

watercourse acreage which that farmer cultivates (with adjustments for time used filling ditches). The farmer is entitled to this turn once every rotation, usually every week.

The sequence in which farmers take their turns depends upon the type of scheduling or Warabundi used on the watercourse. Historically, most watercourses in Pakistan had flexible or kuchha Warabundi meaning that farmers were free to act collectively to adjust individual turns to compensate for low flows during previous turns or to accommodate special individual needs. In addition, farmers were free to arrange for trading partial or whole turns. These systems depended crucially on a timekeeper who both facilitated and monitored trades. But, according to Mirza, et al. (1975), large farmers were able to put effective pressure on timekeepers, undermining their integrity. Consequently, most kuchha Warabundi systems became so unfair to less influential farmers as to be intolerable.

As a consequence of such inequities and associated conflicts, farmers on most watercourses in Pakistan's Punjab have petitioned the Department of Irrigation to convert their kuchha Warabundies to pukka Warabundies. With pukka schedules, farmers take their turns in the same sequence and at the same time every rotation (Mirza, et al. 1975).[1] Under this system trading of turns is illegal.[2] A variation of the pukka Warabundi may occur where farmers share a common field outlet (each of which serves a twenty-five acre square). These farmers may elect to retain a flexible schedule for their square within the pukka Warabundi of the overall watercourse. This is termed kuchha internal Warabundi. If the schedule inside the square is also fixed, then the farmers will be said to practice pukka internal Warabundi. Renfro found that of the 129 farmers he interviewed, seventy-seven used kuchha internal Warabundi while fifty-two used pukka internal Warabundi.

STUDY POPULATION

Renfro's study was initially designed to describe and analyze water trading on Punjab watercourses. Subsequently a second objective was added, which was to measure effects of Pakistan's watercourse improvement program. That program was begun in 1977 in order to reduce significant water losses from poorly maintained watercourses. Teams of government technicians were organized to select watercourses for improvement. If farmers agreed to cooperate with the government team, the government would supply technical supervision and some capital while farmers were obligated to supply labor for rehabilitation of their watercourse.

Measurement of watercourse improvement dictated that the sample survey included both improved and unimproved watercourses. Furthermore, an effort was made to avoid saline or waterlogged areas to decrease the number of explanatory variables. The sample was stratified in order to identify differences between head, middle, and tail farmers. As a result, the sampled population cannot be considered representative of Punjab farmers, but rather as representative of watercourses on non-waterlogged, non-saline ground water areas in the vicinity of Faisalibad.

Table 11.1 gives a statistical sketch of the twenty watercourses sampled. Tubewell water use is a dominant feature on most of these watercourses. On ten of the twenty watercourses measured, tubewell discharge capacity exceeded authorized discharge from canals.[3] This is consistent with the massive spread of private tubewell investment which has taken place over the past twenty years. That growth is partly explained by the forces of population pressure and the diffusion of high yielding grain varieties. A further explanation of farmer enthusiasm for private tubewells lies in the combination of a rigid canal water allocation system and erratic weather patterns during months when crops are in their vulnerable early growth stages.

UNCERTAIN PLANT WATER NEEDS AND FLEXIBLE SUPPLIES

To illustrate the effect of erratic weather patterns on crop demands for water, the water deficit of sugarcane in Pakistan's Punjab for a representative year, 1975, is shown in Figure 11.1. This graph shows the weekly deficit between evapotranspiration and the sum of rainfall and canal water available at the rootzone. It is assumed that 2 acre cm of canal water are available at the rootzone each week. Since water delivery efficiency and irrigation efficiency are quite low, the centimeters of water at the root zone translate into inches of water from the canal system. In addition, farmers may plan to allocate more than 2 cm of water to sugarcane in any given week so that the deficit may be overstated. The main point to appreciate is the considerable weekly variation in the need for supplemental water which is explained by alternate periods of heavy rainfall and intense heat. The general profile of the deficit will be the same from year to year, but the location of weekly spikes and valleys will be unpredictable. It is the

Major characteristics of sampled watercourses

Total Acres	Total Number Farms on Watercourse	Length Main Watercourse (1000 ft)	Number Tubewells on Watercourse	Ownership of Tubewells[a]	Estimated Tubewell Discharge (cu ft/sec)[b]	Authorized Canal Outlet Discharge (cu ft/sec)	Actual Outlet Discharge (cu ft/sec)[c]	Percent Difference In Last Two Columns
415	104	14.3	2	s,s	.79, .72	1.22	1.45	19
450	114	20.9	0	—	—	1.36	2.10	54
363	73	9.9	1	j	1.57	1.09	1.10	1
245	58	9.9	0	—	—	.65	.85	31
350	83	13.8	0	—	—	.99	2.20	122
275	28	15.4	1	c	1.1	.93	1.13	21.5
465	79	22.0	1	c	1.25	1.4	1.73	24
375	61	17.1	1	c	1.2	1.12	1.40	25
430	87	18.7	1	s	1.2	1.34	2.40	79
363	102	15.4	2	s,s	1.45, 1.48	1.03	.85	-17
500	130	30.6	1	s	1.2	1.56	2.60	67
475	107	19.2	0	—	—	1.5	2.45	63
388	117	19.2	1	j	1.2	1.13	1.20	6
284	54	7.7	0	—	—	.79	.70	-11
375	84	18.0	0	—	—	1.00	1.30	30
354	70	20.9	2	s,s	1.1, .8	1.05	1.84	75
392	78	13.2	1	s	1.2	1.11	1.40	26
325	73	13.2	1	s	1.2	1.05	1.65	57
371	111	16.5	1	j	.9	1.16	1.00	-14
350	94	13.5	1	j	1.2	1.07	1.35	26

[a]S = single family; j = joint ownership; c = cooperative ownership.

[b]Measured by using 8" x 3' cut-throat flumes.

[c]Measured by using the Purdue coordinate method.

197

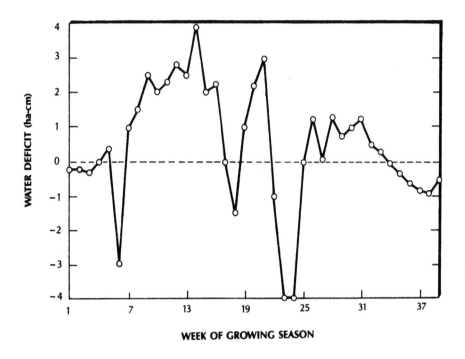

Figure 11.1   **Plant water deficit for sugarcane, Sargodha District, Pakistan 1975**

variability of this weekly profile which motivates the demand for flexible water supplies.

To the extent that soil stores water from week to week, the profile of deficits may differ from farmer to farmer depending on which farmers have most recently irrigated their sugarcane or whether a farmer is growing cane. If these differences between potential trading partners are significant, then there is potential for increasing overall productivity through trading water toward its highest value use. However, if differences are not significant, or if the transactions costs of arranging trades are higher than the benefits to be gained, there will be little incentive for trading. It will be seen below that the transactions costs of trading canal water turns may be quite high.

WATER TRANSACTIONS AND TRADING

The Canal and Drainage Act states that it is illegal to
sell or sublet the whole or any portion of one's authorized
right to canal water under the pukka Warabundi without the
permission of an Irrigation Department official. The one
exception to this is when one's canal water right is sold
simultaneously with the land to which the water right
applies. This stricture has been expanded in case law to a
general prohibition of any exchange of canal water (Nasir
1981).

Despite these legal prohibitions irrigators do trade
canal water turns and occasionally sell and buy water. When
a tubewell is present, they may also infrequently trade
canal water for tubewell water (Lowdermilk, et al. 1975,
1978; Gustafson and Reidinger 1971). When two or more tubewells are present on a watercourse, owners of these tubewells could trade tubewell water with each other, although
there is little incentive for doing this unless one of the
tubewells is out of order.

Apart from legal restrictions on water trading, the
pukka Warabundi system creates significant obstacles to
trading of turns. If farmers wish extra water during a
particular week, they can accomplish this easily only if
they can arrange with farmers immediately adjacent to them
on the watercourse. Otherwise, they must involve intervening farmers in a more complicated adjustment of turns.
The potential complexity of such transactions can be appre-
ciated by considering a hypothetical trade.

A Hypothetical Trade of Canal Water

Suppose two trading partners are separated by two
intervening irrigators on a watercourse. The upstream
trader is designated as i and the downstream irrigator as
i+3. The two intervening irrigators, also with canal water
turns, are designated as i+1 and i+2, proceeding in a downstream direction. Further, suppose that the irrigated
acreage for each of these four cultivators is the same and
that their sanctioned turns based on acreage are two hours
each per week. If the farmers are subject to pukka
Warabundi, their respective turns occur at the same time
each week. To obtain some extra water, irrigator i+3
strikes an agreement with irrigator i to borrow one hour's
worth of i's turn, with an understanding (often unspoken)
that i is entitled to reclaim an hour's worth of water at a
future time. The exchange, however, also requires that i+3

enlist the cooperation of i+1 and i+2 to adjust the timing of their turns forward by an hour.

The general pattern of a transaction of this type is for irrigator i to begin irrigating at the usual time but to release the water one hour early to i+1. Farmer i+1 then turns the water over to i+2 one hour early, who in turn releases the water one hour early, leaving irrigator i+3 with an extra hour's worth of water. Farmer i+3 releases the water to irrigator i+4 at the regularly scheduled time.

Irrigator i may or may not reclaim the hour of Warabundi time. If the hour is reclaimed, the net exchange is balanced out in terms of water supplies, but there is a net gain in water productivity. If the exchange is to be completed, irrigators i+1 and i+2 must again assent to changing their turns, this time starting an hour later as irrigator i reclaims the partial turn.

Such trades will be much more likely to succeed if all four farmers share a kuchha internal Warabundi where their times are flexible. If the four are part of a pukka internal Warabundi, or if they belong to different kuchha Warabundis, intervening irrigators have the legal right to block the trade. Thus, one should expect that trading of canal water turns will tend to be between neighbors sharing the same square.

Indeed, Renfro's findings confirm this conjecture. Table 11.2 summarizes findings concerning the frequency and magnitude of trading by sampled farmers. Among the 113 traders, 75 percent of the trading was done with farmers sharing the same square and, therefore, the same watercourse outlet. Only 3 percent of trades were with farmers outside the immediately adjoining squares. More directly, the most frequent response to the question of significant constraints to trading was non-cooperation of intervening farmers with 65 percent of the 164 responses expressing that concern. Only 23 percent of responses indicated no need to trade, and 4 percent claimed that the length or slope of their watercourse inhibited trading.

The picture which Renfro describes indicates that farmers do recognize the value of exchanging turns but that their trading is restrained by transactions costs due to the need to involve bystanders. Trades are easiest among those sharing the same outlet. Yet, if farmer i's crops are nearing stress, then so will the crops of the immediate neighbors whose last turn was at approximately the same time as that of farmer i. Consequently, although trading with neighbors may have low transactions costs, there will be little potential for transferring water from fields where its current value is low to those where its current value is

TABLE 11.2
Frequency and magnitude of trading in canal water turns,
including active and inactive traders, 1980–1981

Trading	All Farmers	Active Traders	Inactive Traders
	-- (numbers) --		
Total	129	42	71
Mean partial turns traded	6	7	6
Mean full turns traded	1	4	1
Mean times traded	6.3	16.5	2.5
Mean trading partners	3	4	3
Mean hours traded	5.3 hr	12.4 hr	2.2 hr

high. This picture is altered when there is supplemental
tubewell water for sale on the watercourse or there are significant differences in soil water holding capacities or
crops grown.

Tubewell Water Sales and Trading Canal Turns

Private tubewells alter the flexibility of water supplies for their owners. But the typical private tubewell
has far more capacity than can be used by its owner. Therefore, most private tubewell owners must count on selling
water to cover the costs of their investment.

The nature of delivering tubewell water to buyers also
tends to encourage trade of irrigation turns. Buyers of
tubewell water arrange with an upstream tubewell owner to
pump into the watercourse during their turn. The most ob-
vious reason for this procedure is the limitation placed on
use of the watercourse by the Warabundi system. The only

time outside of the user's turn during which the watercourse
could be used for tubewell water would be when the canal
water flow is being diverted above the tubewell. But even
then, if the renter uses tubewell water without canal water,
there is the disadvantage of having a low head and,
therefore, difficulty in covering higher (and drier) spots.

Availability of tubewell water to a particular outlet
will increase incentives to borrow as well as willingness to
lend partial turns. Incentives to trade turns will be
stronger because tubewell water availability may not exactly
correspond to a farmer's Warabundi turn. Therefore, farmers
may wish to adjust their turns. Yet, it will not generally
be necessary to adjust this time by much so that nearby
farmers will be attractive trading partners. From the
lender's perspective, the availability of this supplemental
water reduces the uncertainty in their water supplies. They
face less risk in releasing a part of a turn to a neighbor
because they can obtain a supplemental supply of tubewell
water in their next turn if weather is particularly hot and
dry. Furthermore, such a favor naturally implies a recip-
rocal obligation which increases the lender's future
flexibility.

It follows from the above reasoning that farmers who
use private tubewell water will be more likely to trade
canal water turns. Furthermore, farmers who share a kuchha
internal Warabundi will find it more convenient to use
tubewell water than will farmers sharing a rigid internal
Warabundi. Renfro's data on timing of canal water turns
supports this hypothesis. Canal water trading is highest in
May and June (44 percent of all trades) and in October to
December (36 percent of all trades). These are the seasons
of highest irrigation demand and of highest tubewell use.
This correspondence is consistent with the argument that
trading and tubewell rental go hand in hand. Statistical
significance of this correspondence and more complicated
two- and three-way interactions can be formally tested using
analysis of variance (ANOVA).

Canal Water Trading and Tubewells

Table 11.3 shows the sum of squares of an ANOVA relating five variables to per acre gross income. The ANOVA is
based on observations from the 129 farms. Tubewell water
use includes use of water under three categories; single-
owner tubewells, joint-owner tubewells, and non-use of
tubewell water. Trading is categorized as none, inactive
trading, and active trading. Active traders are those who

TABLE 11.3

Analysis of variance relating type of tubewell, trading, internal Warabundi and watercourse and collective project numbers to gross income

Source of Variation	Sum of Squares (000)	D.F.	Mean Square (000)	Significance of F
MAIN EFFECTS				
Joint effect	38,253	7	5,460	.01
Type of tubewell water use	15,000	2	7,500	.02
Type of trading	12,690	2	6,340	.04
Type of internal Warabundi	246	1	246	.71
Type of watercourse	796	1	796	.51
Number of collective projects	a	1	a	.99
TWO-WAY INTERACTIONS				
Joint effect	46,135	19	2,420	.19
Tubewell and trading	19,645	4	4,910	.04
Tubewell and Warabundi	4,490	2	2,240	.30
Tubewell and watercourse	6,277	2	3,130	.19
Tubewell and collective projects	9,564	2	4,780	.08
Trading and Warabundi	918	2	459	.78
Trading and watercourse	2,364	2	1,180	.53
Trading and collective projects	350	2	175	.91
Warabundi and watercourse	454	1	454	.62
Warabundi and collective projects	53	1	53	.87
Watercourse and collective projects	1,588	1	1,580	.34
THREE-WAY INTERACTIONS				
Joint effect	25,398	14	1,810	.47
Tubewell, trading, and Warabundi	14,737	4	3,680	.10
Tubewell, trading, and watercourse	409	2	204	.89
Tubewell, trading, and collective projects	6,722	2	3,360	.16
Tubewell, Warabundi, and watercourse	3,903	1	3,900	.15
Tubewell, watercourse, and collective projects	12	1	12	.94
Trading, Warabundi, and watercourse	341	1	341	.67
Trading, Warabundi, and collective projects	3,979	1	3,970	.14
Trading, watercourse, and collective projects	4,892	2	2,440	.27
FOUR-WAY INTERACTIONS				
Tubewell, trading, Warabundi, and watercourse	8,009	1	8,000	.04
Explained	109,780	40	2,740	.06
Residual	160,500	88	1,820	

aThe sum of squares and mean square was only 339.

had traded more than 7 percent or more than six hours of their Warabundi time. Type of internal Warabundi is classed as kuchha or pukka. Type of watercourse involves classification of watercourses as either improved or unimproved. Number of collective projects is a watercourse level variable with two categories; fewer than two collective projects and two or more collective projects.

In the analysis, both tubewell water use and trading are significant at the .05 level or better. The two-way interactions show that the tubewell water use and trading variable is significant at the .04 level. The mean gross income per acre display the expected differences in every category (Table 11.4). The differences between mean gross income per acre among categories of tubewell users is conditioned by the degree of trading (Table 11.5). Tubewell users who are also active traders have higher mean incomes per acre than do tubewell users who are not active traders. Among non-tubewell users there appears to be no significant difference in gross income per acre for those who are active traders and those who are not. This last result is worth noting because it supports the contention of Malhotra (1980) that farmers have little incentive for trading Warabundi turns. Malhotra appears to be right if there are no private tubewells on the watercourse.

Private Tubewells and Cooperation

The number of collective projects is a necessarily im- precise measure of cooperation. Nevertheless, it is of interest to note that of the 129 farmers, those who used private tubewells were more likely to reside on a water- course with two or more collective projects than were farms not using tubewells (Table 11.6). The frequencies do tend to verify our tentative hypothesis that private tubewell use indirectly encourages intra-watercourse cooperation. Fur- thermore, the F-test associated with this relationship is significant at the .08 level (Table 11.3). Two things make these results subject to question: (1) the impreciseness of the measure of collective action, and (2) the non-randomness of farmer selection due to other study requirements. The result is, however, consistent with data presented by Mirza and Merrey (1979), who studied ten watercourses in Pakistan's Punjab. Of those ten watercourses, four of the five which had multiple private tubewells were also among the five which Mirza and Merrey classed as having had previous cooperation and little or no conflict (Sparling 1981).

TABLE 11.4
Mean gross income per acre by type of tubewell, water
trading, internal Warabundi and watercourse and number of
collective projects

Major Category	Sub-Category	Mean Gross Income Per Acre	Number of Observations
Type of tube-well water use	Singly Owned	4,019	32
	Joint Property	3,157	28
	None	3,018	69
Nature of trading	Active	3,828	42
	Inactive	3,048	71
	None	3,007	16
Type of internal Warabundi	Kuchha	3,343	77
	Pukka	3,228	52
Type of watercourse	Improved	3,482	65
	Unimproved	3,108	64
Number of collective projects	2+	3,441	53
	0 or 1	3,196	76
Total sample		3,297	129

TABLE 11.5
Average gross income per acre for active traders, tubewell
users, and other farmers

	Tubewell Users	Other Farmers
Active traders	4,505 (25)[a]	3,027 (19)
Other farmers	3,112 (35)	3,015 (50)

[a]Number of observations.

TABLE 11.6
Average gross income per acre for farmers by number of
collective projects and tubewell use

Number of Collective Projects	Tubewell Users	Other Farmers
2+	3,785 (36)[a]	2,715 (17)
0 or 1	3,365 (24)	3,118 (52)

[a]Number of observations.

If one is willing to accept the significance of the
collective projects/tubewell use interaction, there still is
no strong evidence that the causality runs predominantly in
one direction or the other. It probably runs both ways.
Farmers with cooperative neighbors are more likely to invest
in tubewells, and the presence of private tubewells gives
farmers new reasons to cooperate with each other. But
regardless of the direction of causality, this relationship
suggests that using the criteria of farmer cooperation in
choosing watercourses for rehabilitation may be a mistake.
On the average, those are watercourses on which private
tubewells are located and, therefore, farmers need the
additional water less than do those served by watercourses
where there is little cooperation and few private tubewells.

Markets and Cooperation

The empirical evidence suggests that private tubewells
tend to encourage cooperation among farmers on Pakistani
watercourses. Since these ideas were first presented, it
has been pointed out that the argument is really just a
special case of an old idea that market trade tends to be a
civilizing force in society because market exchange always
implies gains to both sides of each transaction (Hirschman
1982). While it is true that the market seems to have

opposing effects as well, the older <u>doux commerce</u> thesis appears to apply in the context of Pakistan's watercourses. A cautionary note needs to be sounded, however, lest anyone interpret this chapter as endorsing wholesale encouragement of investment in private tubewells. It is perhaps enough to end by listing the mean gross income per acre for several categories of tubewell users and let readers draw their own inferences (Tables 11.7 and 11.8).

TABLE 11.7
Gross income of sample farmers by tubewell use

		Gross Income Per Acre	
User Category	Number	Mean	Standard Deviations
Tubewell users	60	3,617	1,744
Non-users	69	3,019	1,081
Tubewell owners	10	4,659	2,029
Tubewell renters	50	3,408	

n.a. = not available.

TABLE 11.8
Two-way table of mean gross income per acre by type of
tubewell, trading, internal Warabundi and watercourse, and
number of collective projects

| | Type of Tubewell Water Use | | |
	Singly-Owned	Joint Property	None
(a) Degree of Trading			
Active	4,919 (16)[a]	3,769 (9)	3,027 (19)
Inactive	3,351 (12)	2,966 (13)	2,915 (44)
None	2,425 (4)	2,656 (6)	3,748 (6)
(b) Type of Internal Warabundi			
Kuchha	4,000 (22)	3,345 (22)	2,905 (33)
Pukka	4,062 (10)	2,471 (6)	3,123 (36)
(c) Type of Watercourse			
Improved	3,995 (18)	3,317 (21)	3,261 (26)
Unimproved	4,050 (14)	2,678 (7)	2,872 (43)
(d) Number of Collective Projects			
2+	4,087 (18)	3,482 (18)	2,715 (17)
0 or 1	3,932 (14)	2,572 (10)	3,118 (52)

[a]Number of observations.

NOTES

1. Seckler (1981) cites a study in north India which chronicles a similar change to pukka Warabundi. Renfro (1982) found only a handful of watercourses, all comprising a relatively small number of farms, retaining kuchha Warabundi in his study area.
    2. It will be seen that this legal prohibition is ineffective. Lowdermilk, et al. (1978) found widespread canal water trading in their survey of forty watercourses.
    3. Actual canal outlet discharge is rarely the same as authorized discharge. Often this is due to informal arrangements with irrigation officers. See Lowdermilk, et al. (1978) for details.

REFERENCES

Gustafson, W.E., and R.B. Reidinger. 1971. "Delivery of canal water in north India and west Pakistan." Economic and Political Weekly, December 25, pp. A157-162.
Hirschman, A.O. 1982. "River interpretations of the market society: Civilizing, destructive, or feeble?" Journal of Economic Literature 20(4):1463-84.
Lowdermilk, M.K., A.C. Early, and D.M. Freeman. 1978. Farm Irrigation Constraints and Farmers' Responses: Comprehensive Field Survey in Pakistan. Water Management Technical Report No. 48, Vol. I-IV, Water Management Research Project, Colorado State University, Fort Collins, Colorado.
Lowdermilk, M.K., W. Clyma, and A.C. Early. 1975. Physical and Socioeconomic Dynamics of a Watercourse in Pakistan's Punjab: System Constraints and Farmer Responses. Water Management Technical Report No. 42, Water Management Research Project, Colorado State University, Fort Collins, Colorado.
Malhotra, S.P. 1980. "Discovery of the Warabandi system and its infrastructure, 1980." Draft Report, The Ford Foundation, New Delhi, India.
Mirza, A.H., D.M. Freeman, and J.B. Eckert. 1975. Village Organizational Factors Affecting Water Management Decision Making Among Punjab Farmers. Water Management Technical Report No. 35, Water Management Research Project, Colorado State University, Fort Collins, Colorado.

Mirza, A.H., and D.J. Merrey. 1979. Organizational
Problems and Their Consequences on Improved
Watercourses in Punjab. Water Management Technical
Report No. 55, Water Management Research Project,
Colorado State University, Fort Collins, Colorado.

Nasir, S.A.D. 1981. A Practical Treatise and Analytical
Study of the Canal and Drainage Act (VII of 1873) with
Punjab Minor Canal Act, 1905, Sind Irrigation Act,
1879, Soil Reclamation Act, 1952, and Detailed
Commentary with Up-to-Date Case Law, Notifications,
Circular Letters and Instructions, etc. Mansoor Book
House, Lahore, Pakistan.

Renfro, R.Z.H. 1982. "Economics of local control of
irrigation water in Pakistan: A pilot study."
Unpublished Ph.D. Dissertation, Colorado State
University, Fort Collins, Colorado.

Seckler, D. 1981. "The new era of irrigation management in
India." Draft Report, The Ford Foundation, New Delhi,
India.

Shaner, W.W., and N.E. Landgren. 1983. "Monitoring and
evaluation of the on-farm water management program."
Mimeo of Report for Pakistan's Ministry of Food,
Agriculture, and Cooperatives, and for CID, Islamabad.

Sparling, E.W. 1981. "Watercourse maintenance and the
value of the going concern." Mimeo, Economics
Department, Colorado State University, Fort Collins,
Colorado.

CHAPTER 12

ALLOCATIVE IMPACTS OF ALTERNATIVE METHODS OF CHARGING FOR IRRIGATION WATER IN EGYPT

Richard L. Bowen and Robert A. Young[1]

In Egypt, as in many countries where public irrigation is important, the system of pricing or charging for water is of concern for its impact on resource allocation and income distribution, and as a source of revenue. Currently, the major type of agricultural taxation in Egypt is a form of commodity tax, imposed on the major crops. The revenue flows into the government's general fund from which the Ministry of Irrigation must obtain its budget for operating, maintaining, and expanding the irrigation system. Ministry officials have expressed interest in obtaining revenue directly from farmers.

The impact water of charges on water conservation is also a concern of officials in the Ministry of Irrigation although official forecasts do not indicate water shortages in the near future (Ministry of Irrigation 1981). Contrary to the more optimistic forecasts of government planners, Waterbury (1979) has argued that water shortages could occur before the end of the century. Over the past several years the drought in the Nile headwater regions, particularly in Ethiopia, has significantly reduced Nile river flows. Reservoir managers have drawn down the level of Lake Nasser, primarily to maintain hydropower production. Continuation of the drought could produce a shortage of water for agriculture. The once pessimistic scenario for Egypt of serious water shortages in the near future has become a realistic possibility.

The objective of this chapter is to assess how alternative methods of charging for irrigation water in Egypt impact allocative efficiency. With the exception of Seagraves and Ochoa (1978) previous studies have been prescriptive without providing empirical analyses of the effects of pricing policies on societal objectives. Furthermore, transactions costs in implementing water pricing policies is often acknowledged but none of the surveyed studies have provided empirical support of its importance. (See Chapter 3 for a brief review of water pricing alternatives.)

EVALUATING CHARGING SYSTEMS

Milliman (1972) was one of the first to attempt a synthesis of the three major strands of economic literature which deal with pricing of public products. The public finance literature has historically stressed the equity (fairness) and long-run efficiency benefits of beneficiaries paying for the benefits received from government projects. But little attention has been devoted to how payment should be extracted.

On the other hand, the public utility literature has been concerned with designing rate structures appropriate to the financial and legal constraints of privately-run, publicly-regulated utilities. As a result, utility rates are generally designed to recover historical costs and reflect average cost of services rather than marginal cost of supply.

Welfare economists have developed the theory of marginal cost pricing, which maintains that public prices be set equal to marginal social (opportunity) costs. In the presence of decreasing costs, marginal cost pricing can produce financial deficits.

In addition to recovering costs and satisfying efficiency objectives, water charges have also been used by governments to pursue income redistribution objectives. Thus, the problem of designing appropriate water rate structures is one of satisfying multiple social objectives. The major societal objectives in the literature can be placed in two categories: allocative efficiency and equity.

Allocative Efficiency

The allocative efficiency objective is concerned with the classic economic problem of allocating scarce resources to maximize net social benefits. The major concern of the efficiency objective is resource allocation under scarcity, including the provision of appropriate signals for investment and innovation. To maximize allocative efficiency the effective price of irrigation water should be set at marginal social cost, defined as opportunity cost rather than historical cost. Where the competitive conditions of markets do not exist to ensure this condition, optimal resource allocation must be encouraged by government set rules and charges. Davis and Hanke (1972) use a static model to illustrate the case of short-run marginal cost pricing. A dynamic model of resource pricing in the long-run is found in Howe (1979).

To achieve greater efficiency in irrigation requires increased administration to yield more precise measuring, monitoring, policing, and price differentiation with respect to place, time, and quality. Incremental administrative costs have usually been assumed to be trivial in studies of pricing of publicly-supplied goods. However, when the value of water is low, the transactions costs of bringing about increased efficiency may be greater than the social benefits (Ruttan 1978; Randall 1983).

Equity Objectives

Cost recovery and income redistribution are objectives usually considered in establishment of water charges. The degree of cost recovery is an equity concern because it is considered "fair" that the beneficiary pays all or part of the cost of a service. Still, policy makers may wish to influence the distribution of income of certain groups by either subsidizing or overpricing the services provided. The formulation of equity objectives is assumed to involve political concerns and not be just an economic issue.

Other Concerns Involved with Water Charges

The "unanticipated and unaccepted failure of an agent to serve his principal" (Reder 1975, p. 607) can be pervasive in countries just developing institutional capabilities and can thwart the achievement of both efficiency and equity objectives of water charging systems. Wade (1982) argues that instead of being operated in the farmers' interests, water systems are often operated for the benefit of government officials and raise large sums of illicit revenue for private gain. The method of charging should, therefore, be selected with the possibility of corruption in mind.

An important concern in implementing schemes which involve measurement of water deliveries and/or changes in the level or method of collecting revenues from farmers, is the possible hostile reaction of farmers to such changes. This issue arises, as Boulding (1980) has observed, from the special spiritual and symbolic role water plays in human affairs. People often express the feeling that they should receive all the water they want (regardless of cost or value in alternative use). In Islamic societies such as Egypt, these intangible considerations come from interpretations of Koranic scriptures which appear to forbid direct pricing of water. However, charging for the resources required to provide and deliver water is apparently not an issue.

RESEARCH APPROACH

The general research approach incorporates the following: (a) a social objective function or criterion, (b) policy or controllable variables, (c) non-controllable variables, and (d) a predictive model which forecasts economic behavior and relates the controllable and non-controllable variables to the social objective.

The social objective used in this study is allocative efficiency, constrained by fairness in cost recovery (in the sense that beneficiaries are fully assessed). The policy variables analyzed include seven alternative farm-area-based and volumetric charging rules. The non-controllable variables include behavioral assumptions regarding farmer response to the policy alternatives, technology, government regulations, and price controls. The predictive model is based on a linear programming formulation of the resource allocation of farm situations in Egypt's northern Nile delta. The model reflects potential allocations of land and water resources among a number of alternative crops and irrigation levels, consistent with animal production requirements.

In order to reflect the more important conditions under which irrigation water charging policy might occur, each policy variable is analyzed under several scenarios. Two of the scenarios represent the current and an alternative government pricing policy. Under current Egyptian policy, farmers are subject to mandatory production controls and receive prices for their outputs which are directly or indirectly determined by government price controls. The alternative scenario investigated is the use of markets for determining product prices.

Three water supply scenarios are considered which include 1980 supply, and 20 and 40 percent reductions from the 1980 level. The latter represent hypothetical water shortages which could occur during a low flow period of the Nile river.

The transactions costs of implementing the various cost recovery mechanisms is explicitly considered. A presumption of the research was that transactions costs can be a decisive consideration in comparing the desirability of different methods of charging for water.

FARMER RESPONSE TO WATER CHARGING INSTRUMENTS

The Abu Raia cooperative, located in the Kafr El Sheikh district, was selected as the study area because it was thought to be representative of a large portion of the Nile delta and because data were readily available. Cotton, rice, and maize are the major summer crops and berseem (Egyptian clover), wheat, flax, and broadbeans are common in winter. Farms are small, averaging about two hectares.

To simulate the impact of water charges on farm water use and income, a linear programming model of a representative farm in the Kafr El Sheikh district in Egypt's northern delta was developed. (See Bowen and Young (1986) for a full description.) The model was formulated to represent considerable flexibility in allocating water under scarcity. For each crop there are multiple production activities, representing different planting dates and numerous irrigation regimes. The irrigation regimes model the predicted impact of water deficits on irrigation efficiency and crop yields.

The objective function of the farmers is defined as the maximization of returns to fixed farm resources (land and management). Using the concept of a reservation wage, family labor is priced at the estimated opportunity cost of foregone leisure. The model reflects a one year planning horizon.

Fixed monthly constraints are used for water supply, reflecting assumed inflexibility in reallocating water among months and between the summer and winter seasons. The high seasonality of demand for irrigation water from the Aswan dams conflicts with the more stable year-round demand for hydropower. Fixed monthly constraints imply that the farmer knows what monthly quantities of water are available, even though the system is continuous flow (during "on" periods) and water rights are not assigned to farmers. The implicit assumption of the water constraints is that the farmer, over a number of years, comes to expect a certain flow of water.

The impact of water charges are estimated under two sets of institutional assumptions. The first set, used in the government model, represents farm decision making under current government pricing and production policies. The government model represents the incentives which faced the individual farmer under the commodity pricing and production policies that existed in 1980. It employs 1980 financial prices for all inputs and outputs and imposes mandatory production quotas on rice and cotton, the two government-controlled crops in the area. The market model reflects a second set of assumptions, designed to simulate farmer response to a hypothetical free market economy. Accounting prices for fertilizer and for crops, based on international border prices adjusted to the farm level, are used and no government production or marketing constraints are imposed.

Three models are formulated, reflecting alternative locations on the branch canals: head, middle, and tail. To reflect the allocation of water under shortages in a continuous flow delivery system, it is assumed that head-reach farms will be able to divert up to 50 percent of the water flowing past the headgate. Middle-reach farms can divert up to 60 percent of the residual and tail-reach farms can use the remainder. These percentages were derived taking into account conveyance losses and the fact that blocking the flow of water is illegal.

Egypt's unique distribution system delivers the water below the level of the farmer's field, forcing the farmer to lift water approximately one meter to field level. The system was designed to control excessive use of irrigation water by imposing a cost on marginal use. However, when the traditional sakia (Persian water wheel) is used, the short-run marginal cost of lifting water is relatively low. The present below-grade system is effective when water is plentiful. In the future, unplanned water shortages could occur or the cost of water supply projects may become prohibitively expensive. Under water shortage conditions, new institutions to conserve and ration water will be needed to supplement the limited rationing ability of the present delivery system.

The below-grade system of delivery has the advantage of being a self-regulating method of water allocation which saves on the administrative cost of government rationing. Below-grade delivery also reduces canal leakage problems. Some disadvantages are the high cost of maintaining draft animals, including the opportunity cost of utilizing a significant portion of cropland for forage production, and the missed opportunity to substitute improved dairy cattle for draft animals (Walters 1981).

WATER CHARGING METHODS AND INSTITUTIONAL COSTS

From the economic efficiency perspective, benefits from institutional change ought to exceed the costs necessitated by the change (Ruttan 1978). Due to the difficulties involved, our attempt to develop quantitative estimates of technological and administrative costs of instituting water charges must be recognized as preliminary and speculative. Rather wide confidence intervals for the estimates should be assumed. The two broad types of water charges analyzed are area-based and volumetric charges.

The flat land charge would be based on cultivable area. Crop charges are also area-based, but are levied only on cultivated area. Crop changes can be uniform across all crops or can vary according to water use or gross or net income of individual crops. A flat land tax is the easiest area-based pricing instrument to administer since only the existing knowledge of the farmers' landholdings is needed. Flat land taxes are already used in Egypt to generate general revenue. Crop charges require information on the number of feddans irrigated by crop for each farmer. This crop information is currently collected by the Egyptian government for use in allocating fertilizer and would require little incremental expense. It is necessary in most countries to determine which croplands actually receive water. Under the extremely arid conditions in Egypt, all cropland must be irrigated and the single source of irrigation water is the Nile river.

Volumetric pricing requires the ability to measure water with a reasonable degree of accuracy. The method selected for analysis involves a counting meter on the sakia. This water measurement device is simple and relatively low-cost. It would record the number of revolutions, and a specific formula would convert revolutions into volumes of water. The formula would reflect the size, design, and degree of submergence of the sakia. Slack (1981) studied the problem of measuring the discharge of a sakia in Egypt and estimates that discharge measurements with this method are reasonably accurate. The counter would be read at least once a year and the readings converted to volumes for tax assessment. Administrative complexity and costs will increase with more sophistication in volumetric pricing.

The annual cost estimates (Table 12.1) are supported by interviews with knowledgeable engineers and data from the research literature including Slack (1981); Cuddihy (1980); Maass and Anderson (1978); and Coward (1980). The estimated annual incremental administrative costs ranged from less than 1 L.E. per feddan for area-based charges to over 5 L.E. per feddan for volumetric pricing.[2] (See Bowen and Young (1983) for derivation and estimated costs for each type of pricing instrument.) The inability to measure the intan-

TABLE 12.1
Estimated annual budgetary costs of providing
and charging for irrigation water in Egypt

Type of Cost	L.E. per Feddan
Capital Cost	10
O&M Cost	10
Administrative Cost of Charging for Water	
Flat land tax	0.2
Flat crop charges	0.6
Other crop charges	0.8
Volumetric charges	5.1

gible costs noted earlier implies that the transactions
costs are underestimated.

RESULTS: IMPACTS OF WATER CHARGING INSTRUMENTS

The cardinal and ordinal rankings of the two alternative cost recovery instruments were similar whether using
the government or the market model. Both models predicted
similar base period cropping patterns, although the cropping
patterns diverged as the water constraints were tightened.
But the degree to which water charges alone improved water
allocation in the model was rather independent of the output
prices and production controls which differentiate the two
models. For this reason, the following discussion reports
only the findings derived from the market model.
Two levels of cost recovery were evaluated. One level
recovers all capital and operation and maintenance (O&M)
costs of providing irrigation water (the latter includes the
estimated cost of administering the cost recovery instru-

ment). The other level of cost recovery treats capital costs as sunk and seeks to recover only O&M costs (Table 12.1).

Table 12.2 summarizes the efficiency impacts of the alternative cost recovery schemes. The optimal pricing instrument, judged by the efficiency criterion, is the instrument which maximizes social net returns to land and water in the study area. These returns are net of the public costs incurred in providing and charging for the irrigation water. An ordinal ranking of instruments is also provided.

Charging for Water Under Current Supply Conditions

Current irrigation water supply in Egypt has been adequate to meet aggregate demand in the agricultural sector. The first column of Table 12.2 shows the summary results of the efficiency effects of charging for water where water supply does not limit production.

Because of lower administrative cost, area-based charges are more efficient than volumetric charges under current water supply conditions. The flat land tax is the least expensive instrument and has the advantage of being allocatively neutral. Although crop charges theoretically can produce allocative distortions, no misallocations were predicted by the model under the conditions tested. Therefore, the small differences in efficiency ratings among area-based charges are due solely to differences in the costs of administering the charges.

Land taxes are the highest rated pricing instrument and can be recommended as an appropriate method of recovering costs, provided that water shortages do not occur. The conclusion is based on the concern for allocative efficiency. If water charges are used to pursue income redistribution (within the agricultural sector) objectives, crop charges (especially those based on crop income) may be more desirable.

Charging for Water Under Hypothetical Water Shortages

Columns 2 and 3 of Table 12.2 show the summary social returns for two hypothesized water shortage conditions. Area-based water charges did not produce any changes in the cropping patterns of the model farms. The result is surprising since most of the crop charges were varied among the different crops. While some differences in optimal cropping

TABLE 12.2
Evaluation and ranking of water pricing instruments under
alternative water supply scenarios on the basis of the
allocative efficiency criterion[a] - market model

Pricing Instrument	Water Supply Scenarios		
	Actual	20 Percent Reduction	40 Percent Reduction
AREA-BASED CHARGES			
Flat land tax	323 (1)	306 (2)	223 (3)
Crop charges[b]	322 (2)	305 (4)	222 (4)
VOLUMETRIC PRICES			
Flat annual (1)[c]	318 (3)	306 (2)	232 (2)
Flat annual (2)[c]	316 (4)	307 (1)	235 (1)

[a]Allocative efficiency criterion: Economic returns to land
and water per feddan net of tangible institutional costs
of pricing water. Rank given in parentheses.

[b]The crop charges tried include the following: A water
requirements-based crop charge, a gross income-based crop
charge, a net income-based crop charge, and a uniform
charge on all cultivated land.

[c]Flat annual (1) charges recover operation and maintenance
costs; flat annual (2) charges recover full capital,
operating, and maintenance costs.

pattern were hypothesized, apparently at the low rates of
water charges, the relative profitability differences were
insufficient to shift the model solution. This result is
due to the step-function nature of the derived demand for
irrigation water in a linear programming model.

Under a moderate degree of shortage (20 percent), area-
based charges are slightly less efficient than volumetric
charges. However, the intangible administrative and political costs of metering irrigation water use would likely
more than offset this small advantage of volumetric systems
over area-based charges.

Under severe water scarcity (40 percent), volumetric
pricing instruments are shown to bring about an improvement
in allocative efficiency over area-based charges. Flat,
annual volumetric charges, however, are inefficient because
the rates designed to recover historical costs are too low
to produce an efficient allocation of water. On the other
hand, if the rates were set to maximize allocative
efficiency, the result would be overtaxation relative to
cost of providing irrigation water. A flat volumetric
charge can be used to meet either the cost recovery
objective or the allocative efficiency objective, but
generally not both. However, if the volumetric charge can
be varied, both objectives can be achieved under certain
conditions (Seagraves and Easter 1983).

Limitations

The analysis assumed metering would create no special
problems although, in actuality, metering the sakia is an
untried method. To some extent this is a management problem, requiring a sound system of monitoring and enforcement.
Yet, if tampering and destruction of meters were to be widespread, the problem may be unmanageable. Any decision to
use volumetric pricing must be preceded by experimental
trials.

This research does not consider certain present and
potential sources of externalities. The impact of water-
logging and the quantity and quality of irrigation return
flows could not be evaluated due to large information
requirements.

The findings that only limited allocative efficiency
gains can presently be achieved by alternative charging
systems may not be relevant outside the Egyptian context.
The below-grade system which requires farmers to lift water
to their fields is thought to ration water and discourage
extreme waste. This places limits on the potential for

further efficiency gains through water charges. Water charges were assumed to be the only social institutions used to regulate water use. The efficiency measures of area-based pricing instruments would be sensitive to further regulations placed on water use. Research into changes in the method of delivery and the use of rules and regulations for allocating water would broaden our knowledge of methods for managing water shortages.

NOTES

1. We are grateful for aid and assistance provided by M. Abu Zeid, E.W. Richardson, G. Quenemoen, and Hassan Wahby of the Egypt Water Use and Management Project (Cairo and Fort Collins). Farouk Abdel Al, Gamal Ayad, and David Martella assisted with data collection and made useful comments on an earlier version.
2. One Egyptian pound (L.E.) was equal to $1.43 in 1980. One feddan is approximately 1.04 acres.

REFERENCES

Boulding, Kenneth E. 1980. "The implications of improved water allocation policy." In Western Water Resources, (sponsor) Federal Reserve Bank of Kansas City. Westview Press, Boulder, Colorado.

Bowen, Richard L., and Robert A. Young. 1983. Allocative Efficiency and Equity in Charging for Irrigation Water: A Case Study in Egypt. Technical Report No. 37, Egypt Water Use and Management Project, Colorado State University.

_____. 1986. "Financial and economic irrigation net benefit functions for Egypt's northern delta." Water Resources Research (forthcoming).

Coward, E.W., Jr. (ed.). 1980. Irrigation and Agricultural Development in Asia-Perspectives from the Social Sciences, Cornell University Press, Ithaca, New York.

Cuddihy, William. 1980. "Agricultural price management in Egypt." Staff Working Paper No. 388, Agriculture and Rural Development Department, World Bank, Washington, D.C.

223

Davis, Robert K., and Steve H. Hanke. 1972. Pricing and Efficiency in Water Resource Management. U.S. National Water Commission Technical Report, Washington, D.C..

Howe, Charles W. 1979. Natural Resource Economics. John Wiley and Sons, New York.

Maass, Arthur, and Raymond L. Anderson. 1978. ...and the Desert Shall Rejoice: Conflict, Growth, and Justice in Arid Environments. The MIT Press, Cambridge, MA.

Milliman, Jerome W. 1972. "Beneficiary charges -- toward a unified theory." In Public Prices for Public Products, (ed.) Selma Mushkin. The Urban Institute, Washington, D.C..

Ministry of Irrigation. 1981. Master Plan for Water Resource Development and Use. Government of Egypt, Cairo.

Randall, Alan. 1983. "The problem of market failure." Natural Resources Journal 19(1).

Reder, M.W. 1975. "Corruption as a feature of government organizations: Comment." Journal of Law and Economics 18(3).

Ruttan, Vernon W. 1978. "Induced institutional change." In Induced Innovation, (eds.) H. Binswanger and V.W. Ruttan. Johns Hopkins University Press, Baltimore, MD.

Seagraves, James A. and Renan Ochoa. 1978. "Water pricing alternatives for Canete Peru." In Selected Water Management Issues in Latin American Agriculture, (eds.) Pierre R. Crosson, Ronald G. Cummings, and Kenneth D. Frederick. Resources for the Future, Johns Hopkins University Press, Baltimore, MD.

Seagraves, J.A. and K. William Easter. 1983. "Pricing for irrigation water." Water Resources Bulletin 19(6).

Schramm, Gunter and F.V. Gonzales. 1977. "Pricing irrigation water in Mexico: Efficiency, equity and revenue considerations." Annals of Regional Sciences 11(1).

Slack, Roger. 1981. "The volume discharge and mechanical efficiency of the field sakia." Unpublished M.S. thesis, Colorado State University, Fort Collins, CO.

Wade, Robert. 1982. "The system of administrative and political corruption: Canal irrigation in south India." The Journal of Development Studies 18.

Walters, Forrest, 1981. "The livestock enterprise on survey farms in Abu-Raia, Kafr El Sheikh: Selected implications for water distribution and field management." Egyptian Water Use and Management Project Staff Paper No. 68, Ministry of Irrigation, Cairo, Egypt.

Waterbury, John. 1979. Hydropolitics of the Nile Valley. Syracuse University Press, Syracuse, New York.

CHAPTER 13

DIRECT OR INDIRECT ALTERNATIVES FOR IRRIGATION INVESTMENT AND THE CREATION OF PROPERTY

E. Walter Coward, Jr.

Throughout Asia, state investments in irrigation are very large and predicted to remain so. Discussions of irrigation investment often focus on the choice of technology and scale of the systems to be built, (Levine 1980). The usual assumption is that the role of the state is crucial in irrigation investments. Easter and Welsch (1983, p. 29) are explicit on this: "The optimum use of water usually requires some government involvement ranging from credit for private tubewells to actual construction of dams and canals." This chapter discusses a different approach to irrigation investment. Here the emphasis is on the pattern, or structure, of investments being used by the state and the resulting property relations which are created by this pattern. In particular this chapter will contrast two general patterns of investment, direct and indirect.

Everywhere in Asia individual farmers and groups of farmers are making private investments in irrigation. Yet, in general, governments are doing little to induce, sustain, or complement these important investments. The collective objects of property of these local groups include both the physical apparatus of the irrigation works (the dams, canals, division structures, etc.) and the water which the works capture and convey to the agricultural fields. None of this property can be sustained over time without frequent renewal through the investments of labor and capital. Therefore, a community irrigation group must have the capacity to mobilize labor for its initial property creation and the capacity to regularly repeat this labor investment to sustain and elaborate what has initially been created. Thus, the basis for their social action is the common relationship that they have with regard to property objects which they have created. Communal irrigation groups act cooperatively because they are partners or common owners of the important properties of irrigation works and water. In examining traditional irrigation systems one is able to observe various norms, rules, and procedures which reflect these basic property relations. The relationships among the participants in a community irrigation system and between these participants and the group leaders are basically property relationships. Specifically, they reflect the rights and privileges which these parties have to the irrigation works and water.

The significant policy issue which arises from these ideas has to do with irrigation investment. As is well known, governments throughout the Asian region are making large investments in irrigation development, both to create new irrigated hectarage and to improve existing irrigated areas. But, as with other sectors of the economy, it often is useful to distinguish between the formal and the informal sectors. In irrigation development, there is a large informal sector represented by the investments which local groups make in irrigation development, both in the terminal unit level of government-managed systems and in small community-managed ones. These investments are typically not counted in government statistics and often not incorporated in policy decisions.

This ignorance of local investments is especially troublesome in situations when the state initiates irrigation development activities in locations where prior local investments have occurred. The simple technology of traditional irrigation works and the apparent casualness with which they operate often mislead outsiders into assuming that little of value exists. The untrained observer can easily fail to extract from the rude weirs and rough canal structures the sometimes intricate property relations which such prior investments have created.

The basic point is that the fundamental processes of investment now being used by the state, direct rather than indirect investment, fail to create a property relationship among water users. Thus, a social basis for action among local people is not created. In contrast, a strategy of indirect investment in which the state assists local people in making their own investments and in creating their own irrigation property would support the formation of social groups based on their common relationship to irrigation property.

PROPERTY AND SOCIAL ORGANIZATION

There have been several important writings dealing with the relationship between property and social organizations in the context of irrigated agriculture (Leach 1961; Bloch 1975). Leach, in his well-known study of Pul Eliya, found "...it is locality rather than descent which forms the basis of corporate grouping" and that the "...concepts of descent and of affinity are expressions of property relations which endure through time" (Leach 1961, p. 7).

Bloch makes the same point with regard to the Merina, a local group that he observed in Madagascar. He argues that the nature of their property -- in this case scarce rice lands -- enforces a particular kinship formation, endogamy, "to keep outsiders out and stop them getting claims to this highly valued land invested with the work of one's own ancestors" (Bloch 1975, p. 207).

In each case the special nature of irrigated agriculture is a critical variable. As Tamaki (1977) has identified, a key characteristic of irrigation is that it involves terre-capital formation: "In general, the function of terre-capital stock is to integrate labor into land so that 'past labor' can be used to facilitate 'present labor' in the process of production" (Tamaki 1977, p. 11).

Developing irrigated agriculture thus is a property-creating process. And, the most important objects of property that are created are the irrigated fields (shaped, leveled, and bunded to receive the irrigation water), the irrigation works (for acquiring, transporting, and dividing the irrigation water), and the water supply itself.

In this chapter the primary focus is on the irrigation works or facilities. The basic proposition is that creation of the irrigation facilities establishes among the creators, property relations. These relations become the social basis for collective action by irrigators in performing various irrigation tasks. Canal cleaning can be seen as a group action being taken by individuals whose relationships with one another are based, in large part, on the inter-relationships which arise because of their common positions with regard to hydraulic property which they have created or acquired.

Their property relationship is evidenced in their social action as well as in the various normative aspects of their association. Ritual activities may also reflect these basic property relationships. For example, Tan-kim-yong (1983) discusses the annual ritual held following repairs to a system's weir in north Thailand. She notes that the activities of the ritual involve paying respect to both the spirit of the weir and to the former irrigation association leaders. The latter may be seen as representing the original creators. The ritual serves to recount the investment efforts of prior generations and to reconfirm the continuity between those previous property-creating activities and the present ones. This continuity of actions, no doubt, serves as a powerful legitimizer for the various collective efforts which the group will be called on to provide during the next irrigation year. This ritual activity can be analyzed to suggest that the irrigation group finds legitimation for collective action not in common biological ancestors but in common property builders. It is from the actions of that prior group and the relationships which they created among themselves that the present group derives its own relationships, rights, and responsibilities.

This point has important implications for irrigation development policy. Since much irrigation development is focused on the construction of irrigation works, current irrigation investments are actively creating hydraulic property. One question to be explored is whether or not hydraulic property can be created in a way which also contributes to the formation of local property groups with incentives to use and sustain these new facilities.

Before moving to these policy implications in more depth, it is useful to review what is known regarding the nature of hydraulic property in traditional irrigation systems in Asia. There is a rather wide range of types or ownership of irrigation works in Asia. Five examples are:

1. The communal form such as the Balinese subak.
2. The investor's group form of the Batak in north Sumatra.
3. The atar system of the Ilocano region of the Philippines.
4. The local government model of Java.
5. The elite-owned system as found historically in the Lanna Tai region of Thailand.

Communal

The communal irrigation model of Bali is probably the best known of the traditional irrigation works of Asia. The succinct description of the subak which Geertz provides emphasizes the property character of this social form: "The subak was, and is, a technically specialized, cooperatively owned public utility, not a collective farm" (Geertz 1980, p. 74). The property which the "public utility" owns include: "The whole apparatus -- dams, canals, dikes, dividers, tunnels, aqueducts, reservoirs -- upon which any particular landowner depended for his supply" and they were "built, owned, managed, and maintained, ..., by an independent corporation of which he was a full and, in legal terms anyway, equal member" (Geertz 1980, p. 69).

It is this property-owning group, the subak, which is responsible for upkeep and operation of the hydraulic works. While land is held individually, and preservation and improvement of rice lands are the responsibility of individual owners, the hydraulic works are group owned. Their repair and improvement are the responsibility of the joint owners, a responsibility implemented, in part, through the actions of the subak leadership (but acting for the corporate group). While much attention in the literature has been given to the subak as a ritual group, it needs to be remembered that the subak is also a group of joint property owners, some of whose joint actions involve ritual activities.

Investor Group

Lando (1979) has provided a very useful social history of the development of a local irrigation system among the Batak of north Sumatra. Using phrases similar to Geertz, Lando describes Batak irrigation systems in the following terms: "Batak irrigation systems are operated more like public utilities rather than cooperative associations or the irrigation agencies of Wittfogel's hydraulic societies" (1979, p. 9). What distinguishes the Batak from the Balinese case is that the irrigation works, rather than being owned by the entire group of land-owning water users, is owned by a subset of that group. The owners are those who made the original construction investments in the systems and which Lando aptly labels the "proprietary group."

This arrangement, for the ownership of the irrigation works and its operation, is based on three interrelated principles found in traditional Batak thought. First is the idea of suhut; a role which one assumes when underwriting various group activities. As suhut, one assumes the costs of these activities but also assumes the right of directorship or ownership once the activity is completed. The second principle that applies is irrigation-specific. The maintenance responsibility for an irrigation system lies with the owners of that system. Thus, if an individual or group has acted as suhut to underwrite the construction of an irrigation system, they become the owners of that system and the party responsible for its upkeep. The third principle is that of hotopan. This is the idea that inherited property need not be divided but can continue to be owned jointly. Thus, a suhut group which created and owns an irrigation system can transfer that ownership to joint heirs (who will be responsible for its maintenance). While the proprietary group is responsible for organizing and implementing maintenance activities, they do collect irrigation fees from other water users and may require some small amount of their labor. The important point, as with the subak case above, is that the social relationships, which exist among members of the management group, and between the management group and the water users, are based on ownership of the hydraulic property.

Atar

In the Ilocos region of the Philippines, a third interesting ownership model has been documented (Lewis 1971; Siy 1982). Irrigation societies in this region are called zanjeras and appear to be of three broad types, one of which is of particular relevance to this discussion (Coward and Siy 1983). This type, the atar model, was created when a group formed into zanjera society for the purpose of constructing irrigation works and irrigating lands which were owned by others. In exchange for providing this irrigation service, the zanjera group received use rights to a portion of the newly irrigated lands. They were granted continued use of these usufruct lands so long as they continued to provide the irrigation service. And, to continue this service, they had to devote labor and other resources to maintaining and operating the irrigation works, of which they were the owners.

Thus, unlike the Balinese and Batak cases, in Ilocano there is a clear separation in ownership between the owners of land and the owners of the irrigation works. But, as in the other cases, ownership of the hydraulic property and responsibility to sustain it are attached.

Government

In Java, particularly in the Javanese areas but also in the Sundanese regions, village government is relatively well organized and is responsible for the local operation of numerous public functions, including irrigation. In many of these villages, there is a specific member of the village staff responsible for overseeing irrigation matters (Duewel 1980). In this case, the irrigation facilities within the village boundary are viewed as owned by the village assembly and managed by the village government (sometimes with supplemental activities provided by a water user organization). These village irrigation works which are owned and operated by the village may be one of two types: (1) the terminal-level facilities of a larger scheme whose main facilities are owned and managed by the irrigation agency, or (2) all, or part of a "village irrigation system;" one whose ownership and management is solely with the local community.

As in the previous cases, ownership of the hydraulic works coincides with responsibility for them. And it does so "through its power to assess special payments from cultivators, its ability to allocate resources from the annual subsidy funds provided by the national government, and its ability to solicit special funds from the various units of government above it" (Coward 1982, p. 11).

Elite-Owned

North Thailand is another area rich with traditional community irrigation systems such as the so-called muang-fai systems (Bruneau 1968; Potter 1975; Tanabe 1981; Siriwong 1979; and Tan-kim-yong 1983). Not all of the muang-fai systems were initiated as elite-owned, and this appellation probably does not apply to any contemporary systems. Examples from another area include many of the irrigation tanks in south India, discussed in Chapters 5 and 6, which were once elite-owned.

Recently, researchers have been presenting evidence of the extent of involvement of local nobles in the development of muang-fai systems. While there is reported to be a long history of involvement by nobles in the development of canal irrigation, there was a significant increase in irrigation investments by these nobles in the late nineteenth and early twentieth centuries (Tanabe 1979).

In Saraphi District, a nobleman was appointed by the King of Chieng Mai to look after the royal rice lands in two villages. At this time, the nobles still had rights to extract corvee labor from the peasants and, in part, that labor was used to build new irrigation canals and maintain the existing canal networks and the headwork weirs. As Calavan (1974) reports, the nobles appointed a local person who acted as supervisor of the corvee labor used to maintain

the irrigation works and as supervisor of water distribution. Also, Calavan (1974) writes that often the local
irrigation projects were initiated and managed by the
aristocratic administrators of the royal lands who were then
regarded as the owners of the systems. They received part
of the produce from the peasants who also used the irrigation for their own plots.[1]

A similar process occurred in an area about 30 kilo-
meters southwest of Chieng Mai city around 1890 (Cohen
1981). The Chao Muang of Chieng Mai appropriated about
2,000 rai of peasant rice land in the area. He also intervened directly in the existing community irrigation system,
selecting his own appointee as irrigation headman and organizing corvee labor to modify and extend the irrigation works
to better serve his newly acquired lands.

As mentioned above, these elite-owned systems are no
longer found in the region. They have either been incorporated into larger government-managed systems or converted
into community systems owned and operated by the community
of water users. But when these systems did operate, they
were a further example of the relationship between ownership
and system responsibility. In systems which the nobles
owned, they were the "aristocratic administrators" and were
responsible for both maintenance and operations such as
water distribution. They implemented this function by
appointing commoners to serve as irrigation supervisors and
by using their rights to corvee labor to mobilize peasants
for developing and maintaining the irrigation works. With
regard to irrigation activities, the social relations between the nobles and the peasants and among the peasantry
were structured by the hydraulic property rights resulting
from investments by nobles.

Summary

These five cases represent a broad spectrum of types of
ownership found in the reports of traditional local irrigation in the Asian region. There are two generalizations
that can be made from these materials and which provide the
basis for the following discussion of alternative state
irrigation investment strategies.

First, the ownership of and responsibility for the
irrigation works invariably coincides. There is no
alienation of hydraulic property from the ones who are
charged with the responsibility for that property. The
integrity of the irrigation management group is reinforced

by its joint investment actions and its common ownership of the hydraulic property.

Second, if there are water users who are non-owners, they invariably make some payment to the ownership group for the water which they receive. Non-owners who wish to become owners may be asked to make large payments which represent the owning group's assessment of a fair portion of the original investment which newcomers should duplicate (Siriwong 1979; Lewis 1971; and Martin and Yoder 1983).

ALTERNATIVES TO DIRECT IRRIGATION INVESTMENT

A simple but fundamental proposition emerges: investments to create irrigation facilities always simultaneously create, or rearrange, property relationships with regard to those new facilities. One cannot build facilities without establishing property. Now, from this proposition, one can derive an important policy hypothesis about irrigation investment. The irrigation investment ought to proceed in such a way as to create hydraulic property for the group which is intended to operate and maintain the irrigation facilities which are created or improved. When such property relationships are in place, the possibility for collective action in sustaining those property objects is enhanced. This approach would be applied in situations where a local group already owns hydraulic property and investment by the state would be made in a manner which serves to sustain existing property rights. But the approach also would apply in situations where completely new facilities were being created and property rights established.

The Nature and Extent of Local Investments

Two recently completed studies illustrate the nature and extent of investment that local cultivators make in their hydraulic property (Siy 1982; Meinzen-Dick 1983). A federation of nine irrigation associations in the Ilocos region of the Philippines (similar to the _atar_ ownership) irrigated an area of approximately 500 hectares which was cultivated by more than 400 farmers (Siy 1982). A major task which the federation faces each year is mobilizing labor (and some other resources) for repair of the brush weir which diverts water to the command area. An enormous amount of labor is required. Table 13.1 shows that a total of nearly 16,000 man-days of labor were provided. This is

TABLE 13.1
Labor contributions for weir repair, 1980

Zanjers	Days Required Per Member	Days Present Per Member	Total Days Provided
San Jose	28	26	1,268
Cabaroan	17	16	975
San Juan	56	56	4,106
Sinigpit	24	23	674
San Pedro	67	64	1,658
Collibeng	32	31	1,247
Surgui	48	42	2,682
Sto. Rosario	40	38	2,618
Nibinib	41	38	748
Total			15,978

Source: Coward and Siy, 1983.

an average of thirty-two days per hectare or approximately forty days per shareholder.

There is little difference between the amount of labor assessed to each shareholder and the amount actually provided. This correspondence can be attributed to the structure of hydraulic property in the federation (Table 13.1).

The second example comes from a study of a tank system in Tamil Nadu (Meinzen-Dick 1983). The tank, Sananeri, is one of a chain of six tanks which receive water from a government anicut (weir) on the Hanuman River. Sananeri tank is the last of three tanks which receive water directly from the anicut and serves a registered command area of 174 hectares. In this tank as with many others in Tamil Nadu (as discussed in Chapter 6), irrigation water from the tank is supplemented with water from private wells within the command area, particularly in the dry period.

While the anicut diverting water from the river and the main channel delivering water to the first three tanks are government facilities, Sananeri tank is locally operated and the below-tank irrigation facilities are locally owned. The costs of operation and repair, provided by the cultivators, are considerable. The major costs include payments to the local association's staff for maintenance and water distribution activities, provision of their own labor for repair work, and cash contributions to the tank fund for other incidental costs.

The value of the total contributions to the association's operational costs (in terms of the 1982-1983 rice prices in the area) was approximately $35 per hectare (Meinzen-Dick 1983). In addition, cultivators on the best double-cropped soils paid a revenue tax of approximately $8 per hectare. An interesting comparison is to note that Palanisami and Easter (1983) report that the Public Works Department of Tamil Nadu expends approximately $2.50 per hectare on repairs.

These two cases suggest that local groups are capable of mobilizing significant amounts of local resources to create, elaborate, and sustain their irrigation property. This will not be the situation in all cases. There is need for more analysis of situations in which such local mobilization is not achieved, or is insufficient, and the factors related to this lack of investment are identified.

Inducing Local Irrigation Investments

The pattern of irrigation infrastructure development used by Japan suggests strong state inducements for indirect investment (Akino 1979). The investment was through subsidies and low-interest loans to local groups, such as the land improvement associations, which generated local investments to match those of the state but left ownership and control in local hands. The state's support of local investment included three key elements. First, laws were passed to facilitate the ability of landowners to act on irrigation improvements without requiring unanimous agreement. Second, subsidies and low-interest loans were provided. One form of subsidy was agreement to not change the tax assessment of lands which had been improved under this program. Third, the state provided technical assistance to the local association. This indirect approach

was highly dependent upon the existence of strong farmers'
organizations which were able to mobilize communal labor and
manage water effectively.

Another example comes from an Indonesian case (Hafid
and Hayami 1979). Two small community irrigation systems
were assisted through the national program called subsidi
desa. Each of the systems received a subsidy of $250, which
was then matched by locally mobilized resources including
construction materials, direct labor, and some payment for
hired labor. They calculate an investment inducement coefficient of 4.4 and 5.4 for the respective systems, based on
the total investment divided by the government subsidy.

Hafid and Hayami conclude that "the subsidies were substantial inducements to the mobilization of local resources"
and that national policy "...to promote the mobilization of
low-cost resources, chiefly labor, at the village by subsidizing the community construction of social and production
infrastructure can be highly successful" (1979, p. 132).
Furthermore, they conclude that these specific projects were
successful for the following reasons: (1) the benefits were
apparent to the community, (2) the projects do not involve
the dislocation of people, and (3) the projects did not
involve construction of the complete system. But these seem
to be imperfect explanations for success since one can think
of exceptions to the explanations suggested. It is likely
that the success of the projects is highly related to the
fact that the subsidi desa strategy represents what one
might call a "property-enhancing strategy." That is, the
community's use of the subsidi desa funds did not result in
a restructuring of property rights. There is no change in
ownership of the irrigation works from the local group to a
superordinate government agency. This is in direct contrast
to the state's other program to assist village irrigation
systems, the sederhana irrigation program. In this case
assistance results in the ownership of the hydraulic
property shifting away from the community group to the
Irrigation Department.

Similar evidence of the possibilities of a subsidy
approach comes from the Sundanese village in West Java
(Coward 1982). In this village, approximately 180 hectares
of land are irrigated by four small weirs (three of which
are permanent masonry structures). There is no highly
formalized organization of water users. Things are done
somewhat more informally by the cultivators served by each
of the weirs and their associated canal layouts. While
there is little day-to-day involvement in the operational
matters of irrigation by the village government, it does
play an important role in irrigation matters through its

policies for investing in irrigation improvement. It is
able to do so through its power to assess cultivators, to
allocate resources from the annual village subsidy fund
(subsidi desa), and to solicit special funds from the
various units of the government hierarchy.

Three aspects of the pattern of irrigation investment
are of special interest (Table 13.2): (1) investments in
irrigation development were made in each of the three years
for which data was available, (2) the total of the yearly
cash investments is almost equally divided between community
contributions and outside assistance, while the community
also provided labor to the projects, and (3) over the three
year period, an increasingly larger portion of the village
subsidy was assigned to irrigation.

Thus, the findings are consistent with the general
pattern reported earlier by Hafid and Hayami. By assisting
the community to invest in its own irrigation property, the
state is able to induce investment of an even larger absolute bundle of resources in irrigation development.
Furthermore, because the investment process is under local
control, the cultivator group is able to decide priorities,
implement needed projects, and retain autonomous ownership
and control of the irrigation works following completion of
the work.

The two Indonesia cases illustrate the success of an
irrigation investment strategy which respects and preserves
existing property arrangements and the associated social
organization of that property. But, of course, state
investments do not always do so. A recent report from Nepal
illustrates the opposite case.

Intervention in a Community Irrigation System

The Nepal case of state intervention in an existing
irrigation system is filled with issues of hydraulic
property (Pradhan 1982). It involves a small-scale hill
system diverting water with a simple weir to lands which
produce rice in the wet season and wheat in the dry season.

The community system actually is an amalgamation of two
previously independent systems. The consolidation occurred
after one of the systems, let's call it system B, had its
weir destroyed and was unable to replace it. Through a
series of negotiations with the other system, here called
system A, system B was permitted to join its canal network
to the works of system A. System B was originally developed
by two individuals using their own, and some borrowed,
capital to hire construction specialists to build the irri-

238

TABLE 13.2
Irrigation cash investments in Ciperut village, West
Java (rupiahs)[a]

Cash Funds	1978/79	1979/80	1980/81
Total irrigation expenditures	670,000	935,000	1,300,000
Village contributions	320,000	485,000	650,000
Village subsidy	350,000	540,000	650,000
Village contributions as percent of village subsidy	91.5	107.0	100.0
Percent of village subsidy allocated to irrigation	35.0	45.0	65.0

Source: Coward, 1982.

[a]Approximately 650 rupiahs = $1.

gation facilities. After construction was completed, they
sold shares in the system to landowners who could be served.
These shareholders formed into an irrigation association
which owned and operated system B. Though Pradhan does not
discuss it, it is assumed that a similar approach occurred
in system A.

The negotiations which led to the formation of the con-
solidated system, A-B, seem to clearly recognize hydraulic
property and water rights. For the right to join their
system with that of A, the B group agreed to the following:
(1) widen the main canal from the diversion point,
(2) assume all responsibility for routine work and maintenance on the entire system while group A could be called
on in time of emergency, and (3) give group A priority in
water distribution. Originally, the agreement was that
group A would receive water during the day and group B only
at night. Stiff arrangements, indeed, but ones that reflect
the prior investments which group A had made in their system
(the investment costs that were to be "paid" by group B) and

the inferior water rights which these payments produced. It was into this complex situation which the state intervened.

The state implemented a development project which modified the existing main system and extended the canal network beyond group B to serve a completely new area operated by group C. While the modifications to the existing canal system went smoothly (perhaps because it did result in some increase in water supply), the project has not been successful in distributing water to the new area.

> The feeling of ownership of the system entails many consequences in terms of effective resource mobilization and management. (Group B) ... feels that for nearly half a century they have put sweat and toil, life and risks, money and labor into the system. It is a private kulo, not a state-owned or state-constructed one. It is, thus, quite irreconcilable for (group B) people to just give water to (group C) simply because of some development program ... Whatever it is (group B) feels that it is their duty to be responsible for their system and, thus, will take all measures to safeguard it and, moreover, own it (Pradhan 1982).

There is a "property explanation" for the impasse which has developed. The state has attempted to intervene with a strategy which seeks to radically alter the existing hydraulic property rights. It created new rights for previously uninvolved groups and modified the property rights of groups A and B with little compensation to them. It is hardly surprising that resistance has materialized.

Applying the Indirect Investment Approach

There are two investment principles which have been identified. First, those irrigation facilities which local groups are expected to maintain and be responsible for must be owned by those local groups. Second, irrigation group solidarity should be based on ownership of common irrigation property. This will both define the appropriate boundaries of the irrigation group and avoid situations of trying to create water user organizations (WUO) with an insufficient base for social action. These two principles, in combination, can help redefine irrigation investment strategies in important ways. For state assistance to existing community irrigation works, the investment strategy should utilize the proposition that it is important to maintain the hydraulic property relations on which the group is based. If the state decides that the ownership pattern is unjust and unacceptable, efforts to modify it should proceed from a sound understanding of what exists, why it exists that way, and what the organizational implications will be of changing it. In addition, unless new property relationships congruent with the intended responsibilities are substituted, little success in sustaining the new hydraulic property can be expected.

Indirect investment in community irrigation systems would use implementation tools such as subsidies, low-interest loans or grants, tax abatements, technical assistance and regulation of water rights to support investments by the irrigation-owning group. What would be precluded would be institutional or organizational arrangements which would lead to direct governance and ownership of new, or modified, irrigation works built by the state itself.

The indirect investment approach also has implications for the development of large-scale, government-managed systems. Nearly everywhere, the state has operated with the principles that the water users themselves should be responsible for the operation and maintenance of the terminal-level or tertiary facilities (those facilities from the lateral canals to the farmers' fields as shown in Figure 1.3, Chapter 1). In recent years, as agricultural production has been under pressure to intensify, governments (and powerful outside lenders) frequently have become impatient with the pace at which farmers accept their "responsibilities" for tertiary development. This has clearly been the case in the central plain of Thailand and on the north coast of Java. This impatience has led to direct state investment in programs to directly design and construct the tertiary facilities and assign responsibility for operation and maintenance to the cultivators. Usually the matter of ownership is, at best, ambiguous. Cultivators typically assume that, since government built the tertiary facilities, they own them and (consistent with matters of ownership and responsibility) are responsible for them. Government may not explicitly define the property situation with regard to the tertiary facilities but it does indicate its expectation that the farmers will be responsible for their maintenance. Those familiar with these tertiary development efforts will know the numerous problems which are being encountered.

The indirect investment approach to tertiary development would use the principles identified above. It assumes that farmer ownership of the tertiary facilities would enhance the probability of social action by the cultivators and increase the likelihood of their exercising responsibility to protect that investment. As in the case of induced investment, the state would act both to supplement and induce the local mobilization of resources for constructing and improving the tertiary facilities. The state could also be helpful in providing technical advice on layouts and control devices, work with the operators of the main system facilities to ensure that they are operated in a manner which would make tertiary-level investments pay off and, where needed, assist in the formation of WUO.

This last activity, assisting in the formation of WUO, is an especially important one since in the absence of such organizations the indirect strategy is impotent. There is no local entity for the state to subsidize. On the other hand, knowing the lack of success which the state has had in forming such groups, one can be very dubious about future success. However, by using a "property strategy" along with organizing specialists, such as the community organizers of the Philippines (Korten 1982) or the institutional organizers of Sri Lanka (Uphoff 1980), one can greatly enhance the probability of success. Nonetheless, even this strategy may not match the pace of implementation which agencies feel is required. The trade-off may be a slower pace of implementation but a longer period of sustained use and less environmental damage.

Those who recall the "ditches and dikes" program of Thailand (Trung 1979) may have their doubts regarding the likelihood of farmers taking action to develop tertiary facilities. The "ditches and dikes" program was initiated by the state precisely because cultivators had not done so. But there are several points to remember about that case: (1) it was the pace of the tertiary development activities of the cultivators which posed the greatest problem for the authorities and their advisors, (2) very little assistance was available for farmers to do the job (neither subsidies nor technical assistance was offered by the state nor was there assistance with group formation), and (3) the strategy used was not explicitly a property strategy. There was no clear policy indicating that the facilities which farmers built would be theirs and not simply be subsumed as property of the state.

CONCLUSION

The main proposition is that an examination of traditional community irrigation systems suggests that these groups can be seen as property-creating and property-sustaining entities. Their actions in creating hydraulic property (irrigation facilities) establish among them

242

property relationships. These form the basis for their collective action in utilizing and sustaining irrigation facilities.

This proposition has important implications for investment policies which the state uses to create new irrigation facilities or improve existing ones. If the state wishes to have cultivators act jointly to operate and maintain some or all of the hydraulic facilities which they use, it appears that group action based on property relations will be required. The state can invest in a manner compatible with these principles by investing indirectly. That is, it should provide subsidies and other inputs which complement local investments but also ensure that the hydraulic property which is created is owned by those responsible for its continuance.

NOTES

1. In addition to the irrigation investments being made by the nobles at this time, there is also evidence that Chinese merchants were also providing capital for the expansion of irrigation facilities (Tan-kim-yong 1983).

REFERENCES

Akino, Masakatsu. 1979. "Land infrastructure improvement in agricultural development: The Japanese case, 1900-1965." Economic Development and Cultural Change 28(1):97-117.

Bloch, Maurice. 1975. "Property and the end of affinity." In Marxist Analyses and Social Anthropology, (ed.) M. Bloch, pp. 203-28. Malaby Press, London.

Bruneau, M.M. 1968. "Traditional irrigation in northern Thailand: An example from the Chiangmai Basin." Bulletin de l'Association de Geographes Francais 362-63:155-65 (translated).

Calavan, Sharon. 1974. "Aristocrats and commoners in rural northern Thailand." Unpublished Ph.D. Dissertation, University of Illinois, Urbana.

Cohen, Paul T. 1981. "The politics of economic development in northern Thailand, 1967-1978." Thesis, University of London.

243

Coward, E. Walter, Jr., and Robert Y. Siy, Jr. 1983. "Structuring collective action: An irrigation federation in the northern Philippines." Unpublished paper.

Coward, E. Walter, Jr. 1982. "Village irrigation in West Java: Notes from Sukaradja." Unpublished paper.

Duewel, John. 1980. "Cultivating indigenous irrigation institutions in rural Java: A study of the Dharma Tirta water user association model in Central Java, Indonesia." Paper presented at Seminar on the Use of Indigenous Social Structures and Traditional Media in Non-Formal Education and Development, Berlin.

Easter, K. William, and D.E. Welsch. 1983. Socioeconomic Issues in Irrigation Development and Distribution. Economic Report ER83-5, Department of Agricultural and Applied Economics, University of Minnesota.

Geertz, Clifford. 1980. Negara: The Theatre State in Nineteenth-Century Bali. Princeton University Press, Princeton, New Jersey.

Hafid, Anwar, and Yujiro Hayami. 1979. "Mobilizing local resources for irrigation development: The Subsidi Desa Case of Indonesia." In Irrigation Policy and the Management of Irrigation Systems in Southeast Asia, (eds.) D.C. Taylor and T.H. Wickham, pp. 123-42. The Agricultural Development Council, Inc., Bangkok, Thailand.

Korten, Frances F. 1982. "Building national capacity to develop water user associations." Staff Working Paper No. 528, World Bank, Washington, D.C..

Lando, Richard P. 1979. "The gift of land: Irrigation and social structure in a Toba Batak Village." Ph.D. Dissertation, University of California.

Leach, E.R. 1961. Pul Eliya: A Village in Ceylon. Cambridge University Press.

Levine, Gilbert. 1980. "Irrigation development and strategy issues for the Asian region." Draft of Issues paper submitted to USAID, Cornell University.

Lewis, Henry T. 1971. Ilocano Rice Farmers. University of Hawaii Press, Honolulu, Hawaii..

Martin, Edward, and Robert Yoder. 1983. "Water allocation and resource mobilization for irrigation: A comparison of two systems in Nepal." Paper presented at 1983 Annual Meeting of Nepal Studies Association, University of Wisconsin, Madison.

Meinzen-Dick, Ruth S. 1983. "Local management of tank irrigation in south India: Organizations and operation." M.S. Thesis, Cornell University, Ithaca, New York.

244

Palanisami, K., and K. William Easter. 1983. The Tanks of South India: A Potential for Future Expansion in Irrigation. Economic Report ER83-4, Department of Agricultural and Applied Economics, University of Minnesota, St. Paul, Minnesota.

Potter, Jack M. 1975. Thai Peasant Social Structure. University of Chicago Press, Chicago, Illinois.

Pradhan, Ujjwal. 1982. "Irrigation development: Whose panacea?" Unpublished paper.

Siriwong, Abhana Ayutthaya. 1979. "A comparative study of traditional irrigation systems in two communities in northern Thailand." Social Research Institute, Chulalongkorn University, Bangkok, Thailand.

Siy, Robert Y., Jr. 1982. Community Resource Management: Lessons from the Zanjera. University of the Philippines Press, Quezon City.

Tamaki, Akira. 1977. "The development theory of irrigation agriculture." IDE Special Paper No. 7, Institute of Developing Economies, Tokyo, Japan.

Tan-kim-yong, Uraivan. 1983. "Resource mobilization in traditional irrigation systems of northern Thailand: A comparison between the lowland and the upland irrigation communities." Ph.D. Dissertation, Cornell University, Ithaca, New York.

Tanabe, Shigeharu. 1981. "Peasant farming systems in Thailand: A comparative study of rice cultivation and agricultural technology in Chingmai and Ayutthaya." Ph.D. Dissertation, The School of Oriental and African Studies, University of London.

Tanabe, Shigeharu. 1979. "Historical development of irrigation systems in Lannathai (northern Thailand)." Unpublished paper.

Trung, Ngo Quoc. 1979. "Economic analysis of irrigation development in deltaic regions of Asia: The case of central Thailand." In Irrigation Policy and the Management of Irrigation Systems in Southeast Asia, (eds.) D.C. Taylor and T.H. Wickham, pp. 155-64. The Agricultural Development Council, Inc., Bangkok, Thailand.

Uphoff, Norman. 1980. "Contrasting legal and organizational approaches to water management development in Sri Lanka." Manuscript submitted to Third World Legal Studies, International Center for Law and Development, New York.

Wittfogel, Karl. 1957. Oriental Despotism. Yale University Press, New Haven, Connecticut.

CHAPTER 14

IRRIGATION POLICIES FOR FUTURE GROWTH IN AGRICULTURE

K. William Easter

A number of important issues face decision makers, ranging from government strategies for investments in small-scale irrigation projects to the selection of alternative procedures for allocating irrigation water. Many of these issues involved both a concern for efficiency in water use and for an equitable distribution of benefits. It is important to realize that many of the irrigation management problems are difficult to resolve once a project has been designed and constructed. Procedures for operating and maintaining irrigation projects should be included in the planning and design stages of projects. The project design will determine what operation and maintenance options are possible. This is also true of the distribution of project benefits.

Another important theme in irrigation development and managment is the concern for decentralized decision making. At what level can farmers be effectively involved in operating an irrigation system? This is one of the basic issues involved in the choice of small-scale vs. large-scale projects. It is also important in determining the relative share of private vs. public involvement in irrigation development. In the past, except for tubewell irrigation and some river diversion projects, developing countries have tended to error on the side of not involving farmers. More needs to be done to develop incentives, training programs, and institutions that will make better use of the knowledge and management talent available among farmers.

Furthermore, it appears that the evaluation of irrigation investments needs to be strengthened in several respects. First, a consistent and uniform procedure of evaluating government projects should be established. This means an agency independent of the traditional construction agencies should have responsibility for the project planning and evaluation. Second, a criterion needs to be developed for selecting the appropriate procedures for allocating water among farmers, e.g., rotation vs. continuous flow. This should be part of the planning decisions concerning project scale and design. Third, a criterion should be included in the project evaluation to determine if the institutional capacity is adequate or can be developed for implementing the irrigation project. For example, if the water is delivered to an outlet serving 100 farmers, will they be able to organize and allocate the water effectively among themselves?

HIGHLIGHTS

In Chapter 2 we suggest two broad investment questions which will be of prime concern for decision makers over the next few decades. The first is the trade-off between new irrigation projects and rehabilitation and maintenance of old systems. Second is the trade-off between small- and large-scale projects. These two broad questions give rise to a number of additional issues including the following:

1. What should be the frequence and type of maintenance and rehabilitation investments in irrigation systems including on-farm investments?
2. How can the success of communal irrigation systems in obtaining local investment be transferred to government-built irrigation systems?
3. What are the benefits from fish production and domestic water use in irrigation projects?
4. What size management units should operate irrigation projects?
5. Are more socioeconomic problems associated with larger irrigation projects?
6. What are the economic returns and distribution of benefits for alternative sizes of irrigation projects?
7. What are the returns from different levels of water application intensity?
8. What is the appropriate timing and level of development of drainage and terminal infrastructure? There is very little information on the returns from drainage investments even though many studies have identified drainage as a major constraint to improving crop production.

In Chapter 3 we spell out a number of the important water management issues which are plaguing decision makers from Washington, D.C. to Bangkok. These issues include the following:

1. What are the best procedures for allocating water over time and among end uses including the conjunctive use of ground water and surface water?
2. What is the optimum size of irrigated area and distribution system?
3. What are the returns from alternative investments to reduce water losses and improve its distribution (control structure, lining materials, etc.)?
4. What can be done to improve the compatibility of incentives and objectives among farmers and system managers for the efficient allocation of water?
5. What alternative institutions can be developed to facilitate farmer participation in irrigation management? These institutions will need to internalize the externalities involved in water allocation and canal maintenance.
6. How can one build institutions for coordinating government involvement in irrigation development, evaluation, and management?
7. How can procedures for financing water user organizations be improved?
8. What are the impacts of land tenure, water rights, and project financing procedures on the level and distribution of project benefits and on project performance?

Many of the issues discussed in Chapters 2 and 3 are of major concern to developing countries and donor agencies. Our judgment is that investments in small-scale irrigation, farmer participation in management, investments in project rehabilitation and maintenance (including drainage), and incentives for efficient allocation of irrigation water will continue to be major concerns for decades to come. With the current level of investment in irrigation, researchers and policy makers cannot ignore these questions.

In Chapter 4 the authors stress the importance to India of irrigation as a means to meet current and future food demands. They argue that the major focus should be on restructuring existing irrigation systems to improve water use efficiency and the equitable distribution of irrigation benefits. They go on to say that too much emphasis in the past has been placed on water impoundment and the management of reservoirs and canals. Too little attention was given to

the field level water management. In addition, they call
for an irrigation policy that views land and water management problems as a whole. They argue that research on water
resources must focus on the social, economic and political
issues. Finally, they recommend an extensive training
program in both the Irrigation and Agriculture Departments
from the chief engineers to the luscars and agricultural
extension personnel.

After a discussion of the limited potential for expansion of large-scale and pump irrigation, two strategies for
small-scale irrigation development, which include the whole
watershed, are highlighted in Chapter 5. One emphasizes
run-off and erosion control with water collection in small
percolation ponds which recharge the ground water and
facilitate well irrigation. The other suggests improvements
in tank water management by controlling the opening and
closing of the sluice gates based on set rules. A set of
rules for closing sluice gates on rainy days was tested in a
simulation model. They increased the area irrigated by 20
percent while reducing the risk of crop failure by 17
percent and increasing dry season water by 24 percent.

In Chapter 6, the last chapter on Indian irrigation, we
focus on the rehabilitation and management of the almost
40,000 tanks in Tamil Nadu. Many of the tanks have been in
use for over a century and have been declining in productivity, particularly since Independence. Rehabilitation
investments offer good rates of return if appropriate tanks
and investments are selected. The chapter concludes with a
simplified procedure, using secondary data, for identifying
the appropriate tanks for rehabilitation. Out of a sample
of forty-nine tanks, ten to twelve were identified as being
high priority for rehabilitation.

Thailand's past irrigation development efforts are
briefly summarized in Chapter 7. Johnson emphasizes the
need to understand the complementary role of agricultural
policy. Improved irrigation, lower fertilizer prices, and
higher rice prices will all be necessary to obtain major
increases in production. He argues that past irrigation
investments have helped Thailand keep its share of the world
export markets. However, for growth in production to continue, clear land titles will need to be established for
about half of the farmers and water charges will need to be
collected to help pay for maintaining existing irrigation
systems.

In Chapter 8 Tubpun evaluates the small tank program
which the Government of Thailand has implemented in northeast Thailand to provide the basic water needs for household
use, livestock use, fish production, small vegetable

gardens, rice nurseries, and in some cases dry season irrigation. Three small tanks are evaluated. She finds that household and livestock water benefits were not large enough to cover project costs in any of the tanks. However, dry season irrigation benefits made the high performance tank very profitable. Leadership, cooperation, price incentives, and location of the tank near the village were all important in the success of the high performance tank. If other small tanks are to be successful, their leaders will need to be trained, market information about alternative dry season crops will have to be provided, and more attention has to be given to the location of the tanks. This study also suggests new ways of estimating tank benefits based on survey techniques to obtain farmers' willingness to pay for tanks.

The surprising aspect of the results reported in Chapter 9 is the good performance of the four tanks relative to the two river pump systems in northeast Thailand. Wet season rice yields were much lower in the pump projects and their construction costs were high. The dry season returns varied a great deal among crops and projects. Low yields and high labor use resulted in negative net returns to farmers in a number of the projects during the dry season. In general, wet season irrigation was adequate, while only half of the farmers practiced dry season cropping. The dry season cropping was limited by water supply, labor supply and markets for dry season crops. A combination of farmer training, improved markets for dry season crops, and technical and financial assistance for water user organizations (WUO), to help them manage and maintain their irrigation systems, is needed to improve project performance.

The last chapter on Thailand, Chapter 10, includes a review of a pilot Asian Development Bank project for improving the performance of a large irrigation scheme. The large pilot project, in combination with technical assistance, was very successful in helping achieve the irrigation production targets. Cropping intensity increased from 98 percent to 163 percent during 1981-1983, while family income jumped from $340 to $855. Nagnju recommends that the same approach be used in other projects to speed up irrigation development. Yet for the approach to be successful three factors are necessary: (1) 20 to 30 percent of the service area should be irrigated before the large pilot project is started, (2) adequate funds and staff must be available for the pilot project, and (3) a team of technical experts must be at the sight working together with counterpart staff.

The study reported on in Chapter 11 focuses on twenty watercourses in the Pakistan Punjab and how they are operated and maintained. Water trading and cooperation in some

of the watercourses suggests that there is a greater potential for cooperative use of the system than is being
exploited. The potential conflicts and disproportionate
distribution of benefits from watercourse improvements have
worked against the improvement program. However, the past
experience of farmers in providing collective goods seems to
help overcome these constraints to watercourse improvement.

Chapter 12 includes a description of a water pricing
study done with representative farms in Egypt's delta
region. A range of pricing schemes including a flat land
tax, a crop charge, and volumetric charges were tested using
a linear programming model. The various pricing systems
were compared under varying levels of water scarcity. Both
the efficiency and economic impacts were compared and the
transactions costs were considered. When water was not
scarce, the area-based charges were the most efficient.
Only when severe water scarcity was introduced into the
model did volumetric pricing provide the most efficient and
equitable pricing system. However, it appears that the
transactions costs of volumetric pricing may be ten times as
high as area-based pricing. Finally, the unusual, below-
ground level canal system which requires water to be lifted
before it can be applied may mean that the results are not
relevant outside Egypt.

In Chapter 13 Coward explores the relationship between
investment in irrigation and the creation of community property in irrigation systems. The ownership of the hydraulic
property and responsibility for sustaining it are held in
common in many successful small-scale irrigation systems.
Investments to create irrigation facilities always create or
rearrange property relationships. Therefore, irrigation
investment ought to proceed in a manner which creates property for the group that will operate and maintain the
irrigation facilities. This gives the incentives to the
appropriate group to sustain the property.

SUSTAINABILITY OF IRRIGATION PROJECTS

Future irrigation investment policy must take a much
broader view than has traditionally been the case. Questions must be asked about the environmental and institutional sustainability of irrigation projects. Policy makers
are now more aware of the need for farmers to participate in
irrigation management and for institutional arrangements to
facilitate water management. In addition, there is a

growing concern about the financial and technical ability of countries to operate and maintain existing irrigation systems given their current level of organization and training. This is all part of the question of sustainability. Even though a project may create more benefits than it costs, a country may not be able to collect any of the economic surplus that the project creates. Thus, the funds required to maintain and operate the project may not be available.

A country's institutional capacity may also not be adequate to support a major expansion in irrigated agriculture. For large-scale, new projects institutional capacity should be a major concern which needs detailed evaluation. In contrast, for small-scale projects and the rehabilitation of large projects, it is less important. Where the expansion is small-scale or the irrigation project already exists (rehabilitation) it will be much easier to judge if the institutional capacity exists or can be created. Yet rehabilitation or small-scale projects may not fit in the existing irrigation bureaucracy which is designed to build large new systems. Thus, a reorganization of the irrigation bureaucracy may be necessary before existing irrigation systems can be improved.

A series of questions must be asked about an irrigation project beyond the basic feasibility analysis (technical, financial, and economic). These questions would be designed to determine if the project is sustainable.

The following are examples of the information the decision maker should have concerning sustainability. Do the farmers have any experience in organizing themselves to provide collective or public goods and what is their record on cooperation? Does the government have the necessary support staff to run the systems and provide technical assistance to farmers? What is the potential for salt accumulation and/or water logging? Will the irrigation cause major changes in land ownership or create uncertainty in land ownership?

As was pointed out in the last chapter, who owns the water can be critical. If the "government owns the water" then farmers are likely to expect them to provide all of the services, i.e., maintain the system and allocate the water among farmers. In contrast, if farmers own the water, they are much more likely to feel obligated to operate and maintain the system.

RESEARCH PRIORITIES

What follows is a review of the water research topics which participants in the UM-CSU-USAID workshop on Water Management and Policy felt were of prime importance. The research topics can be grouped under four headings. Almost half of the topics would involve some evaluation of performance. Another group of issues involved farmer organization and participation. A third group concerns problems related to management and organization. The final group includes those topics concerned with irrigation from the watershed perspective.

Performance

Irrigation project performance can be measured in a number of ways including changes in farm income, total production, distribution of benefits and yields and rates of return. Research issues raised by participants involve all of these measures. What is the yield response to different levels and timing of water applications for different crops? How do different water schedules and crops alter farm income and total production? What are the relative rates of return and risk in irrigated areas relative to rainfed areas? How do different levels and organization of government decision making influence irrigation system performance? Finally, will the type and size of irrigation project influence the distribution of project benefits? If so, why?

Farmer Participation

As mentioned earlier, farmer participation is one of the weak links in many irrigation systems. What can be done about this problem is only partly known. Further research is definitely needed. First, how do farmers view the irrigation system and is this view dependent on project size, how government is organized, water ownership, and the distribution of benefits? A related question involves the appropriate organization for different types of irrigation systems. These questions will involve the classic problems of providing collective goods and the transactions costs involved in group decisions. For example, farmer participation needs to be studied in the context of the theory of group action and the optimum size for effective decision making.

Management and Organization

Many of the irrigation management problems have already been discussed. However, several topics suggested by workshop participants need to be reemphasized. First is the need for a comparative analysis of the operation and maintenance provided for different irrigation systems. Researchers need to compare systems in different countries, across climatic zones, by size and type, and finally by major source of funding (local, state, or central). Second, small tank (reservoir) systems need to be studied to determine how they are organized and controlled to deliver water. Third, a comparative analysis in different countries is needed of irrigation management by project size. In this analysis of irrigation management, the trade-off should be measured between hardware and management. This becomes especially important when farmers are expected to play a larger role in management. Finally a disaggregation and analysis of the government bureaucracy for irrigation is needed. Many irrigation departments were established in a different time and under very different farming conditions but the organizations have not changed. It is, therefore, not surprising that irrigation management is slow to change.

Watersheds

There is growing concern that irrigation projects must be analyzed in a broader physical context. One such framework is the watershed or river basin. Here one can go upstream and include the impacts of forestry, grazing, and farming practices on the irrigation project below. How will these practices affect the quantity and timing of runoff as well as the siltation of reservoirs? The downstream concerns involve water pollution, return flows, and soil erosion. When one considers irrigation within the watershed or river basin it is easier to optimize the combined use of surface water and ground water. This was highlighted in Chapter 5 with the use of small tanks to recharge the ground water.

POLICY RECOMMENDATIONS

It is clear from the above that more research is needed before many of the questions concerning irrigation management and investment can be answered. Still much has been learned over the past decade, although implementation of these lessons has been slow. Thus, it is important to list some of the key policy recommendations coming from past research and experience.

First, irrigation projects must be planned, designed, constructed, operated, and maintained with the firm objective of involving the farmers. Effective top-down management is very expensive and does not work in many cases. Past experience in providing collective goods and strong local leadership are both positive elements in farmer participation in irrigation management.

Second, more attention needs to be given to project rehabilitation and maintenance. The returns from selected project rehabilitation are likely to be higher than from new projects. This is also related to the question of farmer participation since farmers may not be willing to take responsibility for irrigation systems that are in poor condition.

Third, collection of water fees continues to be a problem across many countries. For the farmers in Egypt there is no direct charge for water although farmers must lift the water out of ditches which are below ground level. In Thailand farmers are charged for the cost of pumping water from rivers but pay no fees for water from tanks. Water fees need to be related directly to project operation and maintenance. Farmers need to know that their fees will be used to improve and maintain their irrigation system. If they can see the results from their fees through better service, they are much more likely to pay (Abel 1976).

Fourth, problems of allocating water among farmers and different parts of an irrigation system continue to plague irrigation officials. In many cases, systems have been designed without any concern for how water will be allocated. At least two inputs must be brought into decisions concerning water allocation: first, farmers' and agronomists' knowledge concerning crop and farm water requirements; and second, economic modeling techniques to find more efficient schedules for water allocation.

Fifth, decision makers need to recognize the value of small-scale irrigation and the need for indirect (local) investments. More needs to be done with small-scale projects as highlighted in Chapters 5, 6, 8, 9, and 13. Coward suggests that the property created by irrigation projects must fit in with the ownership patterns traditional to the area. This will have the effect of creating indirect investment over time. The irrigation property should be in the hands of those who must maintain it.

Sixth, irrigation projects will always involve some trade-offs between equity and efficiency. In countries such as India they have lost a great deal of efficiency under the false pretense of achieving greater equity. But as history seems to tell us, irrigation projects are not a very good means of improving income distribution. Thus, one should trade efficiency gains for equity only when income distribution will be improved at a reasonable cost and there is not a better way to do it. This is also related to the water fee issue. The more irrigated farmers pay for water the smaller the economic subsidy they receive.

Seventh, one needs to recognize that other government policies such as food price policy will have a direct impact on project performance. This was brought out in Chapters 7, 8, and 12. If there is a cheap food policy farmers will have a difficult time paying for an irrigation project. Consequently, project planning and operation must be done with a realistic estimate of government policies concerning crop and input prices.

Finally, there is an important role for technical assistance to farmers particularly if farmers are expected to play a significant role in water management. Information concerning crops, crop prices, optimum water application rates, and improved farming practices will all help improve the productivity of irrigation systems. This is brought out in Chapter 10. In addition, farmers will need, in many cases, help and training before they can establish effective WUO as pointed out in Chapters 8 and 9. Agricultural extension and the Irrigation Departments must try to more effectively fill this gap. Sivanappan and Rajagopalan in Chapter 4 argue that training is needed all the way from the chief engineers to the person releasing the water from the headgate.

REFERENCES

Abel, Martin E. 1976. "Irrigation systems in Taiwan: Management of decentralized public enterprise." Water Resources Research 12:341-48.

AUTHOR INDEX

SUBJECT INDEX

Altruistic behavior, 163
Andhra Pradesh, 73,
　75(figure), 76, 91
Asia, 1, 7, 39, 225-226,
　228, 232
Asian Development Bank, 10,
　22, 177-181, 183, 187,
　190, 249
Asian Institute of
　Technology, 147, 167
Aswan dam, 215

Bali, 228
Bangladesh, 25
Benefit distribution, 28,
　48-52, 250
Benefit estimation, 164,
　165(table), 167
based on minimum
　compensation, 135, 137,
　138(table), 139
based on willingness to
　pay, 135, 137,
　138(table), 139, 249
hypothetical approach for,
　137, 138(table), 139
market approach for, 135,
　137, 139
See also economic returns,
　irrigation investment,
　evaluation, tank
　irrigation, and water
　development benefits.
Betterment levy, 51

Cauvery River, 67
Central Groundwater Board
　(India), 67
Central Water Commission
　(India), 66
Collective action, 204, 227-
　228, 233, 242
in maintenance, 44
Collective goods, 19, 250-
　251, 254
Collective projects, 193,
　204, 206
Command area, 46, 80, 82
size of, 37
Command Area Development
　Authority (India), 65-66
Command area development
　(India), 36
Common irrigation property
　ownership of, 239
Common property, 84, 228
Communal systems, 25-26, 45,
　225, 228, 246
Community irrigation, 226,
　232, 239-241
wells for, 93, 98
Community organizers, 241
Conceptual model, 3-9
See also irrigation
　management model.
Conflict management, 26, 250
need for, 94, 104, 152
Conjunctive water use, 26,
　39

261

262

267